IMAGES
of America

WELLSBORO

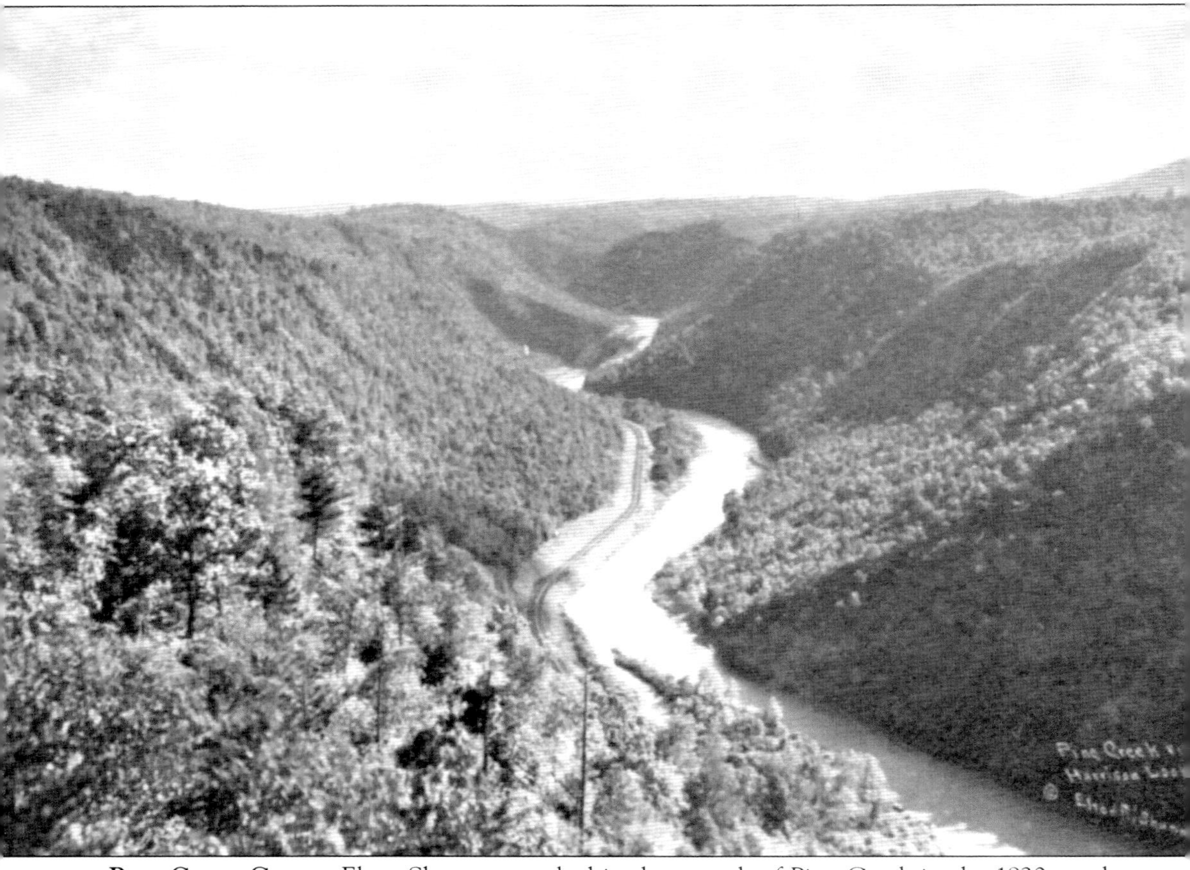

Pine Creek Gorge. Elton Shumway took this photograph of Pine Creek in the 1920s at the request of lumber baron Leonard Harrison, for whom "the Lookout" was named. This iconic view of the gorge, widely known as "Pennsylvania's Grand Canyon," captures the natural beauty that surrounds and sustains the nearby town of Wellsboro. (Courtesy Green Free Library.)

On the Cover: The Wellsboro-Charleston High School Marching Band, directed by Bennie Truax, leads the 1960 Laurel Parade onto Main Street. Majorette Mary Jane Bradley symbolizes the hundreds of students who have proudly represented their hometown at the annual June event. The weeklong Laurel Festival, conceived by businessman and history teacher Larry Woodin, attracts thousands of visitors to Wellsboro each year. (Courtesy Wellsboro Chamber of Commerce.)

IMAGES
of America

WELLSBORO

Ann C. Benjamin and Michael J. Cooney

ARCADIA
PUBLISHING

ISBN 978-1-4671-2252-8

Published by Arcadia Publishing
Charleston, South Carolina

Printed in the United States of America

Library of Congress Control Number: 2014937956

For all general information, please contact Arcadia Publishing:
Telephone 843-853-2070
Fax 843-853-0044
E-mail sales@arcadiapublishing.com
For customer service and orders:
Toll-Free 1-888-313-2665

Visit us on the Internet at www.arcadiapublishing.com

For Billy Cooney and Susanne Benjamin

*"Our darling ones have gone before to meet
us on that distant shore . . . "*

—Epitaph, St. Peter's Cemetery, 1897

Contents

ACKNOWLEDGMENTS

We believed from the outset that Wellsboro would welcome a user-friendly, affordable history of our hometown. Many people affirmed this belief by inviting us into their homes, by sharing their stories, and by trusting us with their cherished family photographs. Individual courtesy lines appear throughout the book; images without credit lines belong to the authors.

We also acknowledge friends and family who encouraged us to press on, no matter the obstacles in our personal lives. In particular, Patricia Benjamin Schwab provided emotional support during a critical period and also drafted the bibliography. Sally Benjamin listened carefully and then responded as a loving sister before responding as a lawyer. Both responses made a positive difference. Skyler Austin and Anne Catherine Feldman offered technical and research assistance, gratefully accepted by their technologically unsophisticated parents.

Former *Wellsboro Gazette* columnists Betty Frazier (Reflections) and the late Arnie Hayden (Woods, Water & Wild Things) provided starting points for numerous research topics. Beverly Markowicz shared original centennial issues of the *Wellsboro Agitator* and the *Wellsboro Gazette*, which proved useful. Numerous people helped identify the individuals in our photographs; special thanks go to Steven Ulsh and Paul Swanson of the Pennsylvania Fish Commission and to Ted and Joan Zuchowski of the US Postal Service. Dr. Ronald Karr, a University of Massachusetts research librarian, helped determine the copyright status of several images.

Thank you as well to Lonnie Campbell, Wellsboro Fire Department (WFD); Kristine Gable, Corning Incorporated Archives; Scott Gitchell, Tioga County Historical Society (TCHS); James Losinger, Pennsylvania Department of Forestry (PDF); Ann Dunham Rawson, Dunham's Department Store; Julie Mosher VanNess, Wellsboro Chamber of Commerce (WCC); and Sandy Webster, Green Free Library (GFL). Each of you represented your organization well, as Wellsboro citizens habitually do.

We hope that the resulting volume successfully communicates our gratitude, our respect, and our affection to the many individuals who helped us, to our childhood friends and classmates, to our families, and—in the broadest sense of the word—to our predecessors, who for over 200 years managed (for the most part) to balance progress with preservation. Despite the unrelenting challenges faced by small towns across America, Wellsboro remains a strikingly beautiful, decidedly historic community, beloved by those who stayed home as well as by those who carried home in their hearts to distant places.

INTRODUCTION

The recorded history of Wellsboro, inextricably linked to the history of Tioga County, begins with the 1784 Treaty of Fort Stanwix, when the Iroquois Confederacy sold northwestern and north-central Pennsylvania to the commonwealth. Historians recount how wealthy investors leapt to purchase land in Pennsylvania's densely forested north before realizing that few settlers wanted to move into a "howling wilderness." As the Honorable Charles Tubbs wrote in 1909, "From the time when men traveled on foot, on horseback, in canoes, in oxcarts down to the period of the stage coach and the railway train, it is and has been difficult of access. It is a true saying, Like Heaven, it is hard to get to."

Apparently, Native Americans agreed. Robert Kennedy Young reported to the Tioga County Historical Society in 1907, "I doubt if any territory in the United States east of the Mississippi . . . is so destitute of Indian interests as that triangle in Pennsylvania bounded north by the New York boundary line, east and southeast by the east branch of the Susquehanna, and west and southwest by the west branch of the Susquehanna. It is mountainous, almost without lakes, and difficult of travel by foot, except in certain narrow trails, few in number."

The Iroquois Confederacy—including the Mohawks, Oneidas, Onondagas, Cayugas, and Senecas—dwelt within the limits of New York State, where inland lakes and agricultural skill sustained them. The Senecas, living closest to what later became Tioga County, ventured south primarily to hunt large game—elk, white-tailed deer, and black bear. Small game also drew the native people south—grey squirrel, rabbits, snowshoe hare, wild turkey, and ruffed grouse abounded in the region's primeval forests.

Evidence exists of seasonal encampments spaced along Pine Creek, for a time called Tiadaghton, meaning "river of pines"—a name later preserved by a lumbering village located south of what are now Colton Point and Leonard Harrison State Parks. All that remain of the ghost town today are the name, a few camps, and an abundance of timber rattlesnakes. Natives also cultivated land at Big Meadows, a fertile floodplain near Ansonia where Marsh Creek empties into Pine Creek. An actual village may have existed where Tioga Point (Athens) now stands. The Indian word *tioga*—originally "di-a-hoga"—refers to "water" and has been interpreted variously as "gateway," "at the headwaters," or "the place where two rivers meet." The "two rivers" were the north branch of the Susquehanna and the Chemung Rivers.

The 1904 Centennial Antiquarian Exhibit, displayed in the historic St. Paul's Episcopalian Church (at that time located on the corner of Charles and Walnut Streets), included a sizable display of Indian relics, including arrowheads, spearheads, and stone axes. Today's locals continue to discuss where artifacts have been found in the region: particularly along Babb's Creek; along the trail through Pine Creek Gorge, where Glen Jenkins, Lamont Satterly's grandfather, once searched the caves for arrowheads; or in Ansonia, where Kevin Webster awaited farmers plowing their fields so that he could search for indigenous treasure.

While Native Americans still dominated the region, King Charles II was in London setting the stage for trouble that eventually exploded in the Connecticut-Pennamite War of the late 18th century. In 1662, the king confirmed to Connecticut a charter that included all the lands between the 41st and 42nd degrees of north latitude extending west to the Pacific Ocean. Then, 19 years later, in his 1681 grant of Pennsylvania to William Penn, he issued a charter that overlapped the Connecticut territory. Prior to the Revolutionary War, Connecticut settlers—or "Yankees"—began to populate the disputed territory. Tensions were set aside during the Revolution, but they reemerged afterward in a way that impacted Wellsboro's earliest settlers.

When a land office opened in Philadelphia in 1785, influential Quakers and the "Delaware elite," many of whom shared connections dating back to their English roots, were among those who invested early. Several speculators together acquired 66,568 acres, including what would later become Tioga County. According to contemporary historian David Hackett Fischer, the founders of the Delaware elite—which included the Morris, Norris, and Waln families—brought substantial capital to the New World. These highly influential Pennsylvanians "rapidly advanced from affluence to wealth, which they achieved primarily by investing in land." They valued hard work and spurned idleness, their motto being, "Up early and busily employed." A visitor to the region in 1768 remarked, "It is almost a proverb in this neighborhood . . . that every great fortune made here within these fifty years has been by land."

Having discovered that little interest existed among buyers, and alarmed by mounting taxes, the investors formulated a two-pronged solution. First, they promoted the idea of building a new road northward "through the heart of the wilderness"; second, they formed a trust called the Pine Creek Company, which ultimately transferred control into the hands of one person. The contractor hired to build the new north-south road and the agent chosen to represent the Pine Creek Company were one and the same: Philadelphia Quaker and Wellsboro founder Benjamin Wistar Morris.

Morris personally oversaw construction of what became known unofficially as "the Benjamin Morris State Road," which approximated today's Route 287. Aware of the difficulties encountered during the 1790s construction of the Williamson Road, which traveled through the region just east of the territory in question, surveyors plotted a course that avoided flood-prone areas while keeping as straight a route as possible. Wellsboro's founding depended on the success of this initiative, begun in 1799 and completed around 1803.

Members of the Society of Friends had long dominated Pennsylvania politics, including elected offices and appointed positions. Quakers also constituted a majority of the colony's economic and social leaders from its founding to the mid-18th century. Against this backdrop, the Pine Creek Company successfully lobbied the Pennsylvania legislature to transform Tioga Township, a part of Lycoming County, into Tioga County.

The legislature passed the bill creating Tioga County on March 26, 1804, with the additional provision that the county seat be located no more than seven miles from the center of the county. The governor was to appoint three persons as trustees who would review proposals for determining the county seat. In accordance with the requirement that the new county have a leader, prior even to locating the seat of governance, William Hill Wells, the brother-in-law of Benjamin Morris, was persuaded to leave an extravagant life in Delaware to assume leadership of the newly created county. Wells, an influential attorney and politician, resigned his seat as the US senator from Delaware, packed up his genteel wife and children, and headed northwest with several black servants. The influence of the Wells family persuaded other families to immigrate to Tioga County from Delaware and Maryland in about 1804. Early adopters posted their favorable observations in the *Republican Argus and County Advertiser* on August 11, 1804, exclaiming over the rich, fertile soil and the well-situated location of their settlement near the state road and "in the vicinity of the place where the county town will most probably be erected."

At the time of Wells's arrival, Tioga County had only one township, also named Tioga, which was earlier populated by Yankees who held all of the county offices. Obviously, this situation was unacceptable to the newcomers and, due to Wells's influence, the Lycoming County Court created a new township in 1805 named Del-Mar, in honor of Delaware and Maryland. Thus freed from domination by Yankee voters, Wells next turned his attention to selecting a county seat.

On October 1, 1805, Governor McKean appointed John Fleming, William Hill Wells, and William Cox Ellis as trustees to accept proposals for the county seat—all three were agents of the Pine Creek Company. On April 7, 1802, Benjamin Morris had purchased property from James Stuart, a wealthy Philadelphia merchant—land that he clearly envisioned as the future county seat. No doubt by previous arrangement, Morris (whose daughter married Ellis's son and whose wife was Wells's sister) proposed a nonexistent entity as the county seat, offering 150 acres to locate the county offices and to develop the town. On March 21, 1806, by legislative act, Wellsborough was founded and simultaneously named as Tioga County's capital.

The naming of the town stirs controversy among locals to this day. One romantic version maintains that Benjamin Morris named the town in honor of his wife, Mary Wells Morris, who arrived with her children in 1805 and remained until her death in 1819. Another more rational version argues that the town was named for the entire Wells family, including Mary's brothers, the influential Gideon Hill Wells, and the town's first leader, William Hill Wells. The latter view is favored by Wellsboro's historians; nevertheless, a life-size bronze statue commemorating Mary Wells Morris was unveiled next to the Robinson House on May 20, 2009.

William Hill Wells returned to Delaware after only three years living in Delmar Township. Although he was the first resident attorney in Tioga County, representing Yankees who were fighting Pennsylvanians' claims on their land, older hostilities may have driven Wells back to Delaware. Local historians generally describe the clash between the Yankees and the "Southerners" as a conflict over land and, later, political power. However, long-standing animosity between the Puritan settlers of New England and the Quakers who settled in Delaware, Maryland, and southeastern Pennsylvania likely contributed to the tension.

Although both groups were of British stock, they carried with them to America radically different ideas about religion, rank, and material wealth. Bluntly stated, the Puritans loathed the Quakers, as did the Anglican Virginians. Fischer states, "However inoffensive the Society of Friends may seem today, they were genuinely hated in their own time as dangerous radicals, disturbers of the peace, and pious frauds and hypocrites who were said to 'pray for their fellow men one day a week, and on them the other six'" (quoting Joshua Evans's 1795 journal). Denominational differences created a deep cultural divide that survived long after the original religious purposes had been forgotten.

Bloodshed and ill will between the two groups lingered into Wellsboro's early history and even beyond. The matter was officially settled in favor of the Pennsylvanians by the Decree of Trenton in 1782, but history suggests that William Hill Wells departed the town that he helped build because a "coolness" had grown up between him and the Yankees he represented. One night, the Wells home was fired upon, an incident that likely caused Wells to return to Delaware. Further evidence of the pernicious effects of the rift can be found in the following remarks included in Josiah Emery's 1879 *Reminiscences* about Wellsboro in the 1820s:

> The Yankees claimed to be the practical element, and preserved among themselves a kind of brotherhood, a 'hail fellow well met' spirit, shook hands heartily, and each one considered himself equal to or no worse than his neighbor. Those who had got it into their heads that those down-country people were aristocratic accused them of being a little too exclusive, of reaching out two fingers for a Yankee to shake, and of thinking of himself as good and a little better than his neighbor, especially if the neighbor happened to be a Yankee.

The complete story of Wellsboro's founding and development has been well told by numerous authors, most recently by Scott Gitchell, director of the Tioga County Historical Society, in the 2008 *Wellsboro Pennsylvania: The First Two Hundred Years, 1806–2006*. Four years earlier, the Tioga County Historical Society Bicentennial Committee published a companion volume, *Tioga County Pennsylvania: The First Two Hundred Years*. Other important references include the 1883 and 1897 histories of Tioga County, both of which inform later accounts written by the Honorable Charles Tubbs in 1909 and the Honorable Charles Webb in 1965. Blossburg newspaperman John Sexton Jr. published numerous articles during the 1870s and 1880s, including those that appear as supplements to the *Elmira Gazette*. Additional resources are listed in the bibliography.

One

WELLSBOROUGH 1805–1894

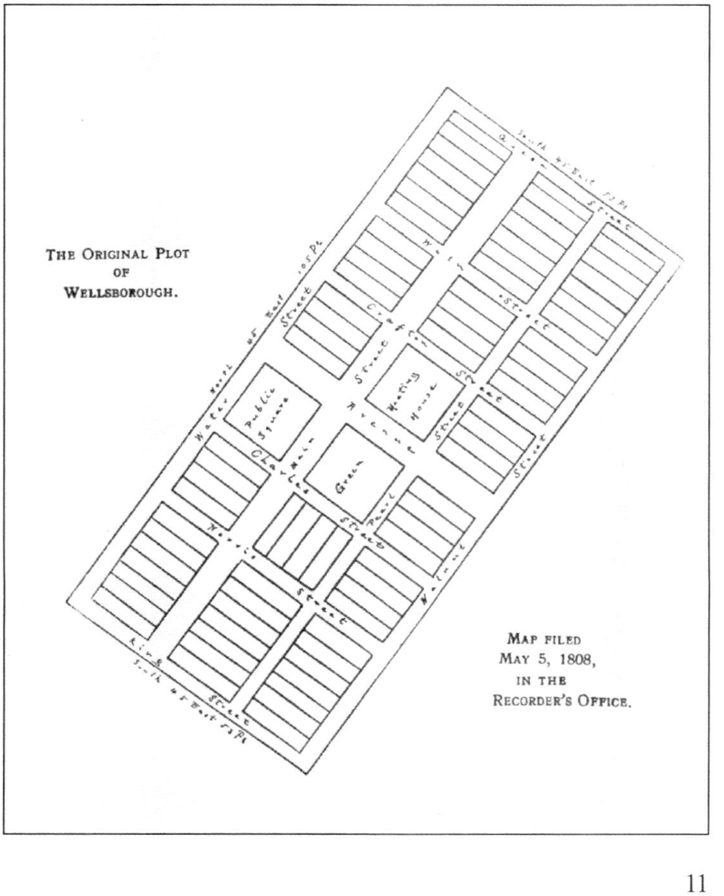

ORIGINAL PLOT. The Pennsylvania legislature created Wellsborough on March 21, 1806. In 1909, Tioga County historian Charles Tubbs described the original plot, surveyed in 1805 by John Norris, as a "town entirely on paper . . . the only gash through the swaying treetops was made by the new State road. Not one of its streets . . . had upon it a single human habitation."

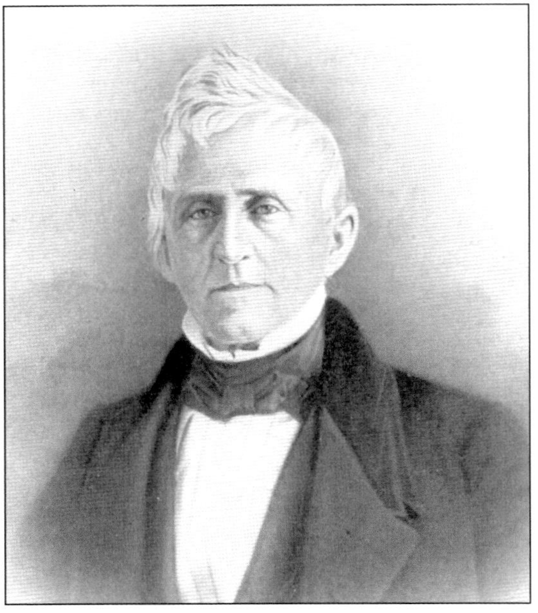

SAMUEL WELLS MORRIS (1786–1847). In 1805, Philadelphia Quakers Benjamin and Mary Wells Morris settled with 19-year-old Samuel and 16-year-old Rebecca on a knoll overlooking the town they envisioned below. Their two-story "Mansion House," constructed of hewed logs, served as the post office, with Samuel Morris becoming postmaster in 1808. After this landmark cabin burned, Morris, now a Princeton-educated judge, replaced it with an impressive frame house built by Alexander J. Brown in 1832.

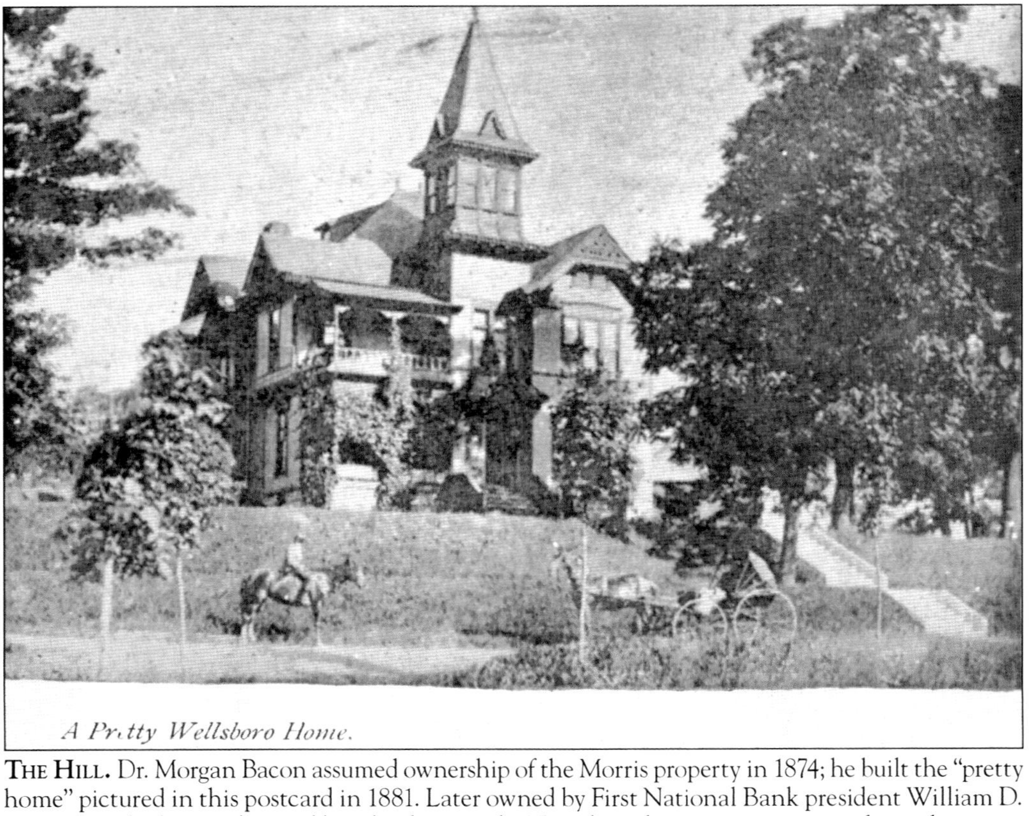

A Pretty Wellsboro Home.

THE HILL. Dr. Morgan Bacon assumed ownership of the Morris property in 1874; he built the "pretty home" pictured in this postcard in 1881. Later owned by First National Bank president William D. VanHorn, the house changed hands often until 1950, when the new owners transformed it into a convalescent home. Today known as the "Shared Home," this lovely Victorian remains standing on what was known as "the Hill," at the intersection of Bacon Street and Morris Lane.

William Bache (1771–1845). Early settlers included several accomplished men, among them Benjamin Morris, John Norris, and William Bache. These individuals set a cultural tone for Wellsboro, identifiable yet today. Bache, born in 1771 in Worcestershire, England, joined relatives in Philadelphia in 1793, established himself as a profiler and perfected his art using his patented physiognotrace, a type of profiling machine. Influenced by Norris, Bache purchased tracts of land in northern Pennsylvania and moved with his wife, Anna Page Bache, to Wellsborough in 1812. He established a general store, operated a whiskey distillery near the northwest corner of Water and Nichols Streets, and served as postmaster from 1822 to 1845. While chopping fuel for a friend, Bache crushed his right arm, thus ending his artistic career. His exquisite silhouettes survive today in the Smithsonian Museum; in the Peabody Essex Museum, in Salem, Massachusetts; and in private collections.

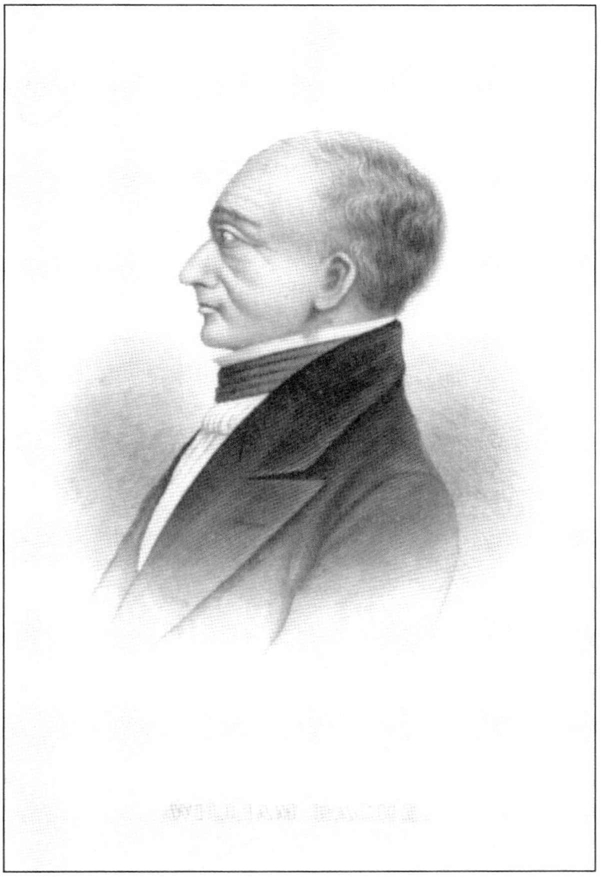

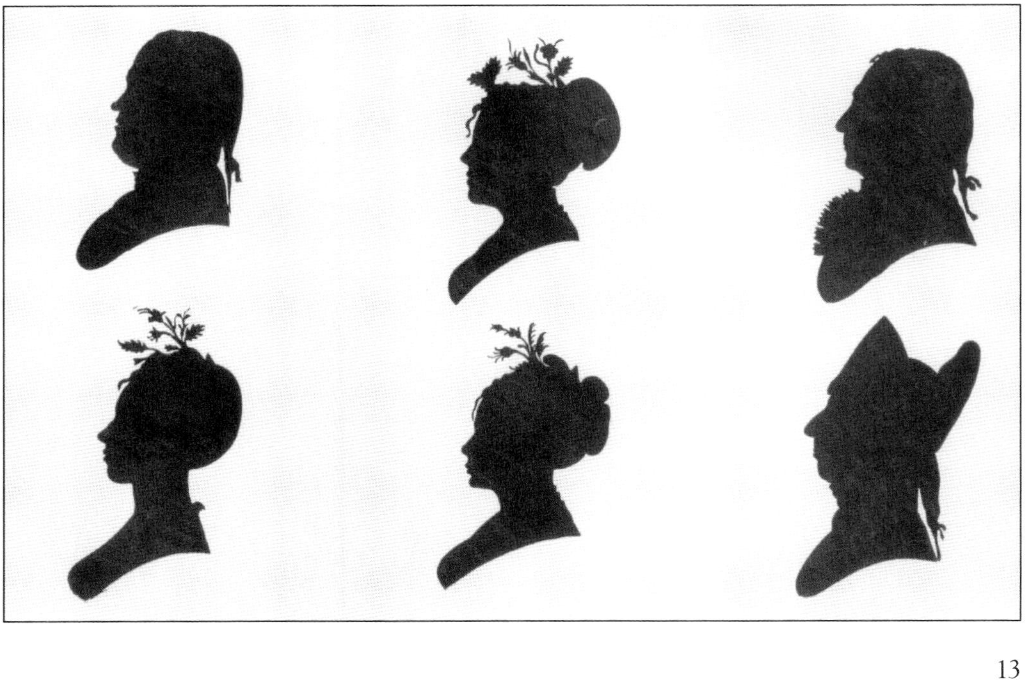

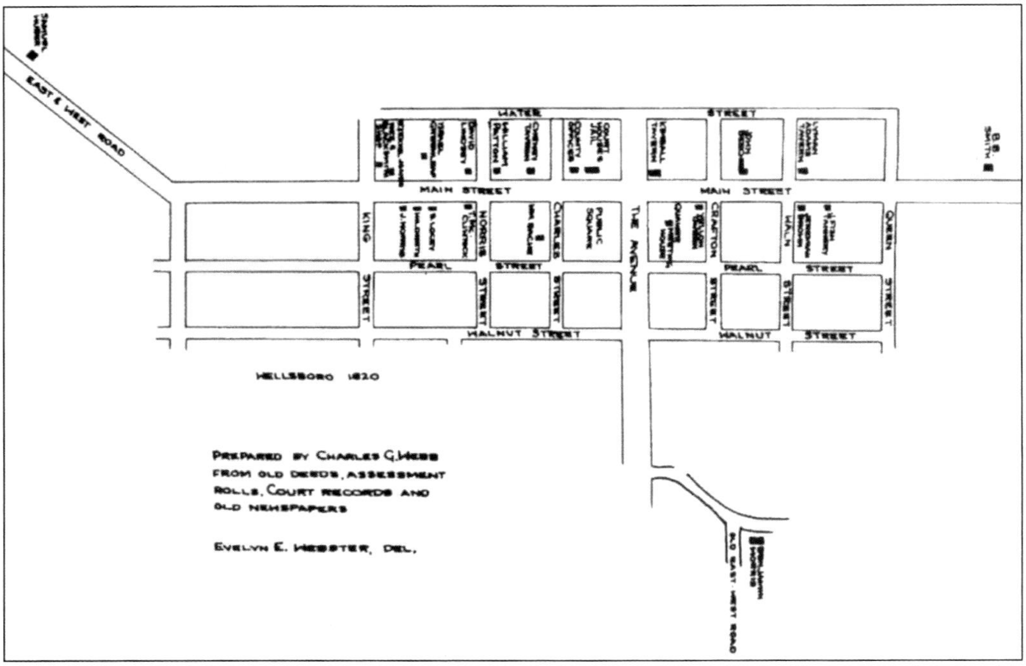

BEGINNINGS. Wellsborough, the county seat, built a log courthouse and jail in 1813, despite the difficulty of procuring nails during the War of 1812. By 1816, fewer than 50 people, living in simple frame houses and log cabins clustered within three blocks of Main Street between Central Avenue and King Street, called Wellsborough home. The town also boasted a county office building, a Quaker Meeting House, and a tavern, although standing timber remained on Pearl Street, Walnut Street, and the Green until about 1818. An influx of German and Swiss settlers arrived in 1819, among them a number of skilled craftspeople. Town leaders successfully lobbied the Pennsylvania General Assembly to establish an educational academy, approved on March 25, 1817, which added greatly to the town's prestige. The former St. Peter's Catholic Church on Pearl Street contains what remains of the original building. Mary Wells Morris died in 1819, was buried in Wellsborough's first cemetery (located alongside the academy), and was later moved to the Wellsboro Cemetery on Nichols Street.

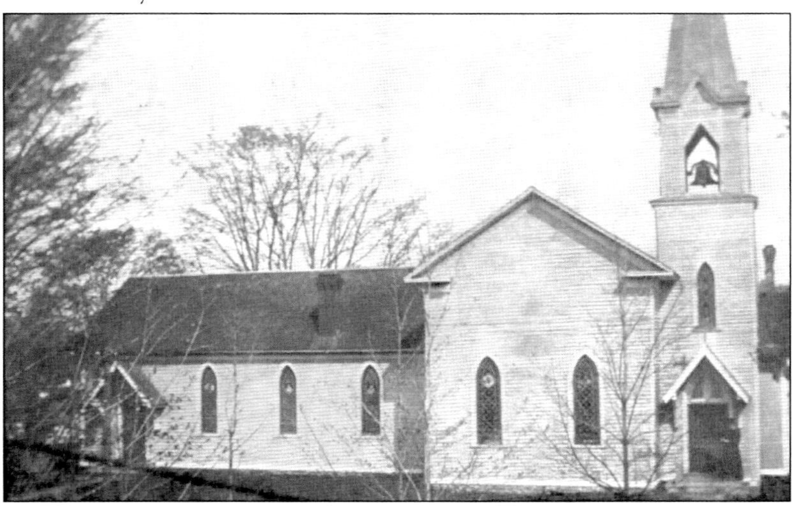

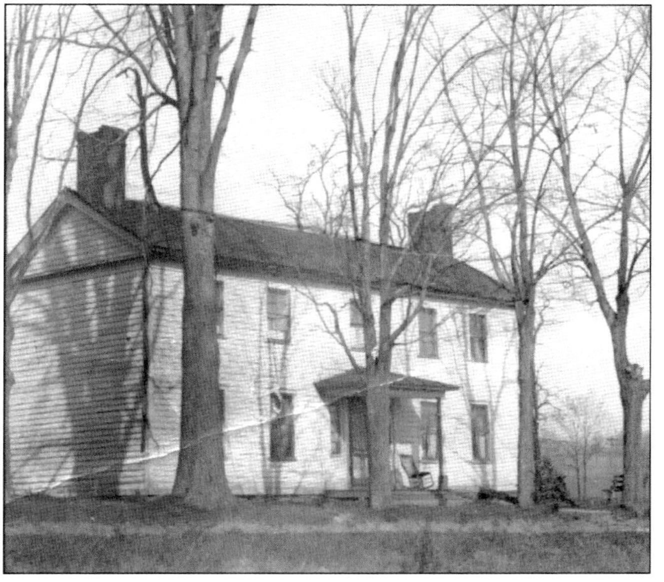

STAGE COACH INN. In 1821, an enterprising Swiss immigrant, Xavier Miller, built a tavern and a stagecoach inn on the far west side of town. Although Miller's intemperance led to loss of his liquor license in 1831, the foundation of his inn survived. The spot later became a popular location for community events, including square dances and the circus. Today, the Old Wellsboro Inn operates at 100 West Avenue, and each of the guest rooms carries the name of a family who once lived there: Miller, Dickinson, Smith, Chadderon, and Niles. (Courtesy Smith-Freeman family.)

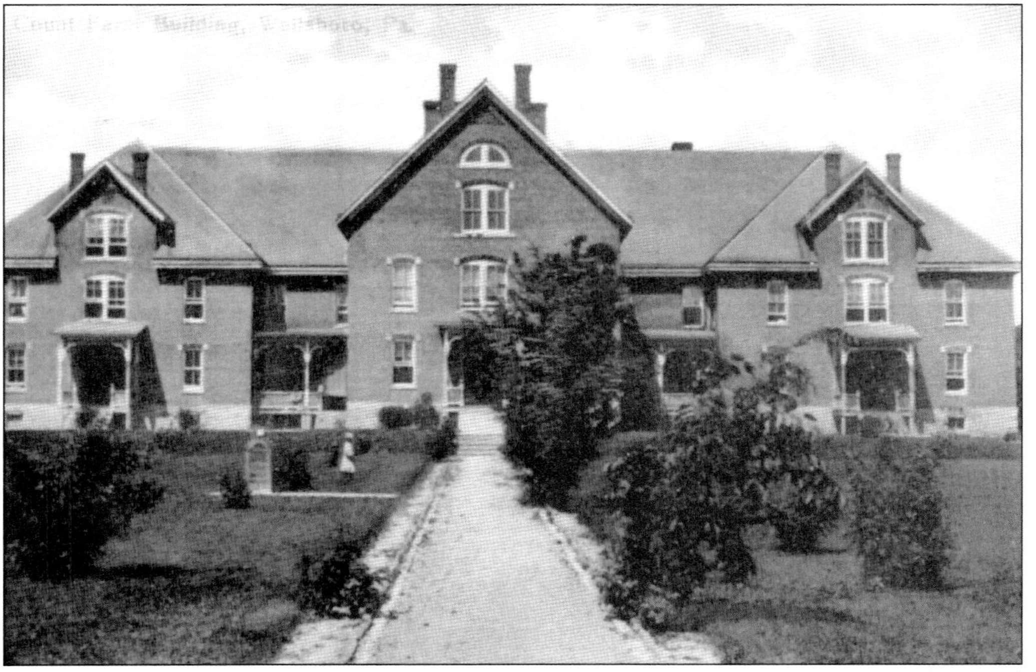

COUNTY FARM. On March 12, 1866, the legislature appointed commissioners to purchase real estate for a county farm to house the indigent, erect suitable buildings, and assess a poor tax. The commissioners purchased 25 acres from Caleb Austin in Charleston Township, later increasing the farm to 315 acres. The original brick structure was replaced in 1888 with the building pictured. A separate edifice was provided for the "insane poor." County commissioner Willard "Dud" Smith constructed Broad Acres following Hurricane Agnes in 1972.

Remodeled Portrait and Eagle (1809–1836)

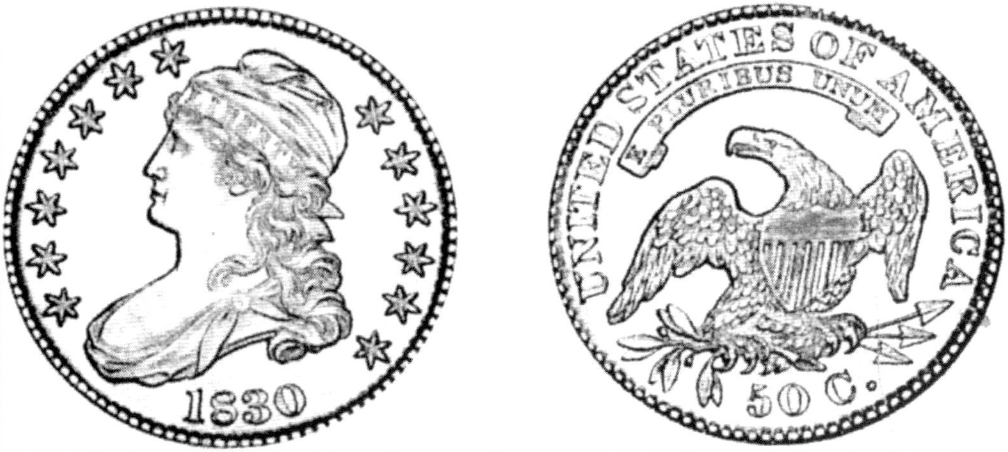

Incorporation. On March 16, 1830, the legislature incorporated Wellsborough as a borough, the first in Tioga County, marking "the end of the beginning." In 1965, Judge Charles Webb summarized the town ordinances, the first of which chose "the Eagle side of an American half-dollar" as the corporate seal of the borough "until an appropriate seal could be obtained." Other ordinances related to horse racing, livestock in the streets, road maintenance, and firing guns within the borough. In December 1894, *Wellsborough* became *Wellsboro* to comply with postal regulations whereby all communities ending in "borough" were shortened to "boro."

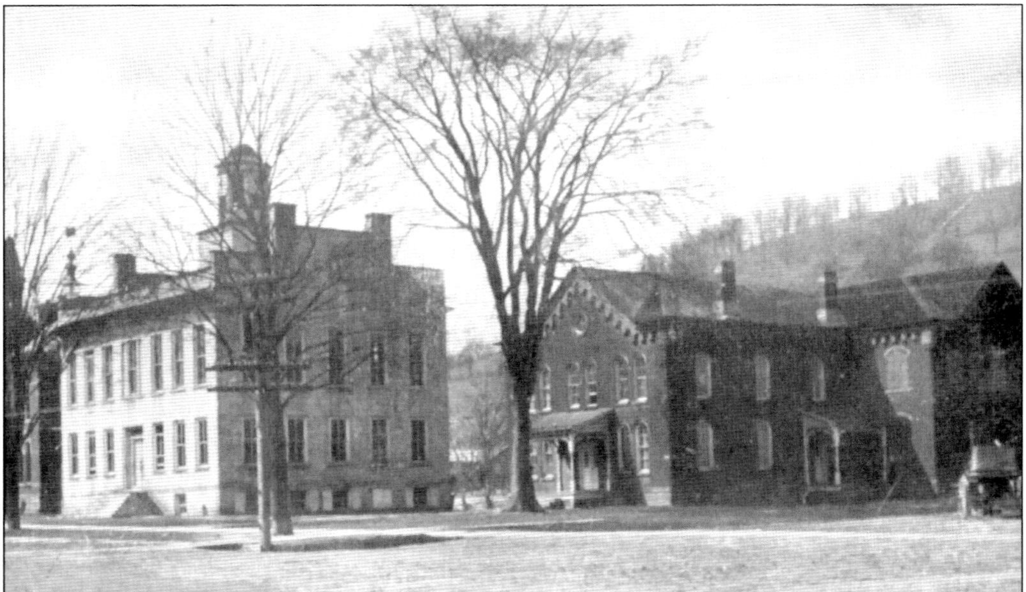

Tioga County Buildings. As the county seat, Wellsborough built a log courthouse and jail between 1813 and 1814 on the public square. Construction of its replacement, made of native sandstone, took place in 1835; the new jail followed in 1860. A local historian described a nearby elm, shown here in 1910, as the "living witness to the entire recorded history of Wellsboro." The Jailhouse Elm remains standing today on Courthouse Square.

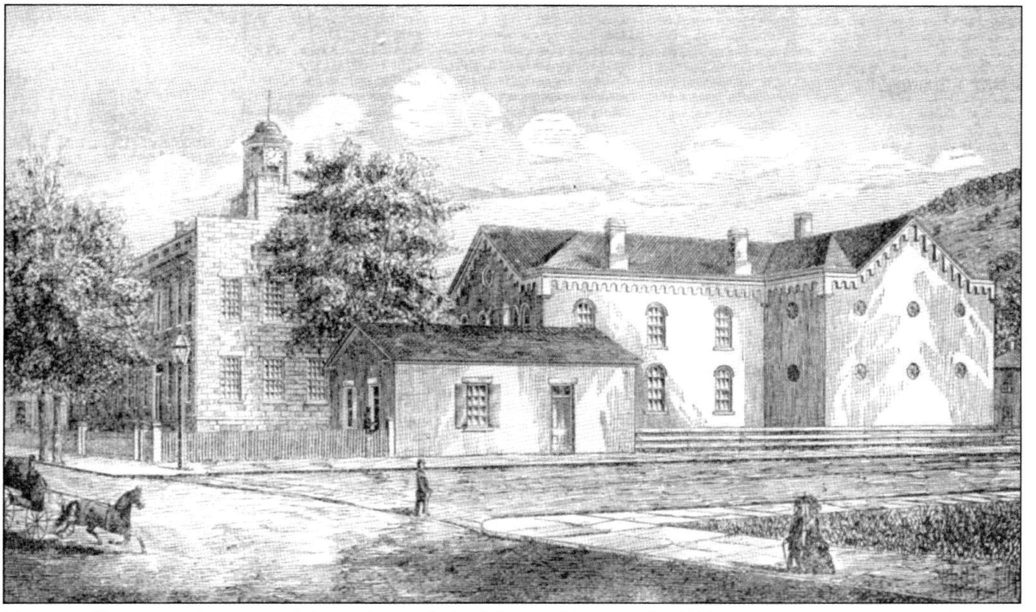

PUBLIC RECORDS STOLEN. This view of the Tioga County buildings appears in a supplement to the *Elmira Gazette* written by John Sexton in 1873. Sexton describes the "great excitement" that ensued following the 1828 theft of the county records in Wellsborough. The records were eventually found, concealed in a hollow log, about a mile east of the borough. Sexton points out that "the excitement . . . awakened the people . . . to the necessity of erecting more substantial and safe depositories for their public records."

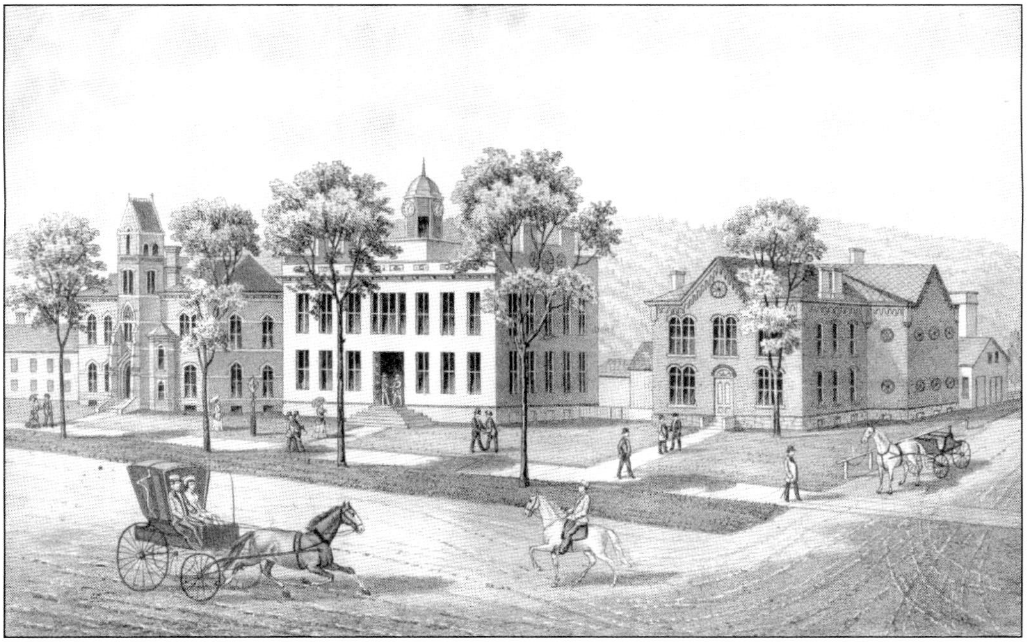

1883 COURTHOUSE SQUARE. The *History of Tioga County 1804–1883* opens with this view of the county buildings, which shows the county office building, built in 1882 to the left of the courthouse. The Tioga County Courthouse Annex replaced the building in 1975.

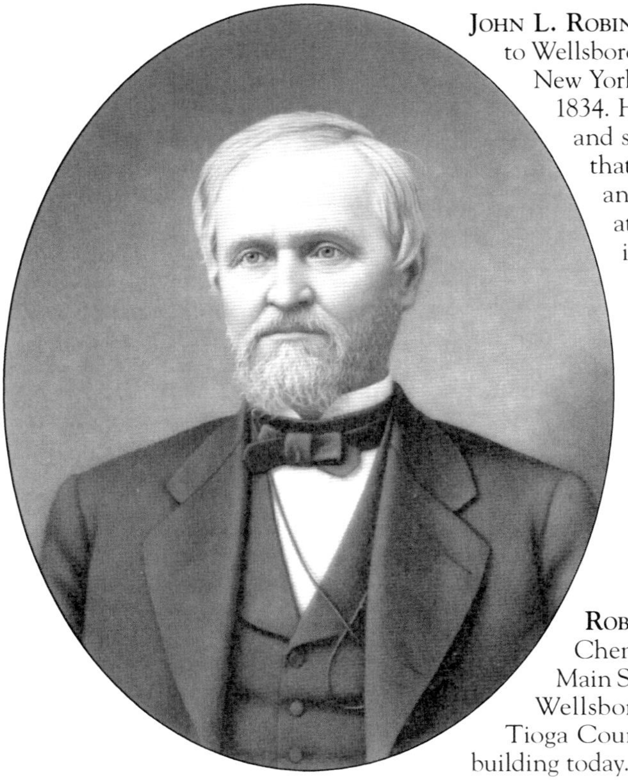

JOHN L. ROBINSON (1813–1893). Robinson moved to Wellsborough from Hartwick, Otsego County, New York, which his parents helped found, in 1834. He purchased the old Cheney Tavern and storehouse on Main Street, owned at that time by Samuel Dickinson. Robinson and his brother Chester operated a store at this site until lumbering caught their interest and in time secured their fortune. The Robinson brothers cofounded the First National Bank of Wellsborough in 1864, thirteen months after Congress passed the National Bank Act of 1863.

ROBINSON HOUSE. First owned by Alpheus Cheney, Tioga County's first sheriff, 120 Main Street is known as the Robinson House, Wellsborough home of J.L. Robinson. The Tioga County Historical Society occupies the building today.

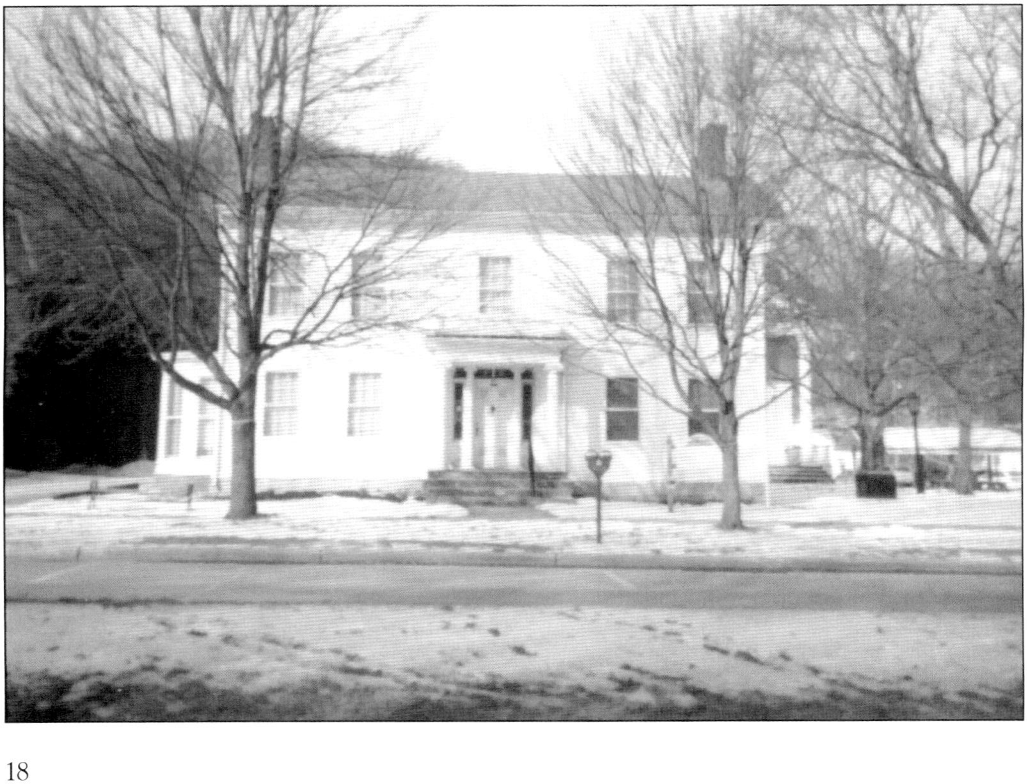

CHESTER ROBINSON (1807–1890). In 1835, Chester Robinson joined his brother John in Wellsborough. Over the course of his long life, Robinson accumulated an "ample fortune" as a merchant, lumberman, and banker. Cofounder and major stockholder of the First National Bank of Wellsborough, Robinson devoted his attention to its success, continuing to visit daily even after he retired in 1880.

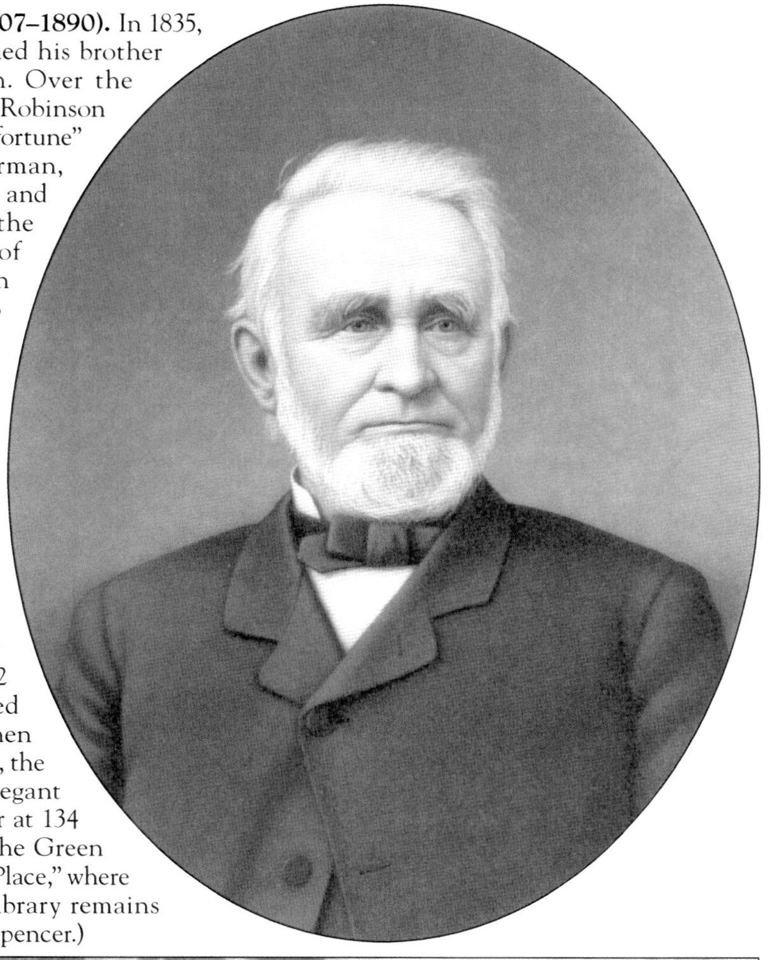

GREEN FREE LIBRARY. Mary "Mazie" Barbour Robinson, Chester Robinson's daughter, served as board president of Wellsboro's first library, endowed by Charles Green in 1912 and temporarily located at 97 Main Street. When she abruptly died in 1913, the library inherited the elegant home built by her father at 134 Main Street. In 1916, the Green Free moved to "Chester Place," where Wellsboro's beautiful library remains today. (Courtesy Mike Spencer.)

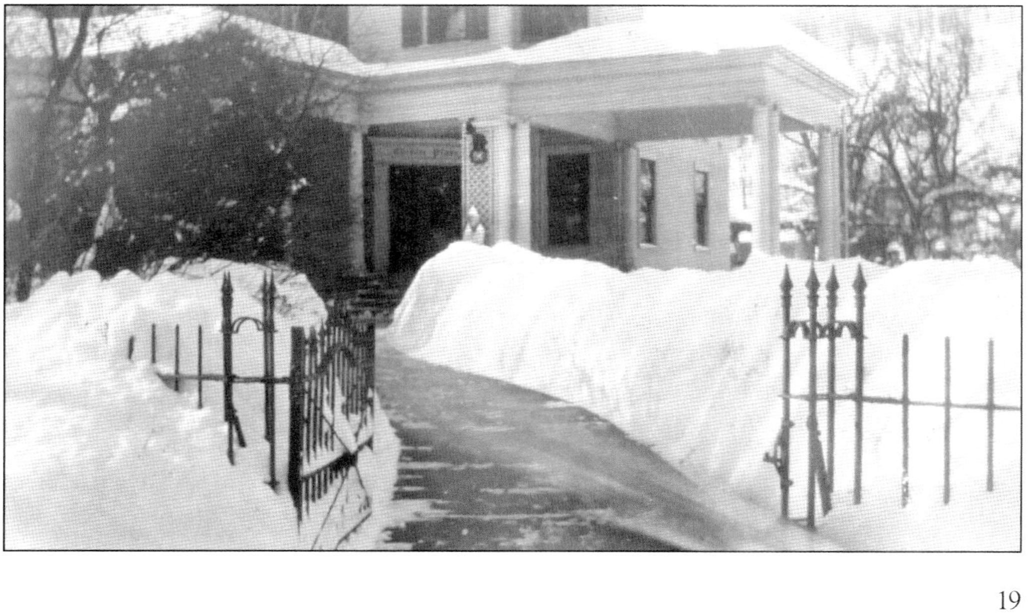

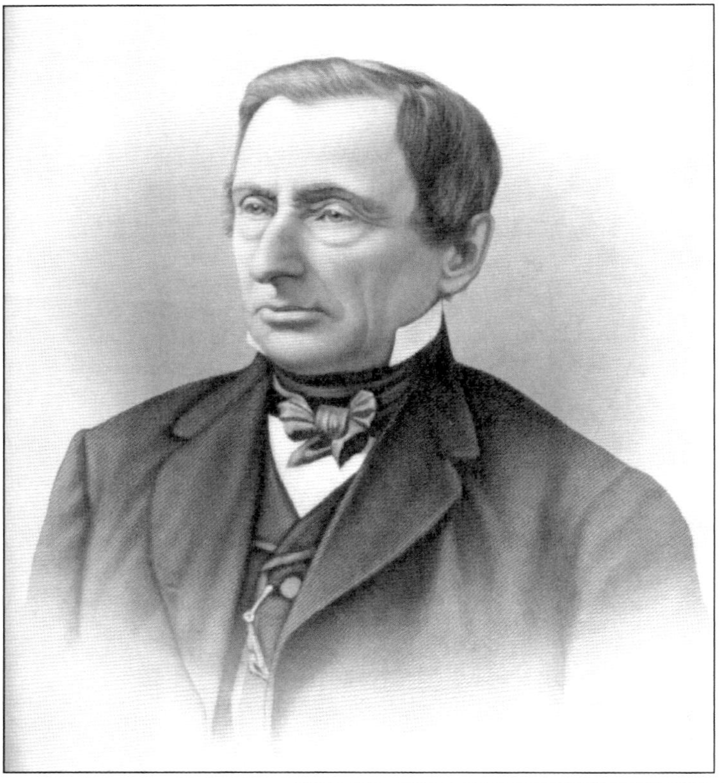

William Bache Jr. (1812–1900). Locally born and educated, Bache accumulated a fortune brokering land sales. He outlived three wives, all of whom were connected to Wellsborough's most affluent families. Bache served as treasurer of the Wellsboro Academy, borough treasurer, manager of the Lawrenceville and Wellsboro Plank Road Company, president of the First National Bank, and president of the Wellsboro Water Company, chartered in 1885. He also influenced construction of the 1870 Wellsboro' and Lawrenceville Railroad.

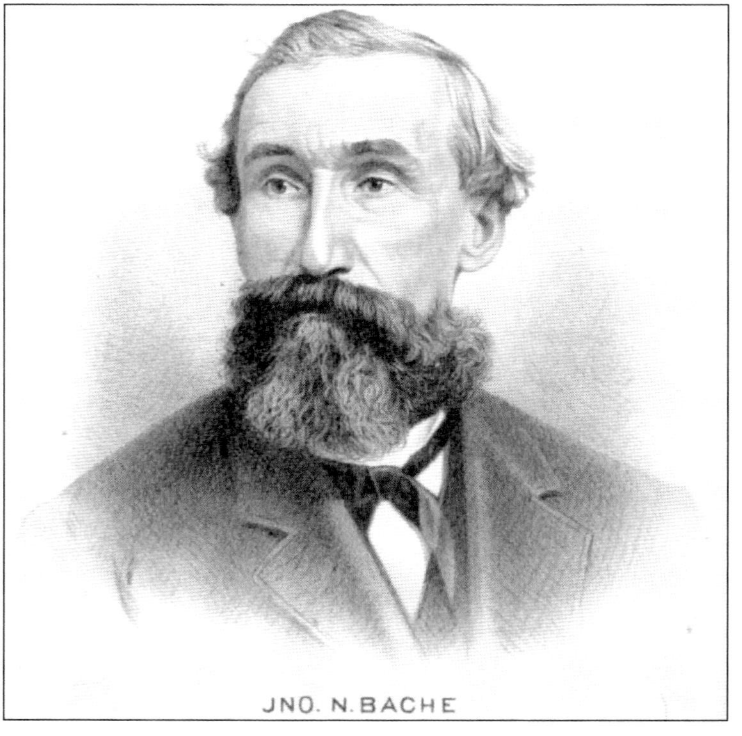

John Norris Bache (1820–1905). Born in the Charles Street log cabin built by his father, John Bache later attended Yale Law School. He was admitted to the Tioga County bar in 1849 but disliked jury trials. Instead, he involved himself in timber, coal, and geological explorations. He and his brother William alerted the Fall Brook Coal Company to the lands later known as the Antrim coalfields, the knowledge of which substantially increased the prosperity of Tioga County.

Henry Sherwood (1813–1896). On Christmas Day 1846, Sherwood moved to Wellsboro, where he was admitted to the bar in 1847. He personally paid expenses for enlisted soldiers traveling to the front during the Civil War. He helped found the Tioga County Agricultural Society in 1854. Sherwood was elected to Congress as a Democrat in 1870. He also advocated for the Wellsboro' & Lawrenceville Railroad, serving as president until its completion in 1872.

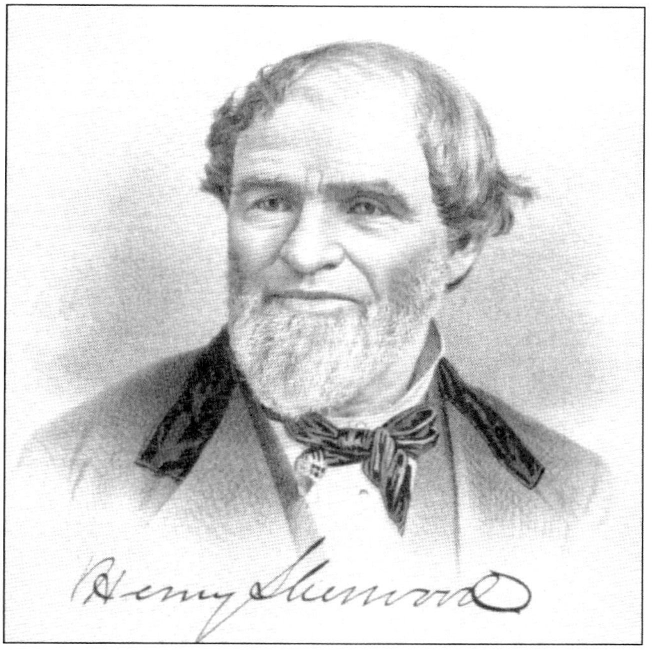

(No. 102.)

WELLSBORO' AND LAWRENCEVILLE.

[For the financial year ending December 31, 1870.]

State of Pennsylvania, }
Tioga County, } ss:

Personally appeared Henry Sherwood, president, and James Heron, treasurer, of the Wellsboro' and Lawrenceville railroad company, and in due form of law made oath, that the statements in the within report are true, to the best of their knowledge and belief.

(Signed) HENRY SHERWOOD, *President.*
JAMES HERON, *Treasurer.*

Sworn and subscribed before me, this }
30th day of January, 1871. }

CHARLES F. VEIL, *Associate Judge.*

Stock and Debt.

Capital stock as authorized by law	$1,000,000 00
Amount of stock subscribed	1,000,000 00
Total amount now paid in of capital stock	248,980 00
Number of shares of stock issued	20,000
Par value of each share	$50 00
Amount paid in on each share	12 44

Cost of Road and Equipment.

	By present report.
Construction, (expended to 1st January, 1871,)	$154,000 00

Characteristics of Road.

The road is in process of construction. There are about 13 miles graded. The masonry of five bridges is completed. About three-fourths of a mile is laid with iron. The work of grading, &c., is now being proceeded with under contract, and the superstructure will be completed by the company's own men.

Wellsboro' & Lawrenceville Railroad. By 1867, Wellsborough citizens began to agitate for a railroad from Lawrenceville to Wellsborough "to overcome the inconveniences of her isolated location." Civil engineer Anton Hardt undertook the survey on September 23, 1867; influential citizens rallied to ensure rapid completion of the project. The first train arrived on December 9, 1871. According to a 19th-century historian, the community celebration on May 22, 1872, punctuated by cannon booms from Fellows Hill, was "a proud day for Wellsboro . . . her cup of pleasure and delight was overflowing."

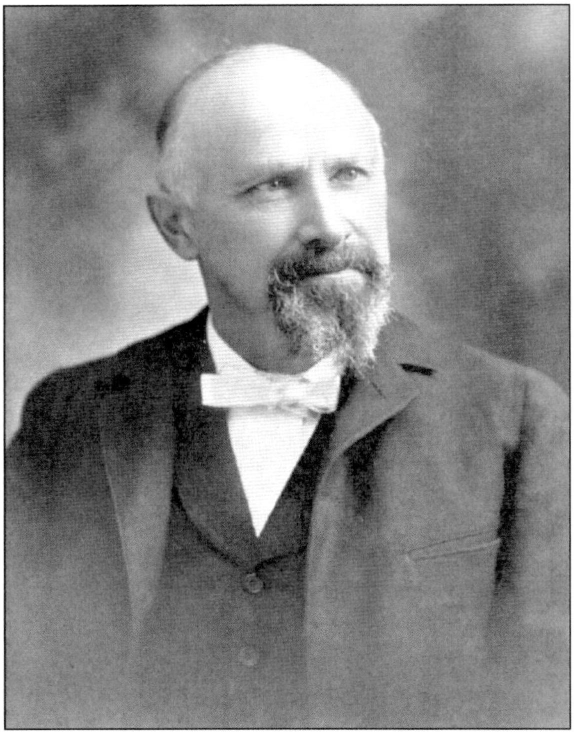

ANTON HARDT (1839–1923). Hardt immigrated to the United States from Austria in 1865, finding employment first as a civil engineer in Williamsport, Pennsylvania. After conducting the survey for the Wellsboro' & Lawrenceville Railroad, he worked for the Fall Brook Coal Company, becoming superintendent of mines at Fall Brook and Antrim. He was elected chief engineer of the Pine Creek Railroad in 1882.

PINE CREEK RAILWAY COMPANY.

Operated by New York Central and Hudson River Railroad Company.
Date of organization: February 17, 1870.
Under laws of what government or state organized: State of Pennsylvania, page 149, pamphlet laws.

DIRECTORS.

Names.	Official Address.	Names.	Official Address.
Wm. K. Vanderbilt, ...	New York, N. Y.	Albert F. Kelly, ...	Philadelphia, Pa.
Chauncey M. Depew, ..	"	Anson Hardt.	Wellsboro, Pa.
H. McK. Twombly, ...	"	George F. Baer, ...	Reading, Pa.
John Magee, ...	Watkins, N. Y.	F. E. Herriman, ...	Philadelphia, Pa.
M. E. Olmsted, ...	Harrisburg, Pa.	W. D. Kelly, ...	"
Charles Miller, ...	Franklin, Pa.	Samuel R. Callaway.	New York, N. Y.

Date of expiration of term: January 14, 1901.
Postoffice address of general office: Wellsboro, Pa.
Date of last meeting of stockholders for election of directors: January 8, 1900.

OFFICERS.

Title.	Name.	Official Address.
President, ...	Jefferson Harrison, ...	Wellsboro, Pa.
Vice President, ...	John Magee, ...	Corning, N. Y.
Secretary and Treasurer, ...	E. V. W. Rossiter, ...	Grand Central S'n., N. Y.

PROPERTY LEASED OR OTHERWISE ASSIGNED FOR OPERATION.

Name.	Terminals.		By what Company Operated.	Under what kind of contract operated.	Miles of line.
	From—	To—			
Pine Creek Railway Company.	Stokesdale Jct., Pa.	Newberry Jct., Pa.	N. Y. C. & H. R. R. R. Co.	Lease, ...	74.8

PINE CREEK RAILWAY REPORT. The Pine Creek route from Ansonia to Stokesdale Junction was effected in January 1882 with the election of Henry Sherwood, president; George Magee, vice president; Anton Hardt, chief engineer; and Cornelius Vanderbilt, treasurer. The road "runs through an exceedingly wild and romantic region, the Pine Creek canon not being excelled in natural grandeur by any other point touched by rail in the Allegheny Mountains."

Pine Creek Railway. Completed and opened June 4, 1883, the train traveled from Williamsport, up Pine Creek, to the mouth of Marsh Creek through Big Meadows to Stokesdale Junction, where it connected with the Corning, Cowanesque & Antrim Railway. The operators once boasted, "As remarkable as it may seem, the company has never killed a passenger." (Courtesy Mike Spencer.)

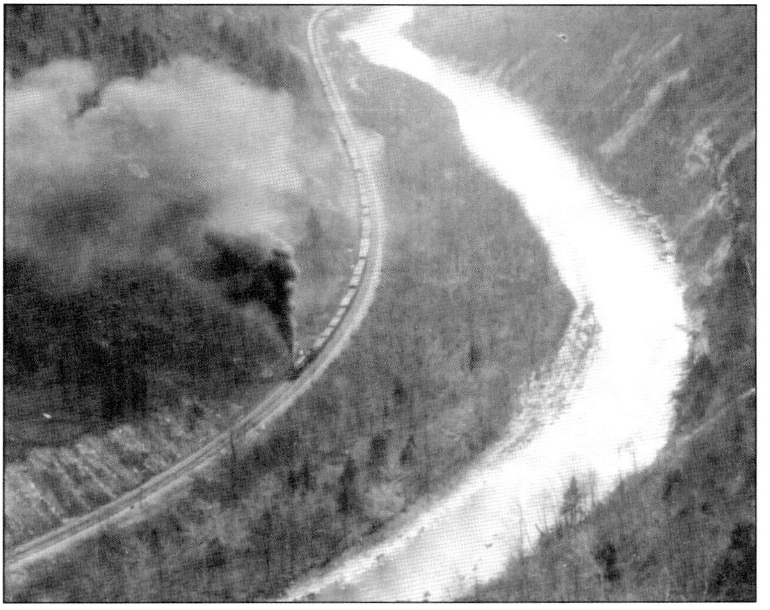

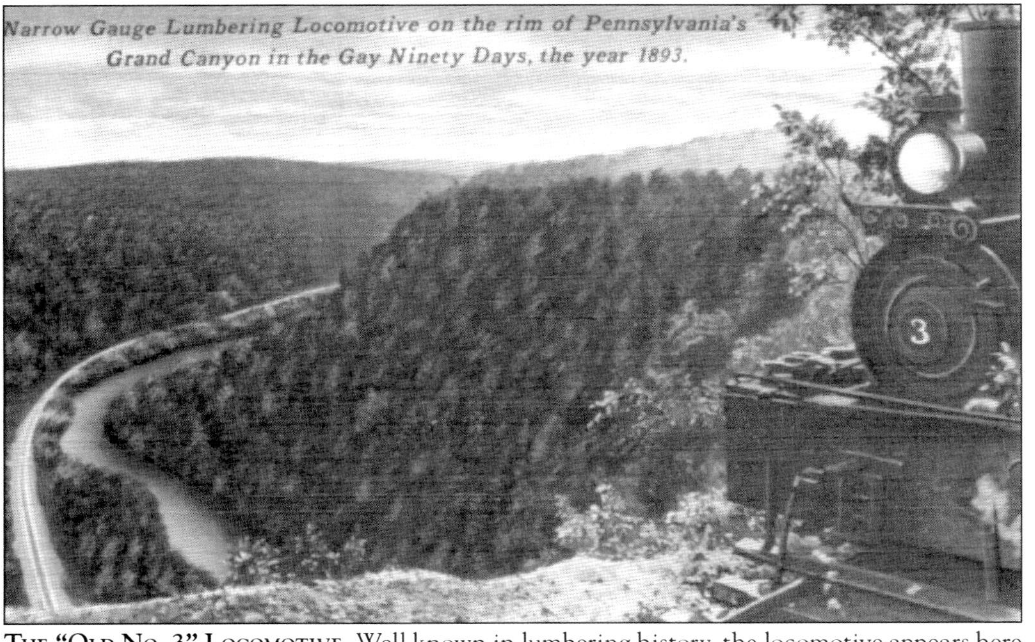

The "Old No. 3" Locomotive. Well known in lumbering history, the locomotive appears here on the west side of the canyon just north of the entrance to Colton Point State Park. In 1893, switchback narrow-gauge railroads operated throughout the mountains as woodhicks removed timber from the virgin forests.

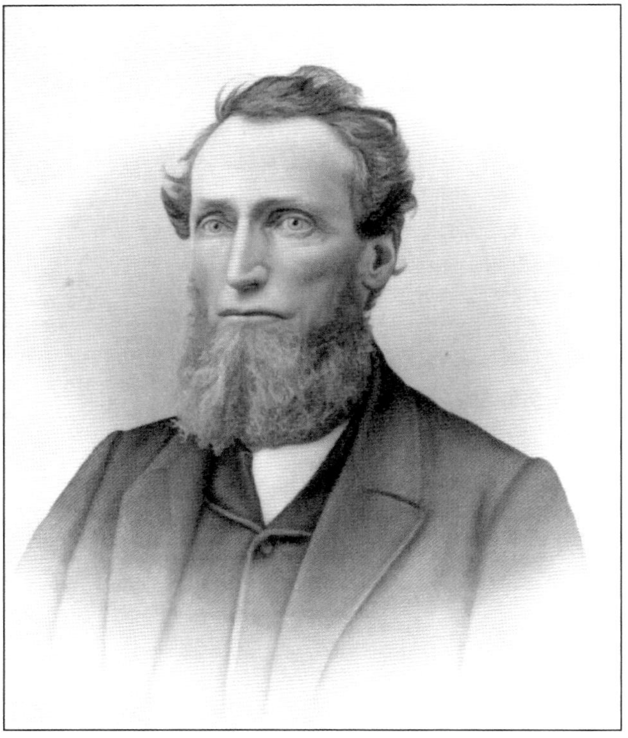

Nelson Packer (1814–1883). After completing medical school in 1838, Nelson Packer moved to Wellsborough. Known as a storyteller with a fine sense of humor, Dr. Packer and his tall bay horse Bob soon became a welcome sight around town. During the Civil War, he served as an assistant surgeon, but, weakened by malaria, he was discharged early. Dr. Packer lived on upper Main Street, where he died on his birthday, February 8, 1883.

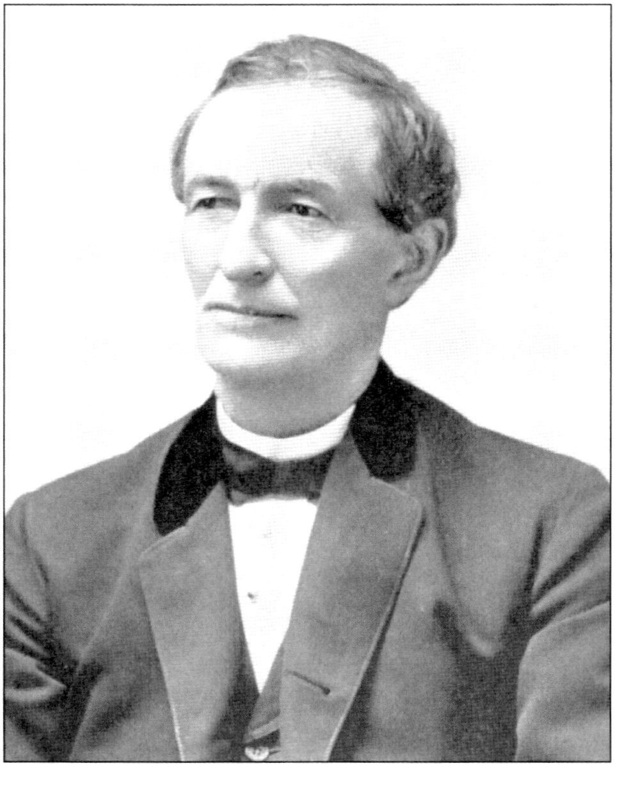

Robert Corson Cox (1823–1901). Brevetted brigadier general in 1865, Gen. R.C. Cox attained the highest rank of any man from Tioga County in the Civil War. Cox, in his 1897 pamphlet *Memories of the War*, describes the alacrity with which county men assembled in response to President Lincoln's call for volunteers. At the close of the war, his regiment observed Lee's surrender at Appomattox. General Cox's beloved horse, Banks, a gift from his regiment, was buried at his home, located on what is known locally as "the Island" behind the West End Market on Main Street, deeded to Fred and Lilia Williams in 1908. In 1872, Cox was elected prothonotary of Tioga County, an office that he held for many years.

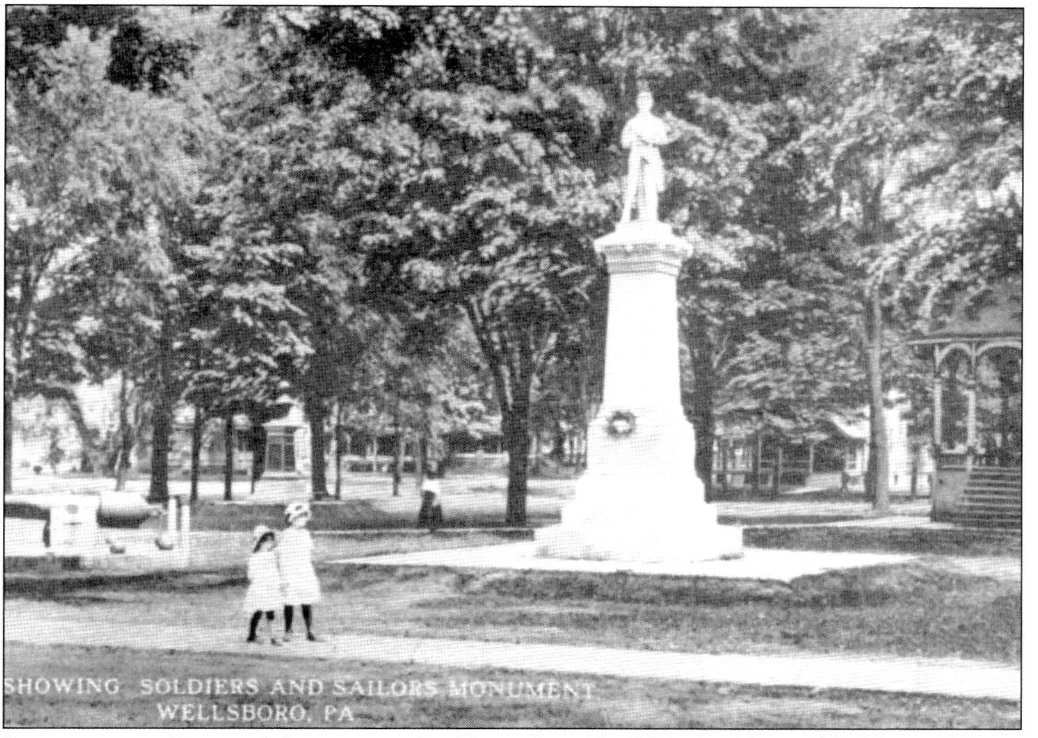

SOLDIERS AND SAILORS MONUMENT. On November 18, 1886, the Honorable Henry Warren Williams presented a memorial, made of Green Mountain granite and weighing 2,000 pounds, to those who died during the "War of Rebellion." The inscription reads, "It is noble to die for one's country." In 1917, Josephine Webb (Alexander) and Elizabeth Rees (Irwin) were photographed strolling past the monument.

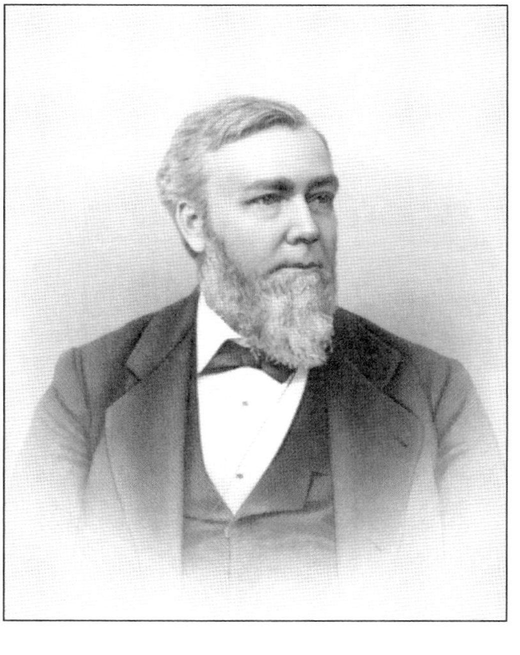

HENRY WARREN WILLIAMS (1830–1899). H.W. Williams was admitted to the bar in 1854, shortly after arriving in Wellsborough. An eloquent speaker, Williams rose rapidly from bar to bench, becoming president judge by 1871 and Pennsylvania Supreme Court justice by 1887. A devout Presbyterian, Williams supported numerous Christian organizations. His splendid brick residence, built in 1885 at 126 Main Street, is currently occupied by the Walrath and Coolidge Law Offices.

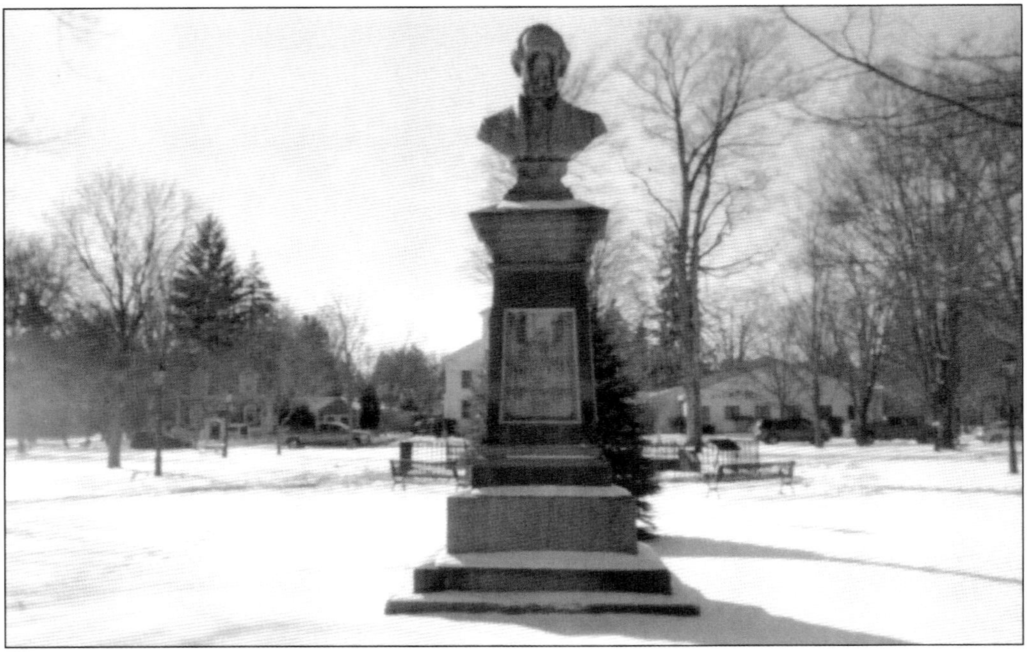

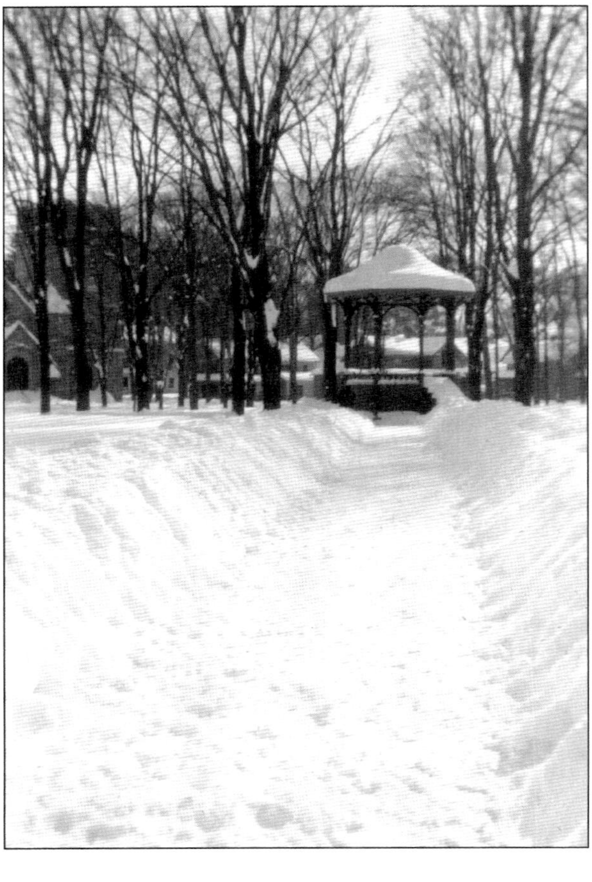

MAGEE MONUMENT. Wellsborough unveiled a memorial bust of John Magee, founder of the Fall Brook Coal Company and Railroad, in December 1886. Inscribed on the monument is the following: "The story of a useful and honored life may be told in these words: his energy and diligence compelled success, his ability and integrity won public confidence, his kindness and liberality drew to him the affectionate regard of rich and poor, permitte divis caetera [leave all else to the gods]."

PAGODA ON THE GREEN. The original design of the Green, graded in 1885, featured four diagonal paths leading to a walkway encircling the pagoda. Wellsborough bands performed in the bandstand; between 1910 and 1920, concerts occurred every Friday night. The St. Peter's Catholics often sold homemade ice cream at these events, giving Wellsborough's delighted children any ice cream that did not sell. (Courtesy Mike Spencer.)

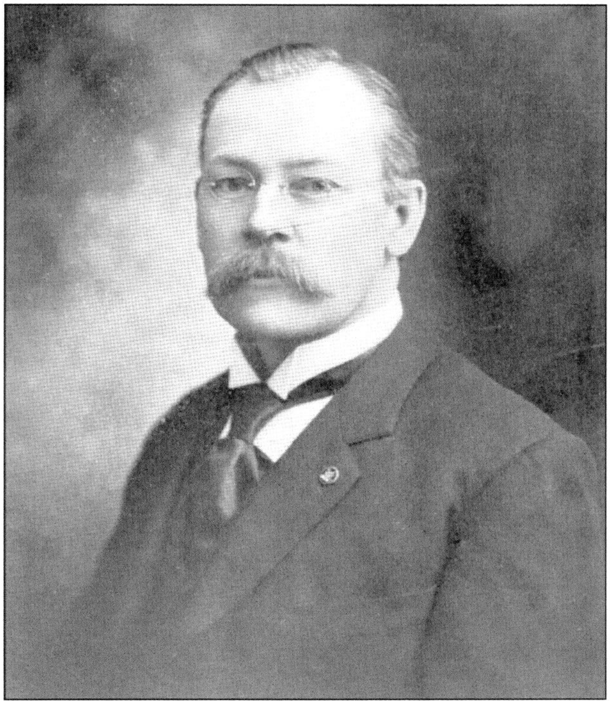

The Wellsborough Military Band. Frank A. Deans, affectionately known as "Pa" Deans, led local bands beginning in 1870. Under his direction, the Wellsborough Military Band achieved fame throughout the region, frequently winning first place at firemen's conventions. After Deans retired, William Woodhouse led the band for several years. Competition from moving pictures eventually led to the band's demise. (Below, courtesy TCHS.)

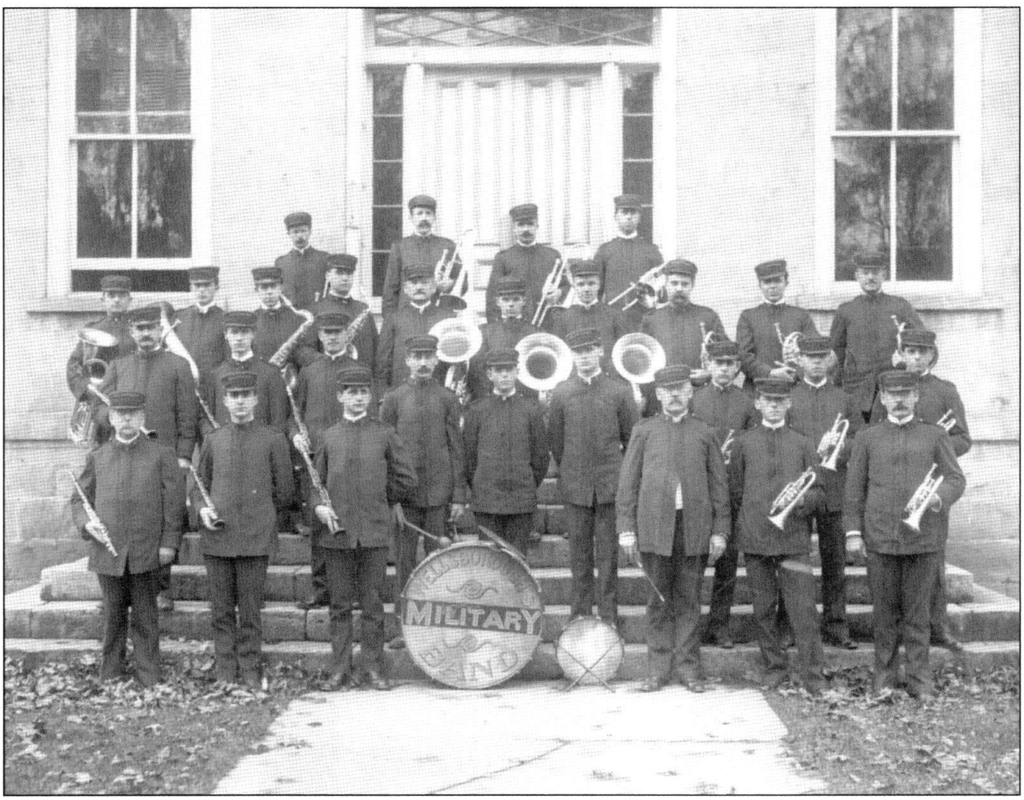

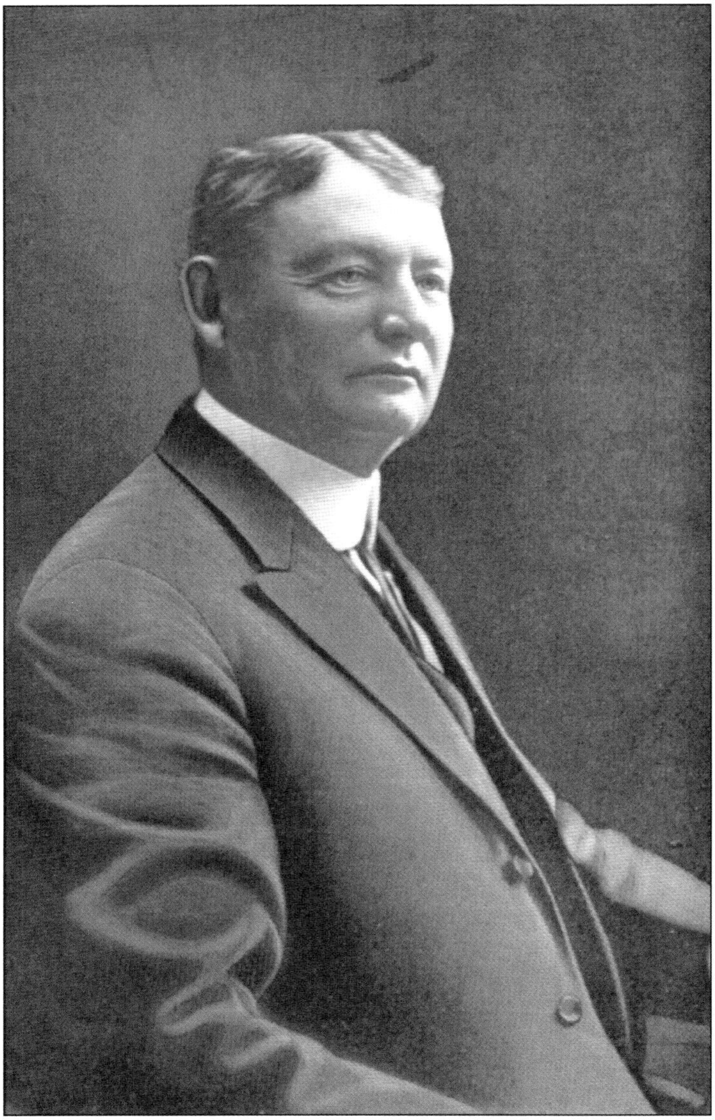

Horace Billings Packer (1851–1940). A Wellsborough native, educated at the academy and at Alfred University, Packer later studied law with Jerome B. Niles. Admitted to the bar in 1873, he shared the Central Avenue office of his mentor. Election to Congress in 1896 secured Packer's fame among Republicans in northern Pennsylvania. After the death of his father in 1883, he lived with his mother, Mary, at 137 Main Street. The Packer home was eventually divided, with each piece sold separately. In 1921, he deeded Packer Field, now the Horace Billings Packer Memorial Park, to Wellsboro. Although Packer wanted his estate to create a home for orphaned boys, his assets instead established the Horace B. Packer Foundation in 1951. The foundation has served innumerable civic purposes, including scholarships for Tioga County citizens.

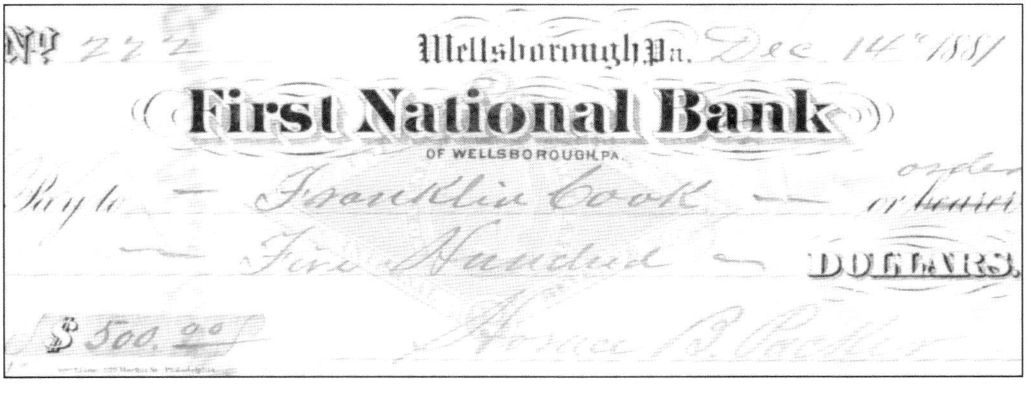

Two

WELLSBORO 1895–1925

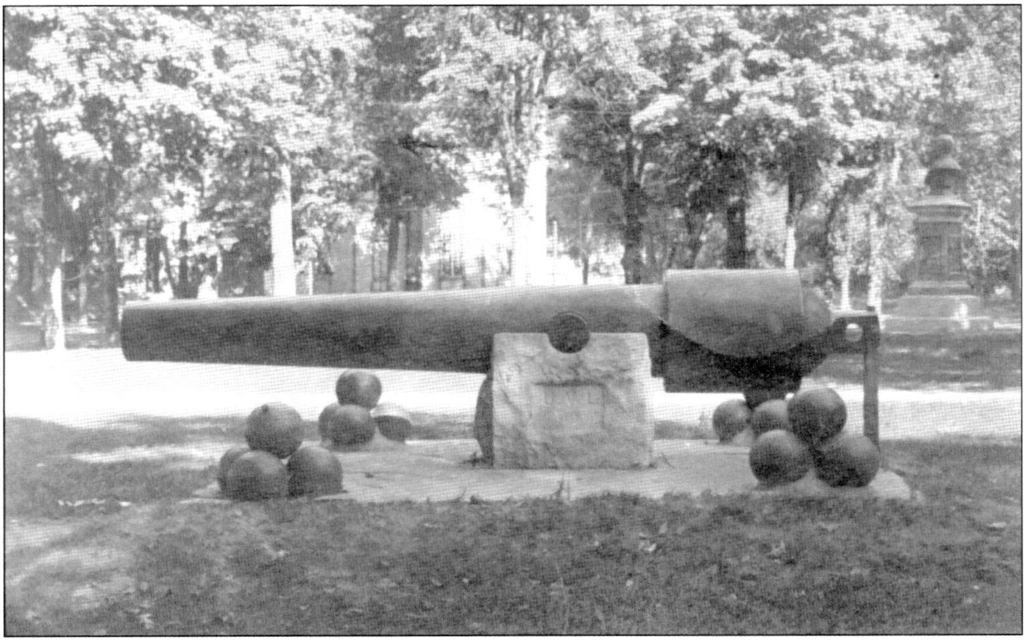

"CANON" ON THE GREEN. In 1897, Congressman Horace B. Packer procured an outdated cannon from West Point as a gift to Tioga County. Generations of Wellsboro children played with the cannon, including "firing" at the nearby Wilcox House. Balls weighing 175 pounds each, intended for a larger gun, surrounded the cannon. In 1942, Clyde Bailey persuaded the town to donate the gun to the war effort as scrap metal. The 9,732-pound cannon left by truck in September for Elmira, New York, later to become casings for the US Navy. The "canon" on the Green was never fired in battle.

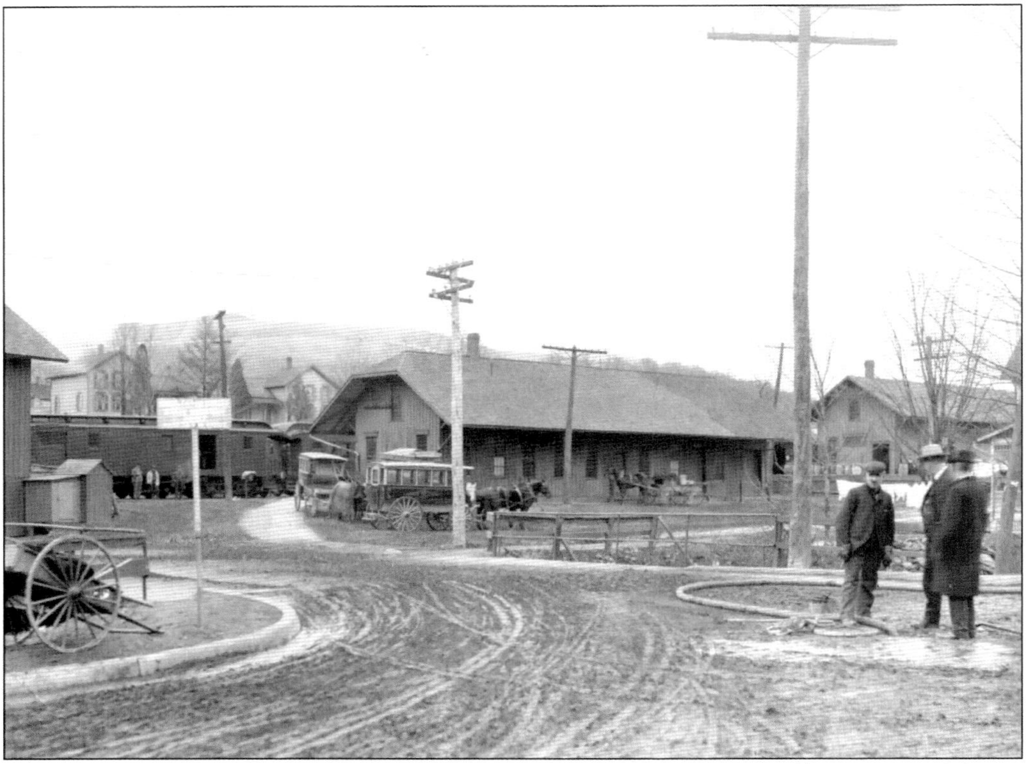

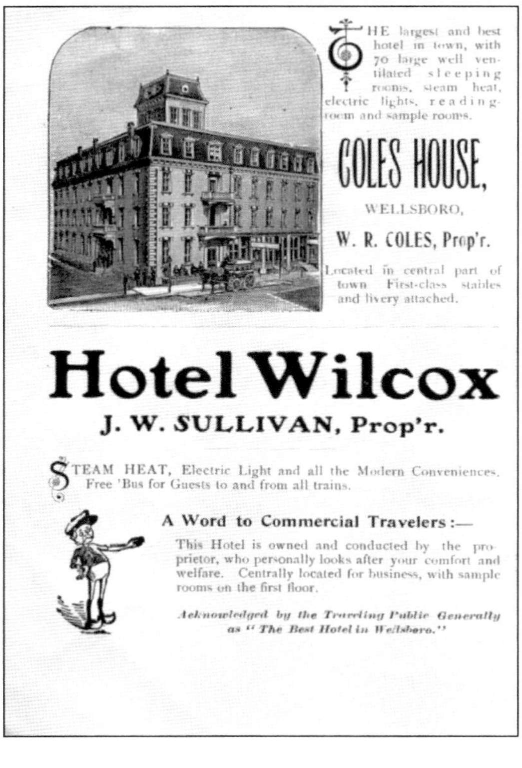

THE DEPOT. Erastus Fellows operated the Fellow's House (later the Farmer's Hotel) on Charleston Street from 1831 to 1870. The railroad company purchased a portion of Fellows's 160-acre farm and erected a depot, a freight house, a coal yard, and "neat and comfortable housing for their employees" nearby in about 1872. This postcard shows the depot soon after the line transitioned from the Fall Brook Coal Company to the New York Central in 1889. Note the horse-drawn hacks that conveyed passengers to local hotels. (Courtesy Donald Root.)

ADVERTISEMENT 1899. The Coles House opened in 1885, although various hostelries had previously occupied the site. Earlier businesses included the Adams Tavern (1820), Murphy's Tavern (1824), the United States House (1843), the Cone House (1869), the Holliday Inn (1873), and the Parkhurst House (1874). Clark Louis Wilcox and J.C. Wheeler built the Hotel Wilcox (later the Parkview Hotel) in 1875; a third floor was added in 1885.

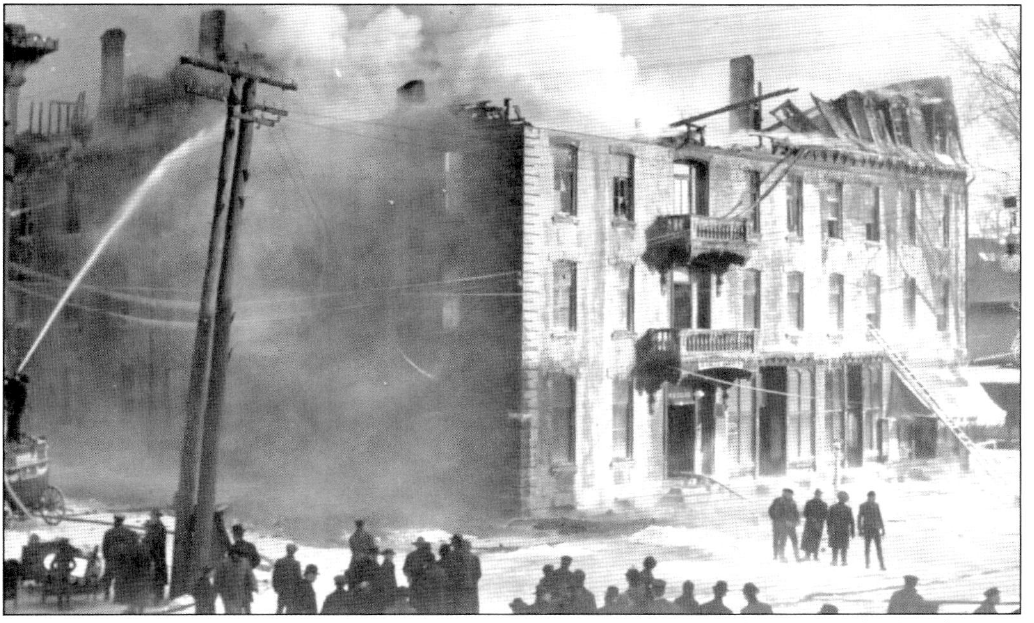

COLES HOUSE FIRE. On March 23, 1906, fire gutted the Coles House, destroying the fourth story. The frigid temperatures hampered firefighters, turning water to ice. The hotel's depot hack was used as a stand from which to fight the blaze.

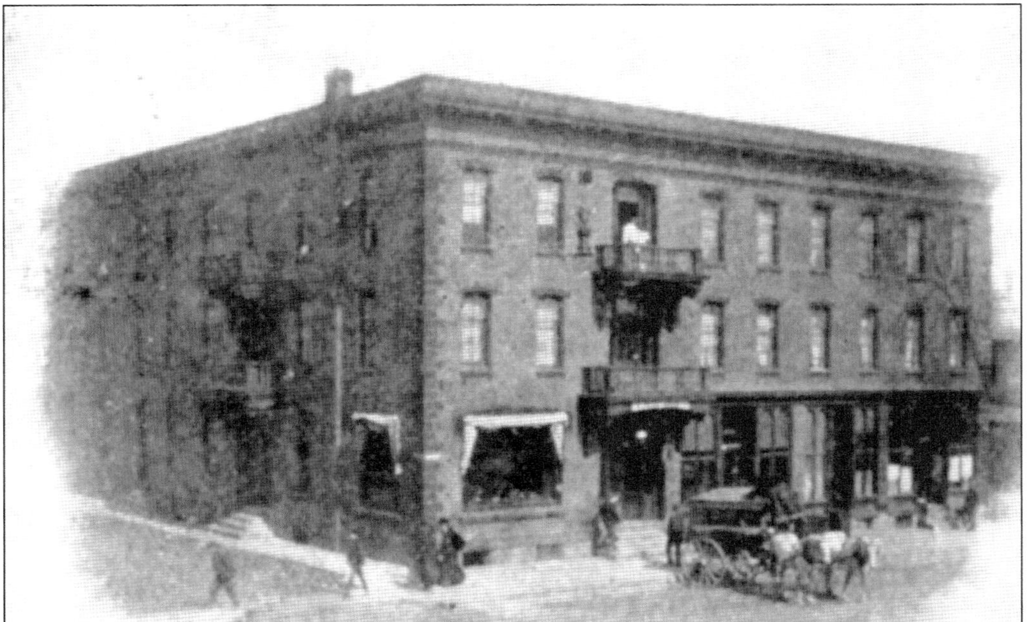

NEW COLES HOUSE. After the 1906 fire, the Coles House was remodeled as a three-story building, known as the New Coles House. The brick walls of the 1869 Cone House (and its successors) today form part of the Penn-Wells Hotel, which opened on this site in 1926.

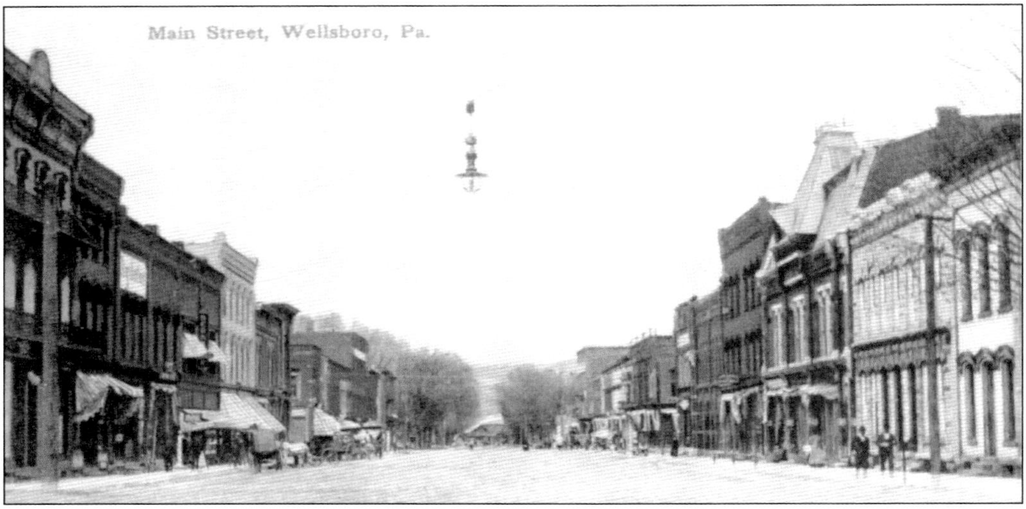

CARBON-ARC LIGHTS. Organized in 1894, the Wellsborough Electric Company established a powerhouse, strung wires, and installed incandescent lighting in dwellings and offices. The company also contracted with the town in 1895 to light the streets. Thirty arc lights were distributed throughout the borough. Each night, an attendant lowered the lights for servicing by using ropes and a pulley attached to a pole on the street corner.

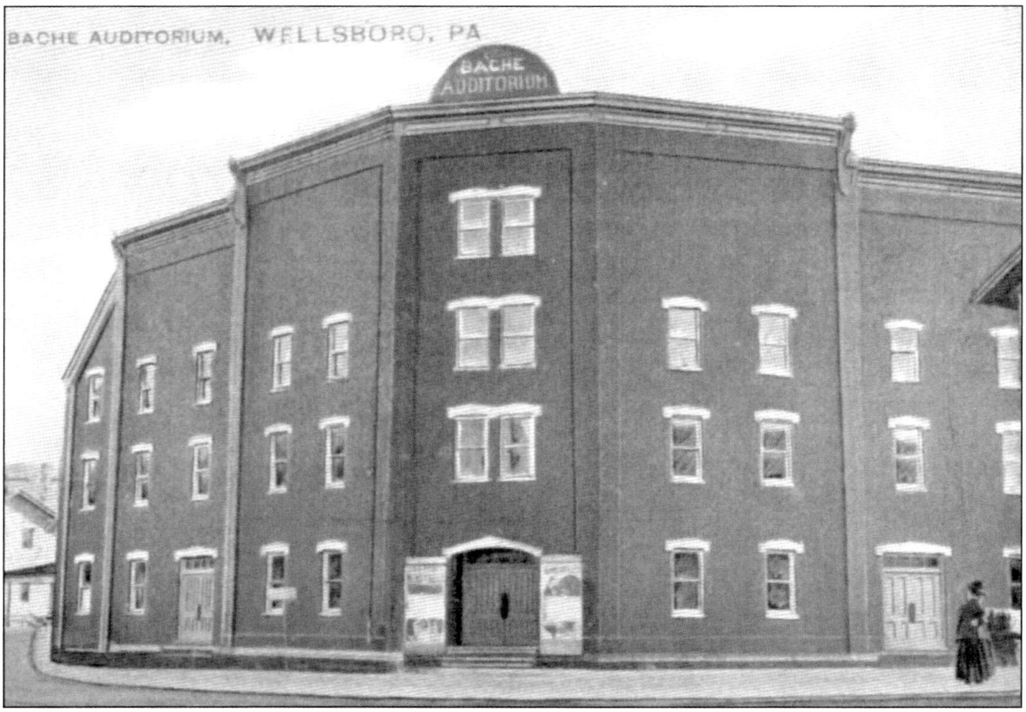

BACHE AUDITORIUM. In 1893, William Bache Jr., age 81, attended a performance in Annandale Hall on Main Street with his family. A performer accidentally caused an inferno by knocking over a kerosene lamp. Although Bache successfully guided 500 people to safety, the hall closed forever. This near-tragic fire motivated Bache to build the Bache Auditorium, lit by 262 incandescent lightbulbs, on the corner of East Avenue and Pearl Street, a gift to the borough in 1894.

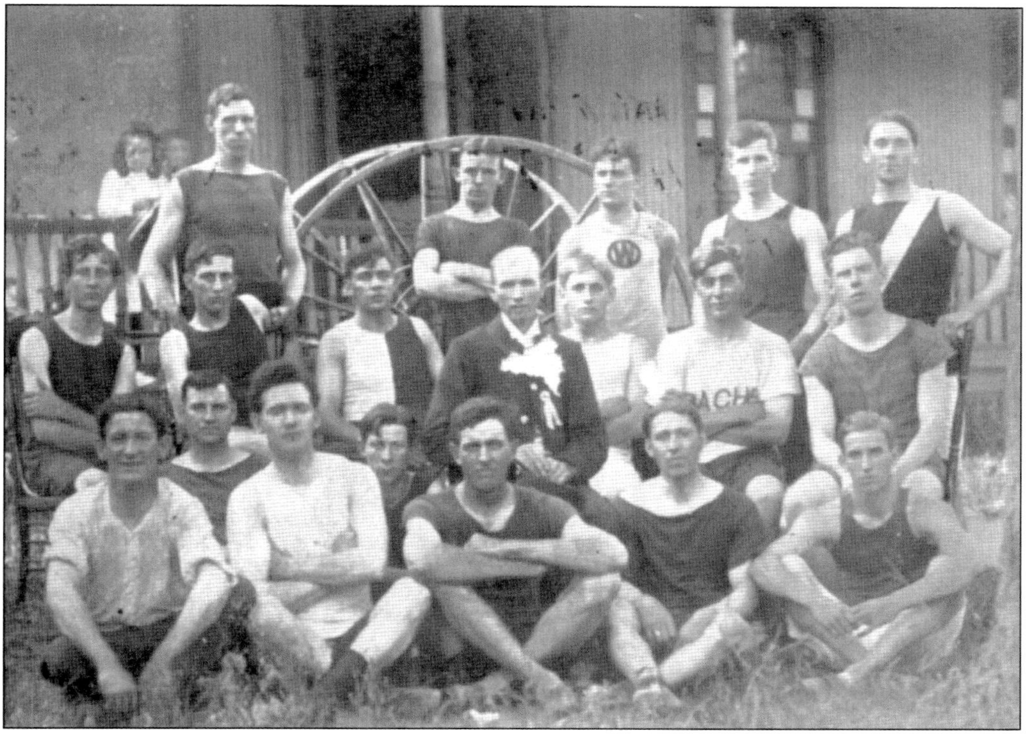

Bache Hose Running Team. When William Bache Jr. completed Wellsboro's waterworks system in 1886, the Lafayette Engine Company (foreman, John Norris Bache) honored him by changing its name to the Bache Hose Company. Intense rivalries between local volunteer fire companies led to competitions that included running with equipment. The Bache Hose Company, led by Howard H. Button (second row, center), produced so many winning teams that it was awarded first place by default at the 1907 firemen's convention in Galeton. The following year, at the Wellsboro convention pictured below, the team nearly broke a world record; it would happily achieve that accomplishment in 1909. The team competed successfully until 1916, when motorizing the department led to an eventual decline in sports and social activities. (Above, courtesy Lamont Satterly; below, courtesy TCHS.)

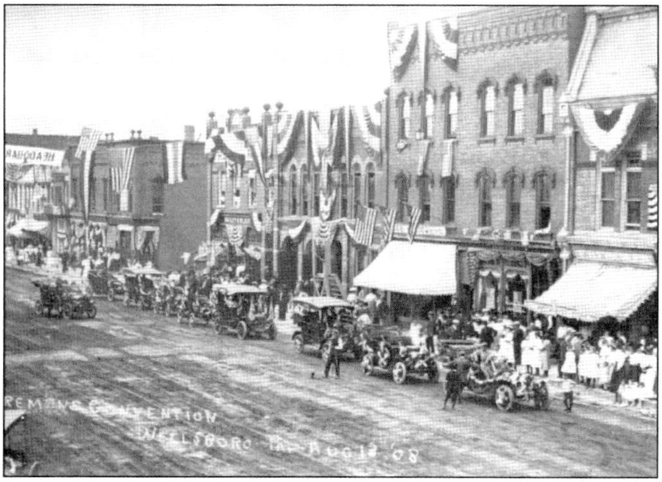

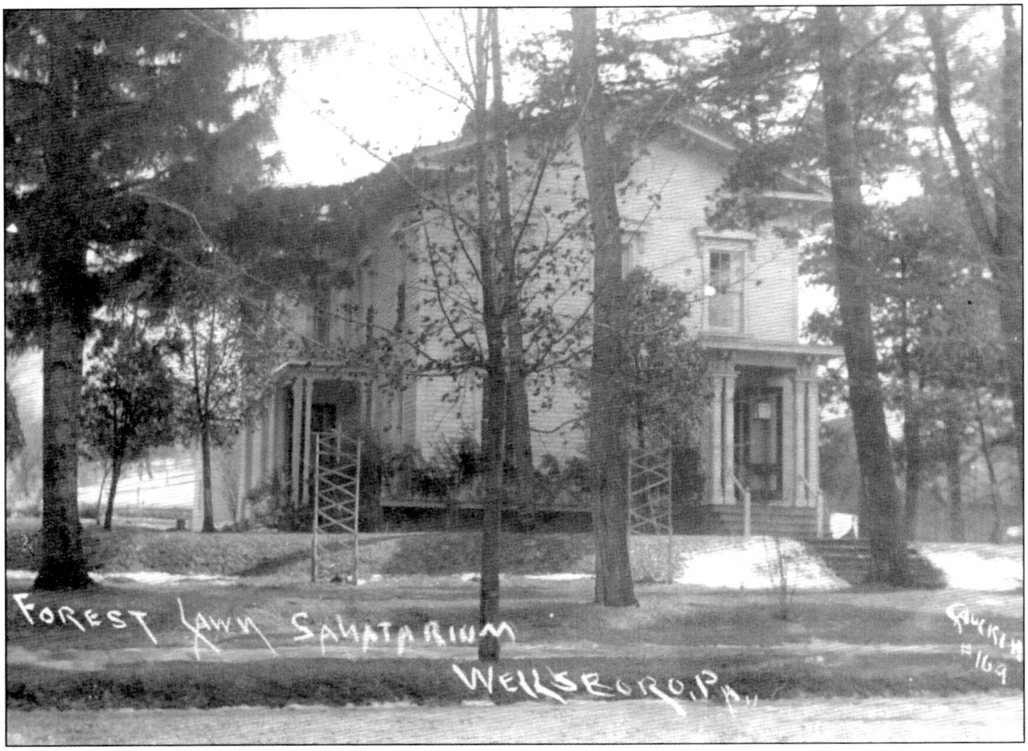

FOREST LAWN SANITARIUM. In 1860, William Bache Jr. built a home for his bride at 55 Pearl Street. In 1910, Dr. Willard G. Lent, who lived at 17 East Avenue, moved his medical practice from above the drugstore on Main Street to this location, founding the Forest Lawn Sanitarium. The building's next occupant, Prof. Alfred Pusy-Keith, an English concert pianist, established the Conservatory of Music. Other owners included Soldiers and Sailors Memorial Hospital Trustees, the IOOF (Odd Fellows Hall), and attorney Thomas Wilcox, whose plan to erect a modern apartment building never materialized. The house was razed in 1965.

WELLSBORO BOROUGH DIRECTORY

FOREST LAWN SANITARIUM

WILLARD G. LENT, M. D.
Proprietor

Complete Equipment, Trained Nurses, Massage, Vibration, Electricity, Surgery, Diseases of Women and Rectal Diseases. Rupture and Hemorrhoids Cured Without Operation. Catarrah and Catarrhal Deafness and all Diseases of Ear, Nose, Throat and Lungs. Cancer Treated by the Alexander Method. Opium and Morphine Habits Cured.

WELLSBORO, PA.

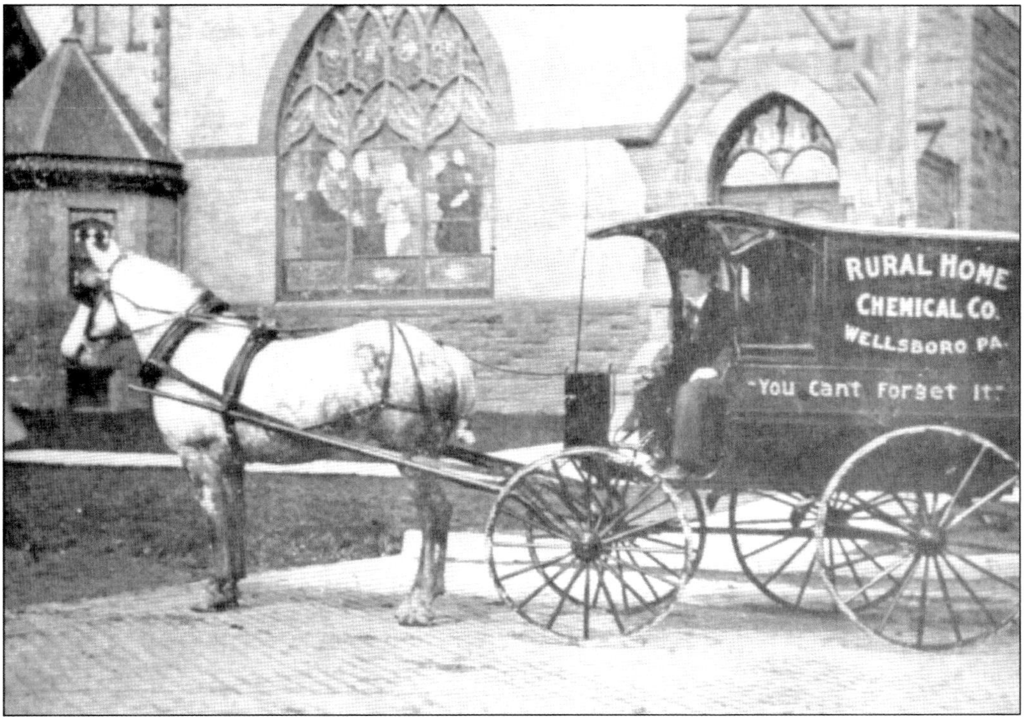

THE RURAL HOME CHEMICAL COMPANY. Located at 101 Courtland Street (today Cortland Street), the Rural Home Chemical Company manufactured an odd assortment of products, including household and veterinary remedies, flavoring extracts, toilet articles, disinfectants, and polishes. It featured a product called Fly-Stick, used to "make your own sticky fly paper and save money." The company wrote its motto, "You Can't Forget It," on horse-drawn advertising wagons.

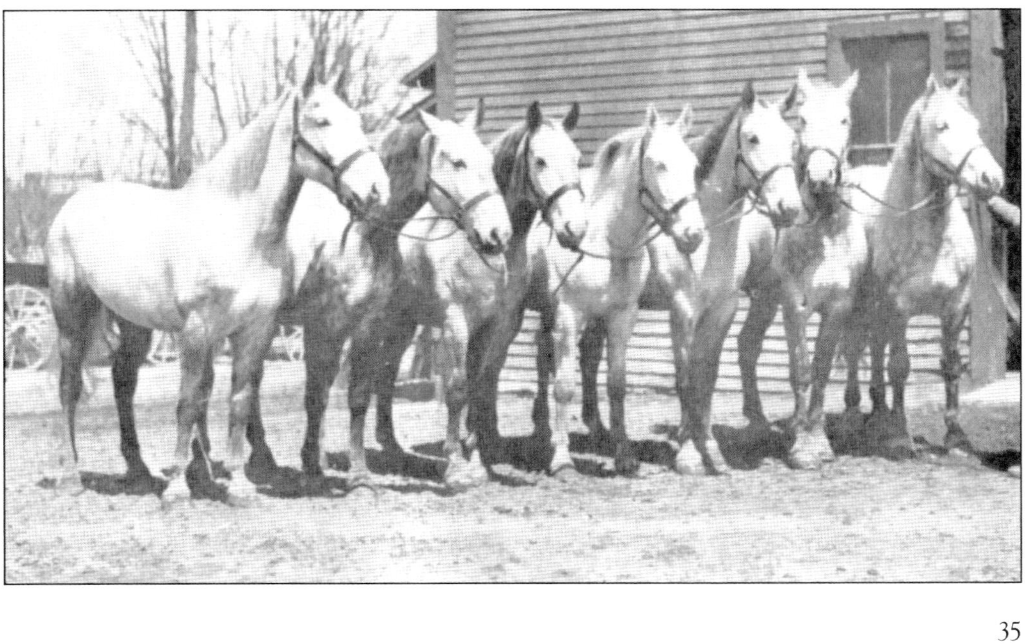

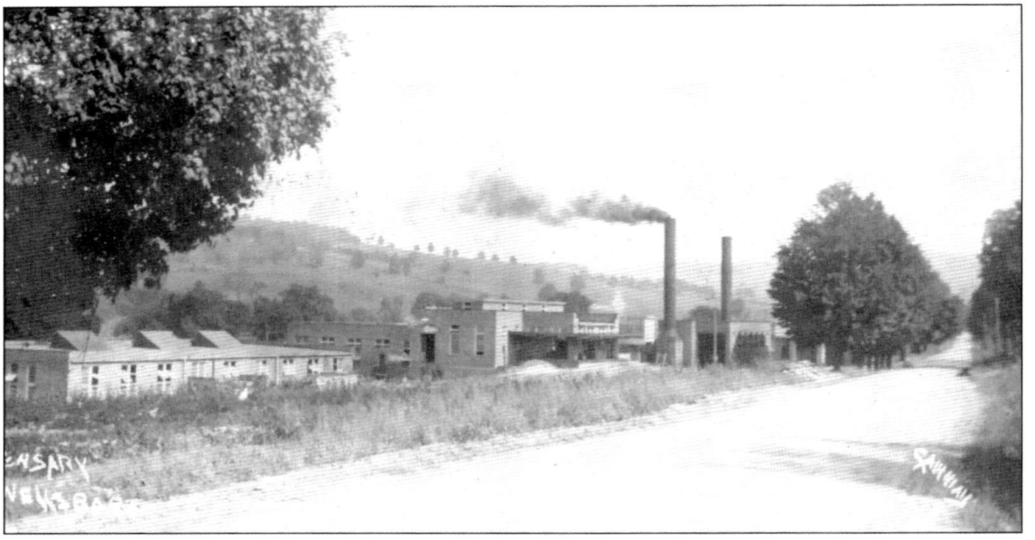

HELVETIA CONDENSERY. For nearly a century, this East Avenue location hosted milk plants. The Helvetia Condensery operated from 1906 to 1925. Pet Milk took over, followed by Borden's in 1927. Local farmers could purchase Holstein cattle at cost from the west, and agriculture became the county's largest industry by 1964. The Eagle Milk Plant ended a century of milk production, closing in 2005. (Courtesy Mike Spencer.)

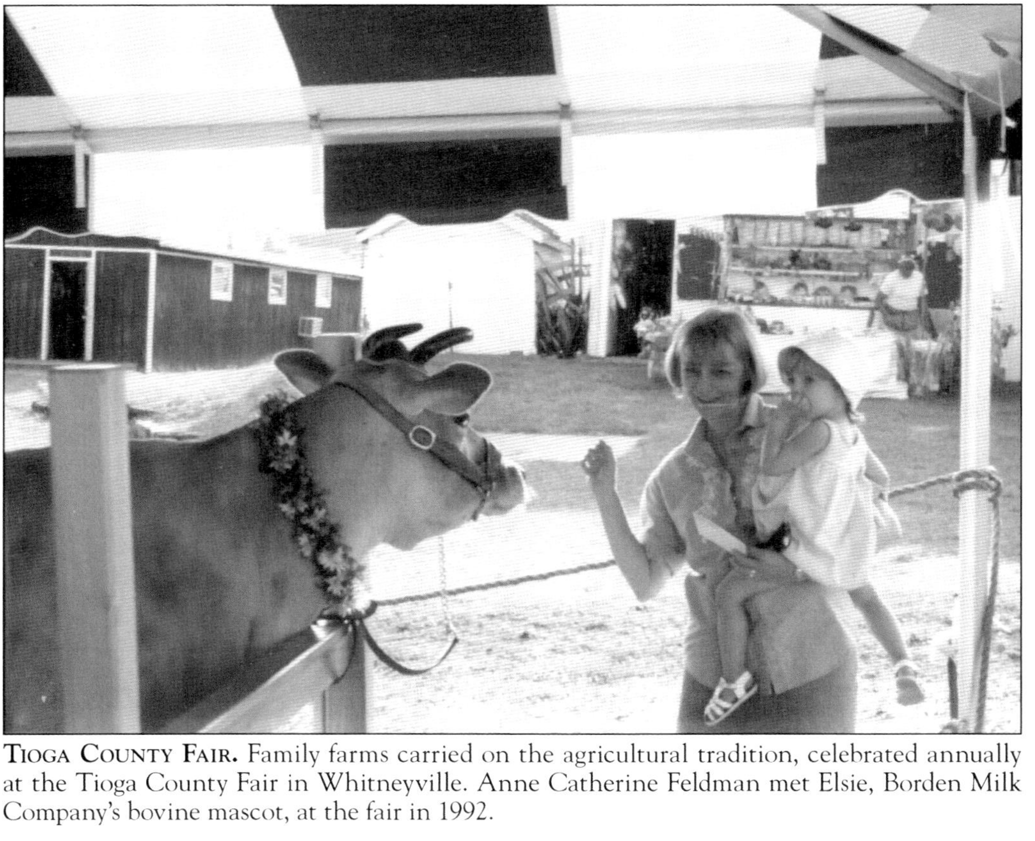

TIOGA COUNTY FAIR. Family farms carried on the agricultural tradition, celebrated annually at the Tioga County Fair in Whitneyville. Anne Catherine Feldman met Elsie, Borden Milk Company's bovine mascot, at the fair in 1992.

Tioga County Centennial Celebration. In 1903, Judge Jerome B. Niles made the case for a birthday extravaganza in Wellsboro, the county seat, saying, "A county so rich in minerals, timber and agriculture, and so long noted for the intelligence of its people, should show a proper appreciation of its development." The celebration occurred June 29–July 1, 1904. A 1905 volume preserves the event, described in the book as a "crowning success."

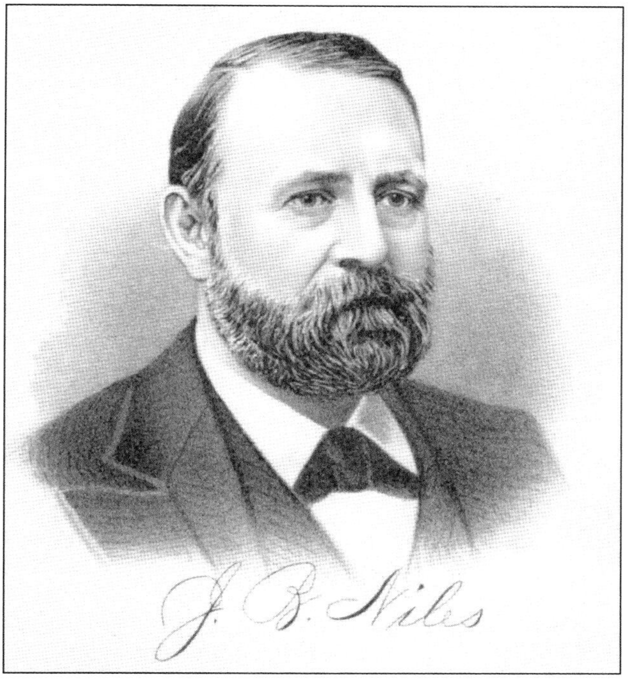

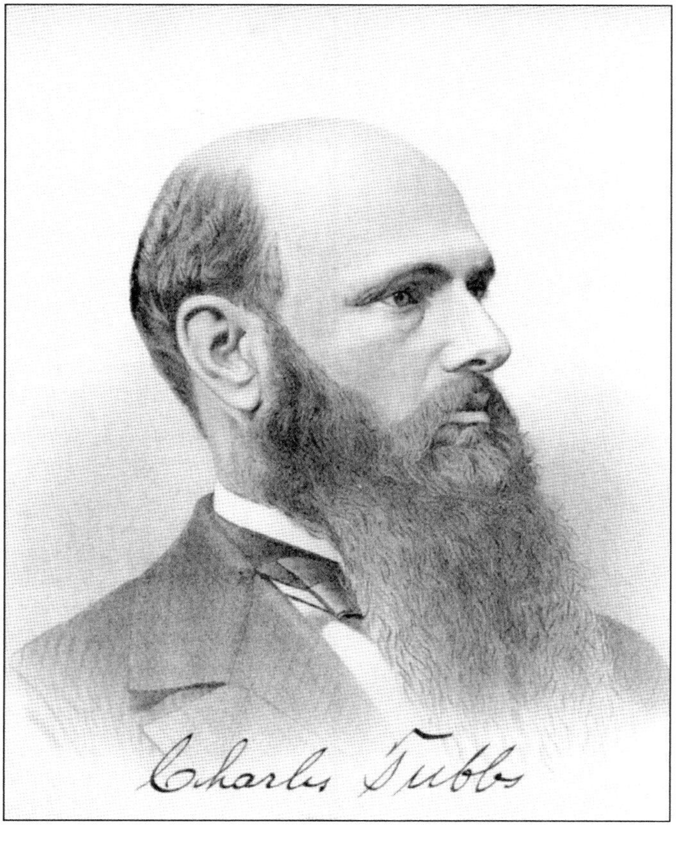

Charles Tubbs (1843–1913). The Honorable Charles Tubbs of Osceola served as president of the 1904 Centennial Commission. Of New England ancestry, Tubbs early on developed a "taste for learning," a "taste for history," and a "taste for politics." Elected to the state legislature in 1880, he stood against the railroad monopolies, favoring instead the "interests of education" and "the rights of labor." Tubbs was the first president of the Tioga County Historical Society, and his 1909 monograph, *Wellsboro and the Wells Family*, placed him among Wellsboro's most authoritative historians.

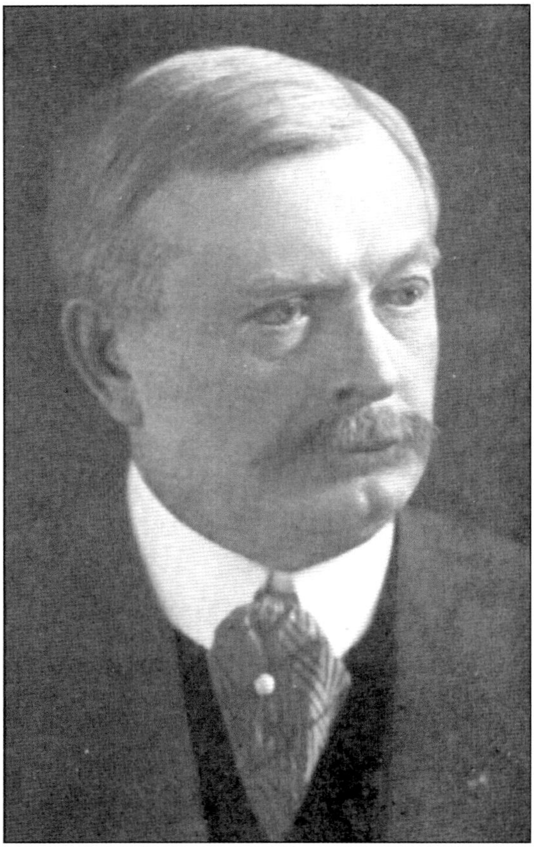

William Alexis Stone (1846–1920). As the former governor of the Commonwealth of Pennsylvania (1899–1903), Stone was invited to deliver the 1904 centennial military address. Born on a farm in Delmar Township, Stone attended local schools. After the "Great Battle of Gettysburg" in 1863, he enlisted at age 17. His regiment escorted Lincoln's body as it traveled through Philadelphia to Springfield. Stone mustered out as a second lieutenant in 1865. Lacking the means for a formal education, he approached Professor Allen of Mansfield Normal School, who arranged for Stone to matriculate. After graduating with high honors in 1868, Stone taught for two terms at the Wellsboro Academy, studied law under the direction of Jerome B. Niles, and was admitted to the bar in 1870. Republican presidents Rutherford B. Hayes, James A . Garfield, and Chester A. Arthur appointed Stone US attorney for the Western District of Pennsylvania. Pres. Grover Cleveland, a Democrat, removed him from office in 1886. Stone represented the 23rd District in Congress from 1891–1898, which he followed with a successful run for governor.

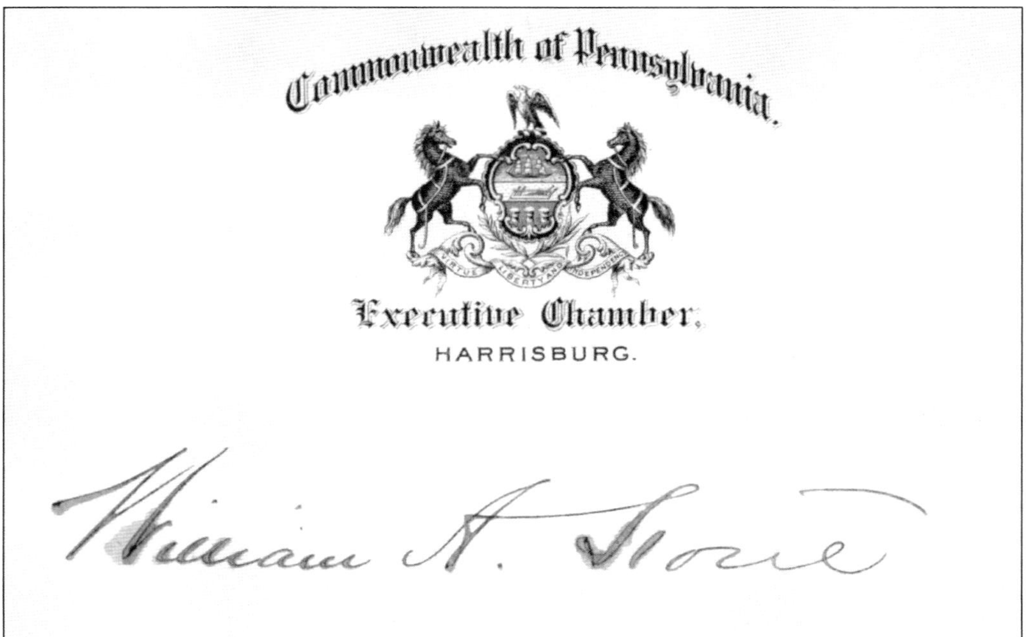

STONE'S HOMESTEAD. Governor Stone wrote his memoir, *The Tale of a Plain Man*, at the request of his children and grandchildren. Demand exceeded the 500 original copies, so Stone sent his manuscript to a Philadelphia publisher, and the second edition appeared in 1918. These photographs show Stone's boyhood home in 1864 and again in 1916. Of his earliest memory, Stone recalls, "Santa did not bring me very much that Christmas morning—two round bull's eye candies and some doughnuts in the shape of elephants and horses. But that was as much as the others got, and it was enough." Later, Stone writes, "It was between 1856 and 1860 that I discovered that our home was an underground railroad station . . . I had never seen a colored person before . . . My father was an anti-slavery man."

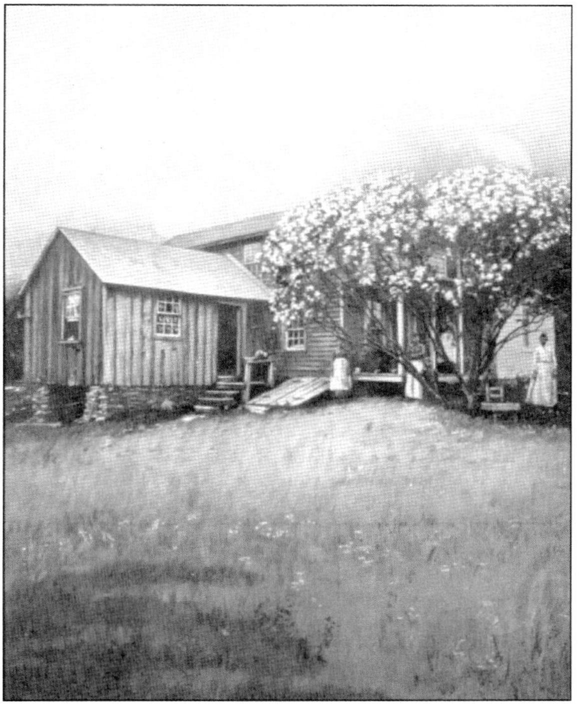

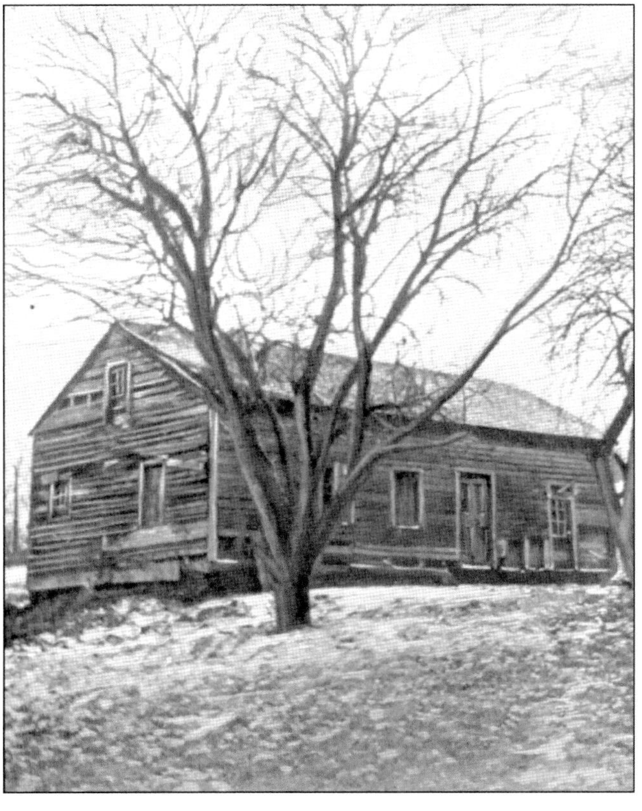

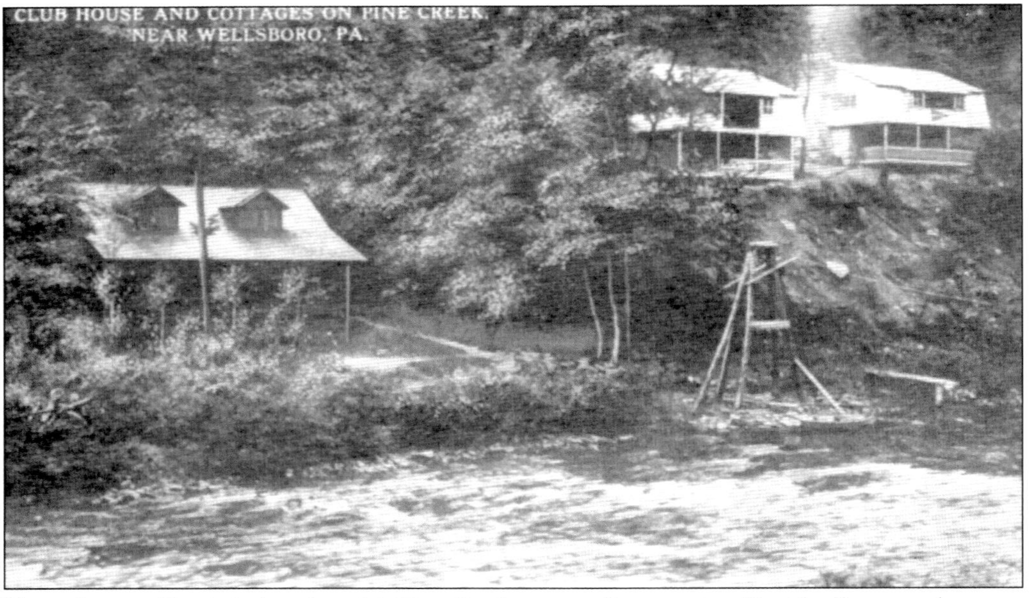

HEART'S-EASE. Reminiscing about his Pine Creek cottage, Stone writes, "I wish all men and women were as contented and happy as I am." Stone spent the time between June and October at Heart's-ease, located on Four-Mile Run, with "Pa" Deans and "Bob" Young staying nearby. Young, in *Tales of Tioga*, recounts his adventures with "the Guv," referring to Wellsboro as "the center of the world." Heart's-ease hosted frequent visits from outdoor enthusiast Pres. Theodore Roosevelt.

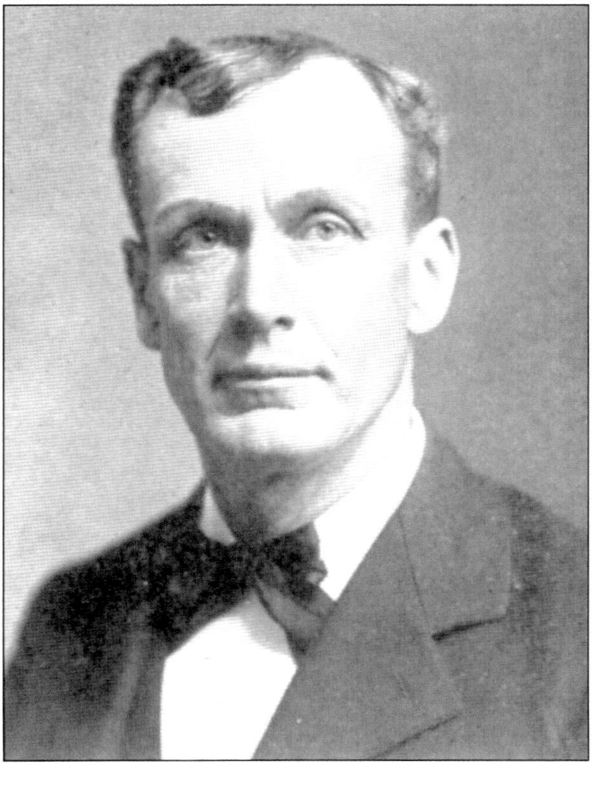

LEONARD HARRISON (1850–1929). Businessman Leonard Harrison built two cottages, Wetumka and Osocosy, opposite Stone's cottage on Four-Mile Run. Young Harrison had worked with his father, William, a carpenter, until about 1878. He later clerked at the courthouse, learning about land, lumber, and coal. Founder of the Tyoga Lumber Company in 1884, Harrison ordered a log slide cut into the side of Pine Creek gorge, choosing to float his product to market rather than relying primarily on trains. Harrison served as first president of the Electric Company (1894) and third president of the First National Bank (1896). Within a decade, he became recognized as one of the most successful businessmen in Tioga County. His magnificent home, located at 10 West Avenue, is today the Carleton Senior Care and Rehabilitation Center.

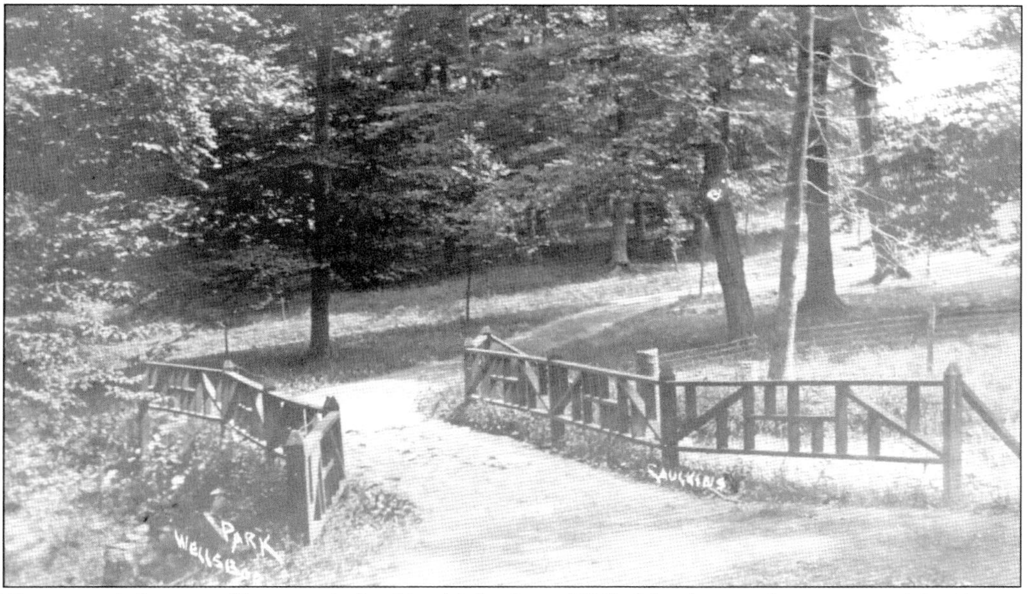

Harrison's Legacy. Harrison helped build the Penn-Wells Hotel, served as trustee of the Green Free Library, and left a bequest to the Soldiers and Sailors Memorial Hospital. A devout Christian, Harrison supervised construction of the First Presbyterian Church on Main Street. In spring 1902, Harrison purchased a wooded area near the reservoir, 16 acres of which became Woodland Park (pictured). Wellsboro newpapers report that Harrison called it "an attractive pleasure resort" and that the community could enjoy the park "so long as they . . . appreciate[d] it and [did] not abuse the privileges so freely offered."

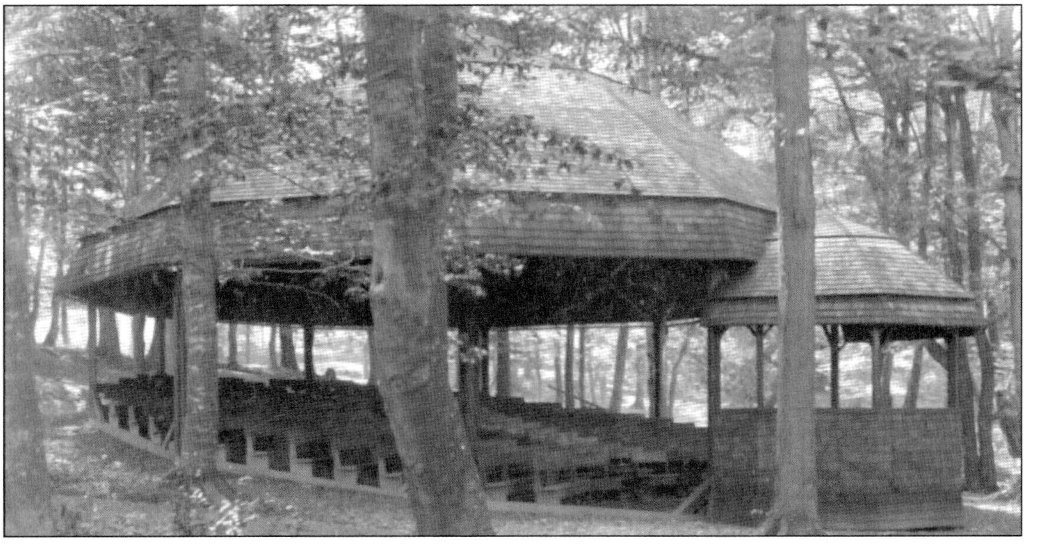

Woodland Park Auditorium. Improvements to Woodland Park included a mile of drives, fountains filled with reservoir overflow, rustic seats and pagodas, and a circular auditorium "with a canopy shaped like an umbrella." The scene of many band concerts, its amphitheater-style seating could accommodate up to 500 persons. Harrison conveyed Woodland Park to the borough in 1916. The borough council voted to demolish the eight-sided auditorium in 1970, although the smaller pagoda remains standing today.

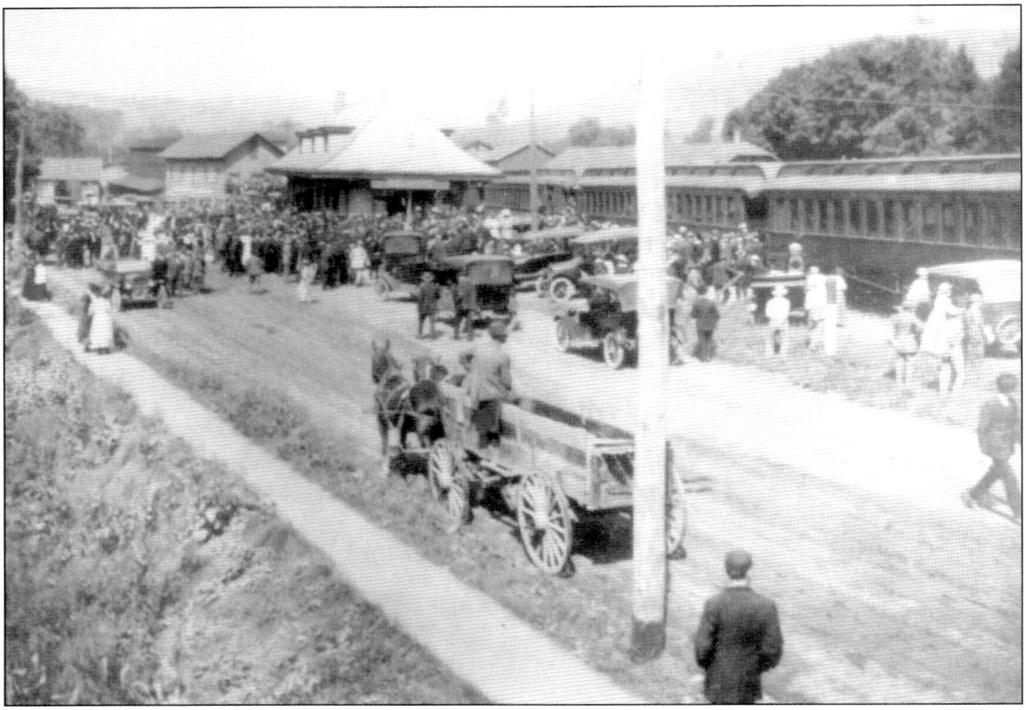

New York Central Depot. The New York Central Railroad took over the Fall Brook line in May 1899. The dedication of the remodeled depot on Charleston Street occurred in 1914. (Courtesy Mike Spencer.)

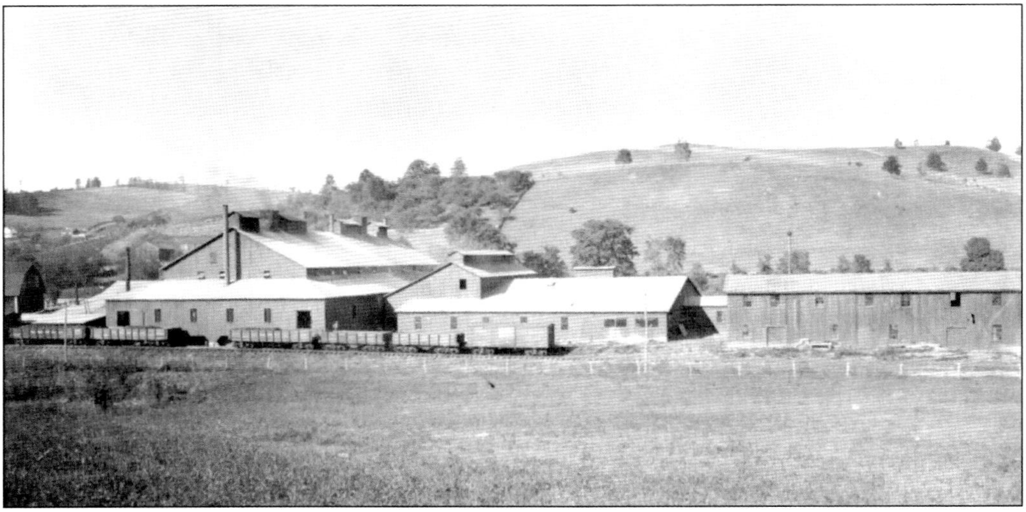

Columbia Glass Works. As early as 1886, Wellsboro industry included glass companies. The Wellsboro Glass Company, Ltd., successfully manufactured window glass until the plant burned in 1888. The company rebuilt, only to burn again in 1892, after which it closed. Columbia Glass Works (pictured) opened at the same site but was prone to shutdowns and late openings. The company was taken over by the First National Bank, only to lie idle for seven years. By 1916, business leaders formed the Wellsboro Chamber of Commerce in order to recruit a new company to operate the plant. (Courtesy Corning Incorporated Archives.)

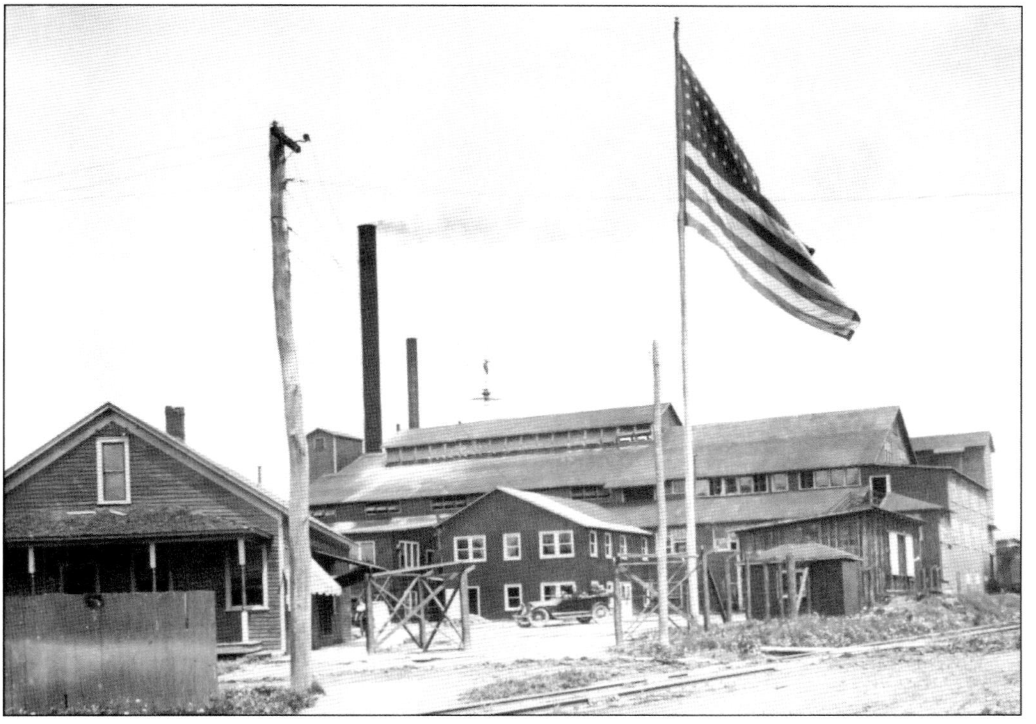

Corning Glass Works. World War I produced a tremendous demand for electric lightbulbs. Chamber representatives approached Corning officials regarding the plant vacated by Columbia Glass Works. In May 1916, Corning Glass Works purchased the plant, renovated the building, and produced the first lightbulb blanks by fall. The factory originally hired 100 workers; the number increased to 600 by 1920. The 1916 supervisory staff includes, from left to right, Charles A. Murray, producer foreman; William J. "Billy" Woods, plant supervisor; George R. Crites, machine shop foreman and (later) plant manager; and Walter R. Keagle, timekeeper and (later) inspection department foreman. (Both, courtesy Corning Incorporated Archives.)

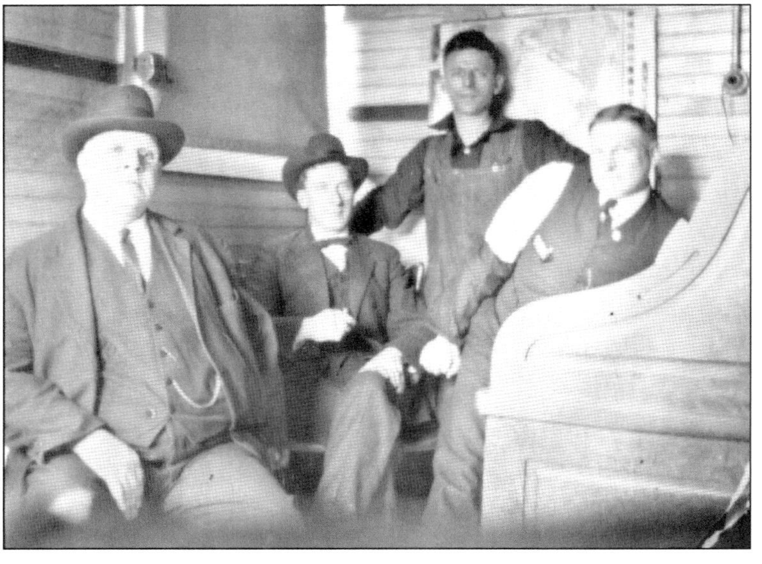

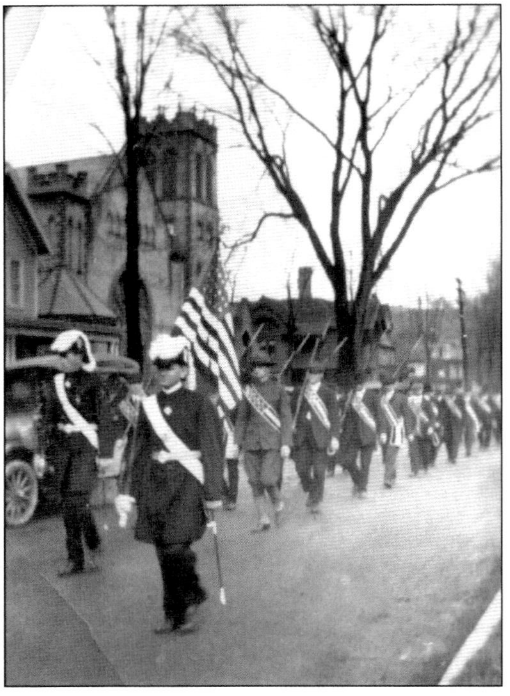

Armistice Day Celebration. Wellsboro received news that World War I had ended on a Thursday afternoon, sending townspeople into frenzied celebration. As a child, former Tioga County commissioner Willard "Dud" Smith reportedly hawked hot roasted peanuts to the revelers. The armistice was not, however, signed until the following Monday, November 11, 1918. Undaunted, the town enthusiastically continued celebrating into the night. In 1919, the town recognized Armistice Day with a grand parade, pictured here. (Courtesy Mike Spencer.)

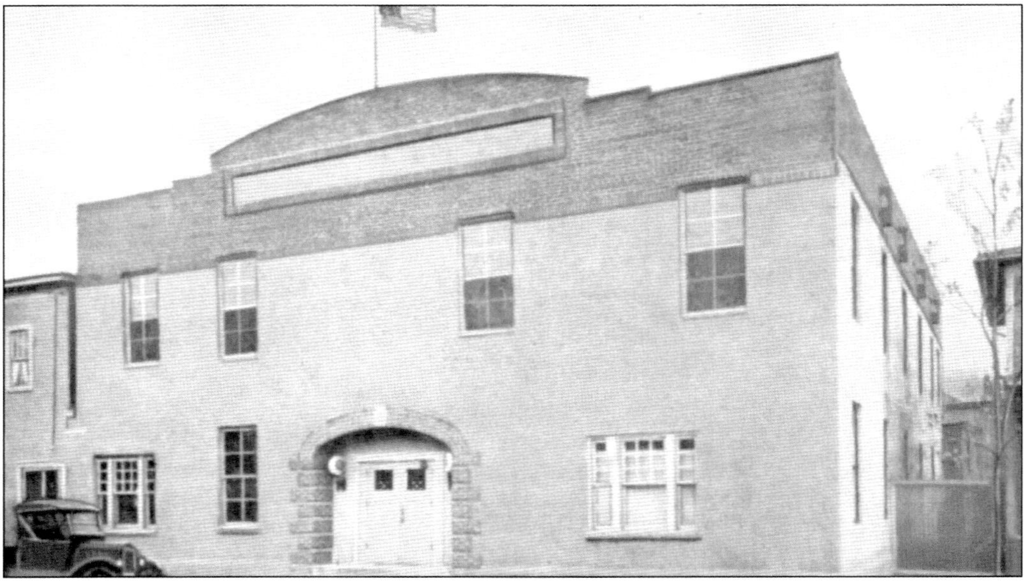

American Legion. In 1920, Leonard Harrison offered Judge Niles's former home on the corner of Walnut Street and Central Avenue to the American Legion for its headquarters. However, if "intoxicating liquors" were permitted on the premises, the property would revert back to Harrison. The home, later owned by Charles Fullwood, was razed in 1973. On December 6, 1921, the W. Earle Champaign Post of the American Legion purchased the concrete building, known as the Equity Building (from the Wellsboro Cooperative Milk Station), located at 16 Pearl Street (pictured here). The building functioned as a community center, often used for basketball or dances. The Pearl Street shops have occupied the site since 1980.

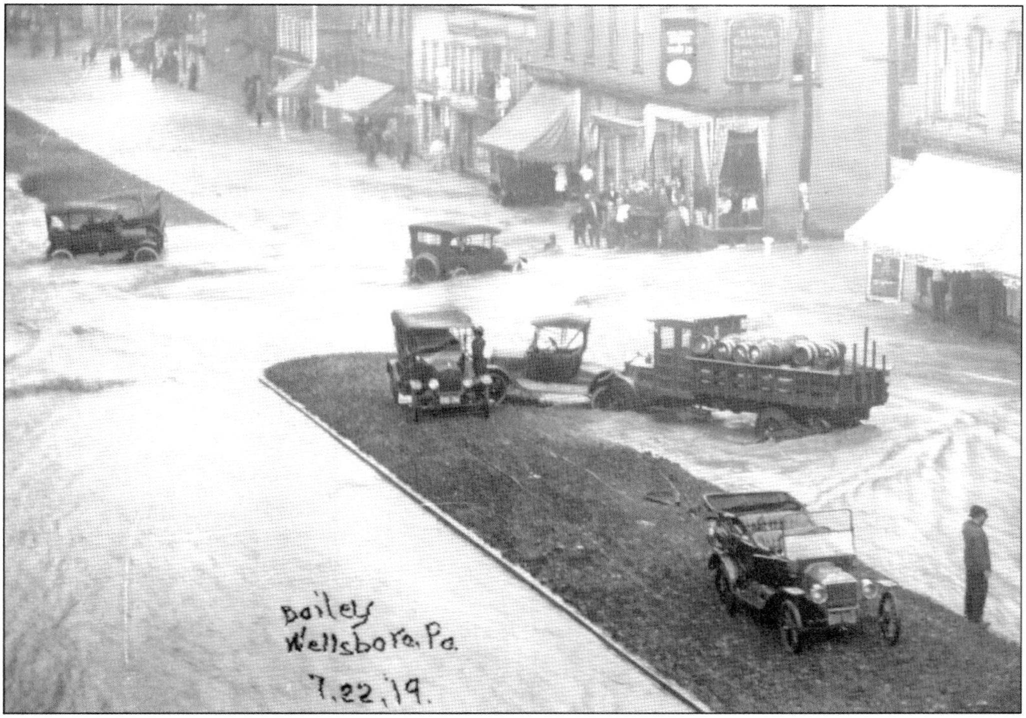

Flood of 1919. On July 22, 1919, between 4:30 p.m. and 6:00 p.m., a series of violent electrical storms hit Wellsboro, causing extensive damage to public and private property. The three creeks running through town—Kelsey, Morris, and Charleston—became raging torrents, flooding the area with amazing rapidity. An eyewitness is quoted in a booklet about the flood: "It was a weird and horrifying sight to see Main Street a turbulent river, with floodtrash floating down—barn roofs, bales of hay, chicken-coops, outhouses, and heavy timbers." (Below, courtesy Lamont Satterly.)

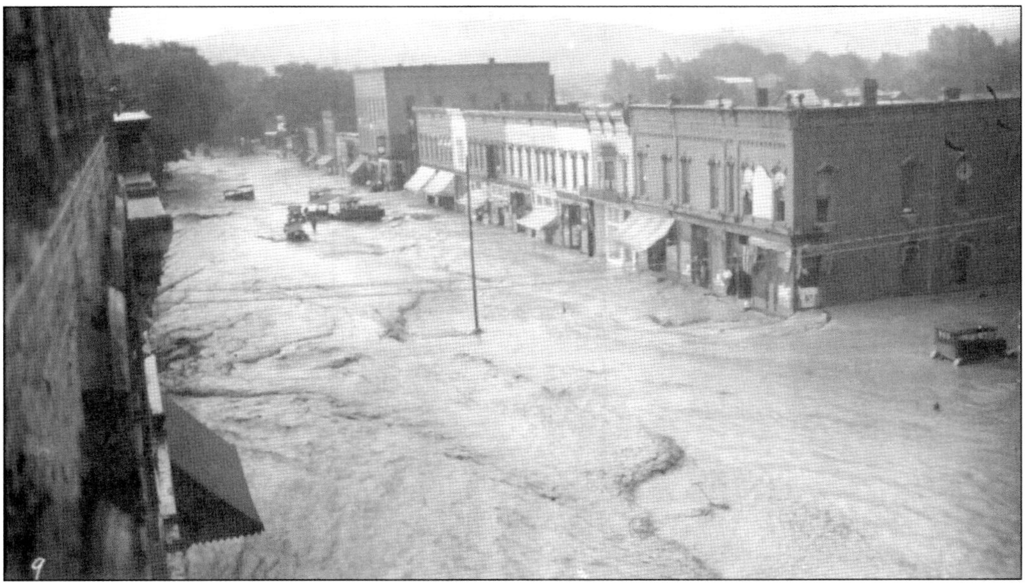

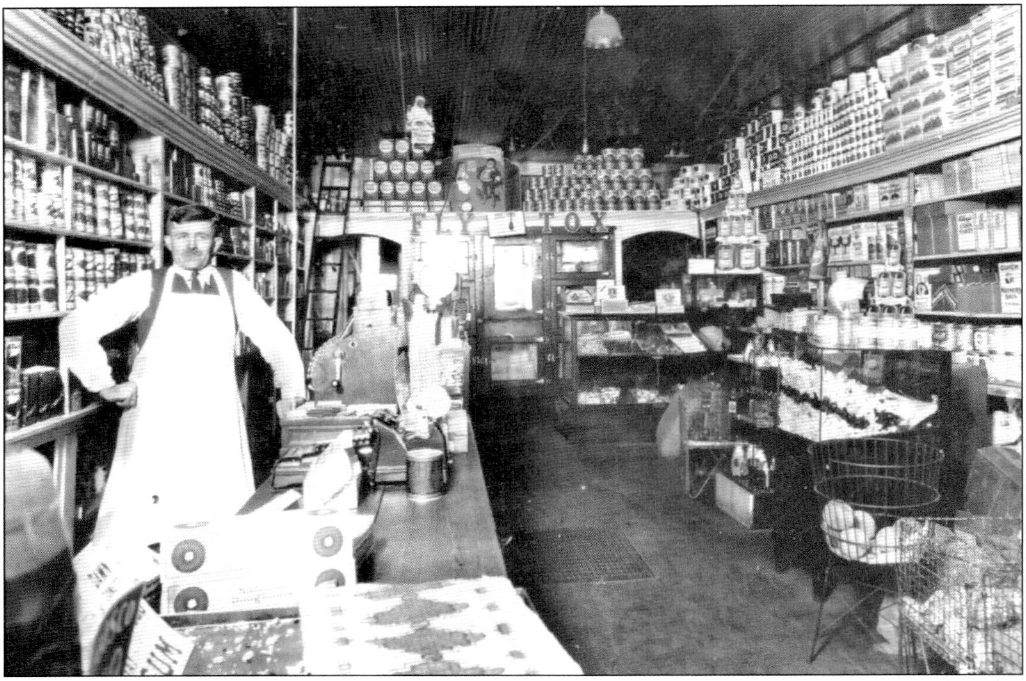

Tunk's Grocery Store. Arthur C. "Tunk" Edwards arrived in Wellsboro in 1923, purchased a milk route from Vern Green, and prepared to open a milk station and grocery store in the space vacated by the Bloise Shoe Company on lower East Avenue. He offered the First Baptist Church five percent of all sales on December 1, 1923. Edwards later sold his milk route to L.A. Shumway but kept his East Avenue store. Here, longtime assistant Martin Scheeley works the counter in this early photograph of Tunk's grocery store. (Courtesy Elgin Sink.)

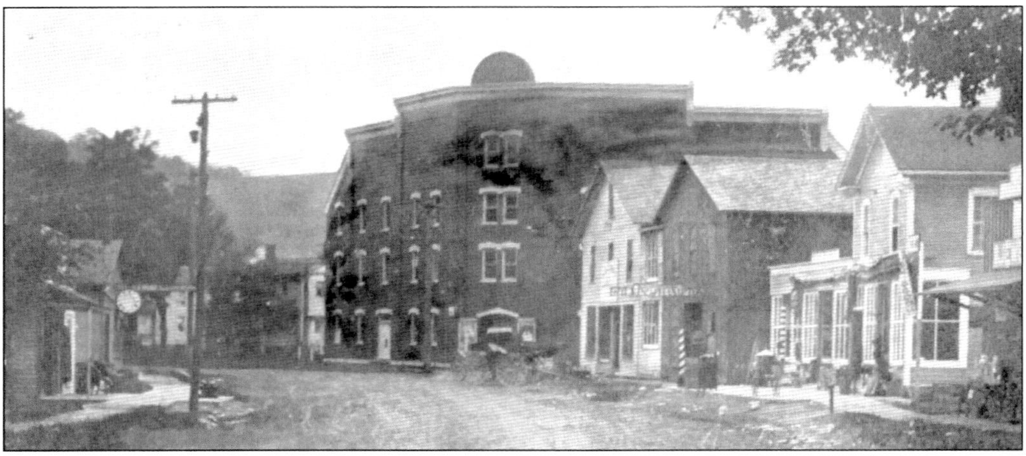

The Bowery. From 1894–1958, the Bache Auditorium anchored the upper side of "the Bowery," a section of East Avenue located between Pearl and Main Streets. Managers included William Kress, the Dartt family, Cecil and Ida Roberts, and the Woodin family. Numerous businesses located here, including the *Wellsboro Gazette*, Spencer's Barber Shop, the Silver Dollar Bar, the NU Way Lunch, Corwin's Dairy Bar, Jimmy Kimble's billiard parlor, Bloise Variety Store, and the Jello (named for owner Angelo Bloise), a popular teen hangout with a snack bar and music. Dunham's parking lot replaced these businesses in 1984.

Three

Bygone Times

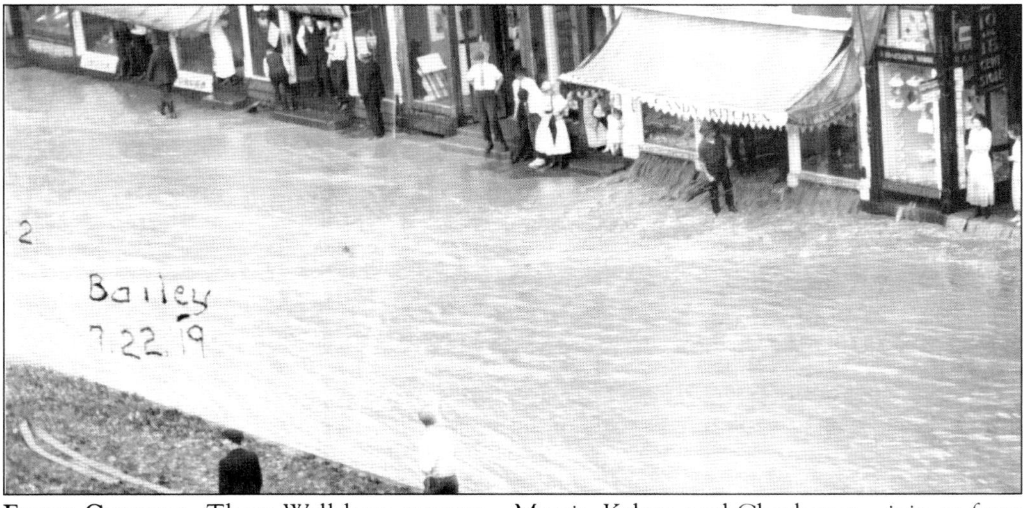

Flood Control. Three Wellsboro streams—Morris, Kelsey, and Charleston—join to form Marsh Creek on the northern edge of town. Disasters such as the flood of 1919, pictured here, led to the Marsh Creek Watershed Project in 1972. Hamilton Dam, completed in Round Top in 1967, can impound 44.526 million gallons of water. The Kelsey Creek Dam was also completed in 1967. Hamilton Lake and Lake Nessmuk, completed the following year, also provide recreational facilities for public use.

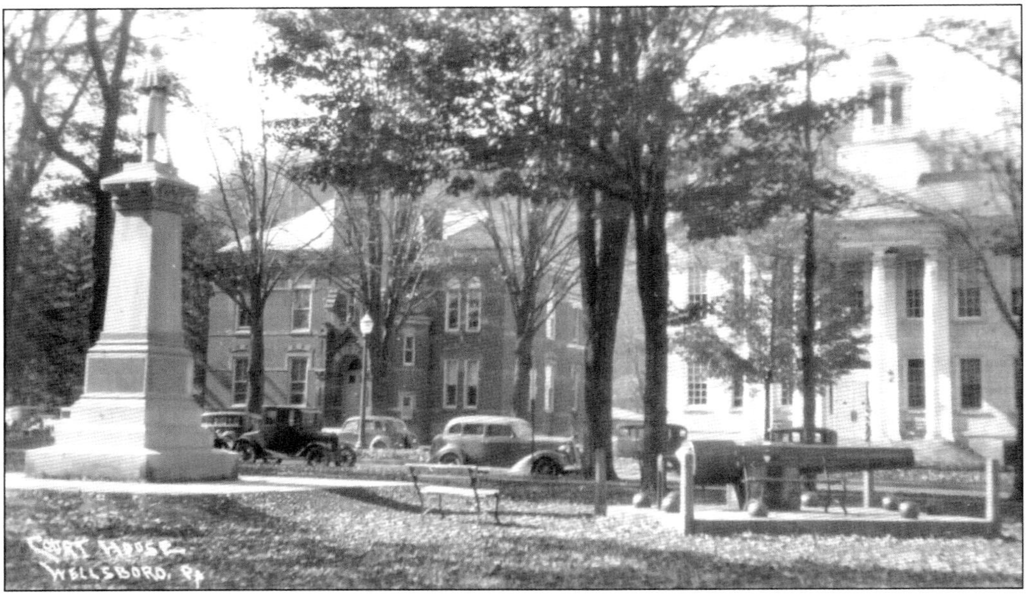

Renovated Courthouse. Despite the displeasure of some residents, columns were added to the Tioga County Courthouse in 1931 when the building was renovated and expanded. Items placed in the cornerstone included a coin from 1776 and a handmade spike from the old jail.

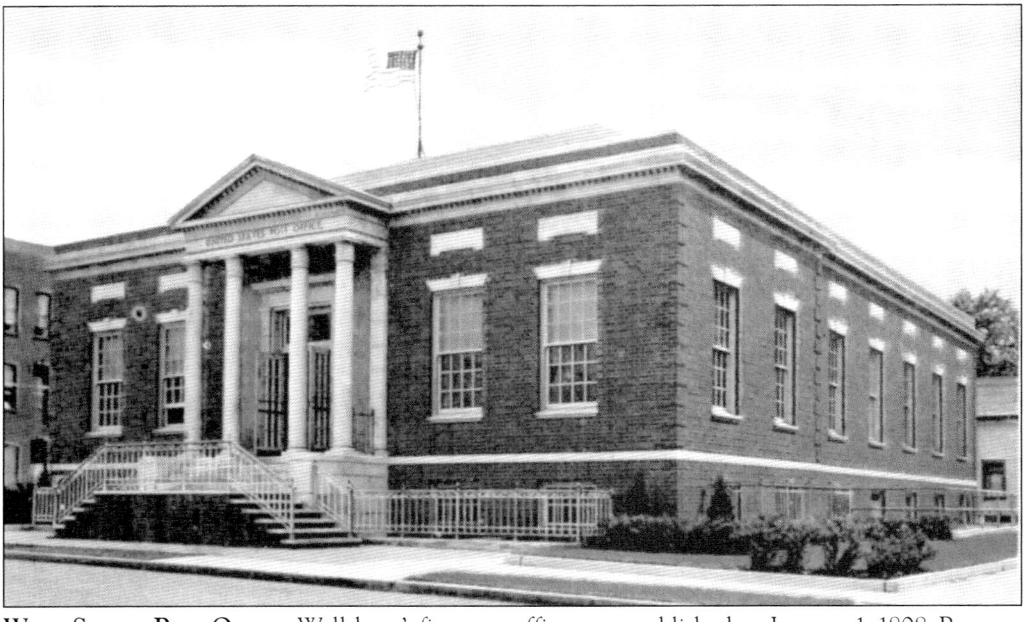

Waln Street Post Office. Wellsboro's first post office was established on January 1, 1808. Because postmasters could choose the site prior to 1930, the location of the post office often changed. On May 30, 1930, Congressman Edgar R. Kiess reported that an $80,000 post office building would be erected on land donated on Waln Street by Leonard Harrison. The office opened on July 1, 1932, with Clyde Bailey as postmaster.

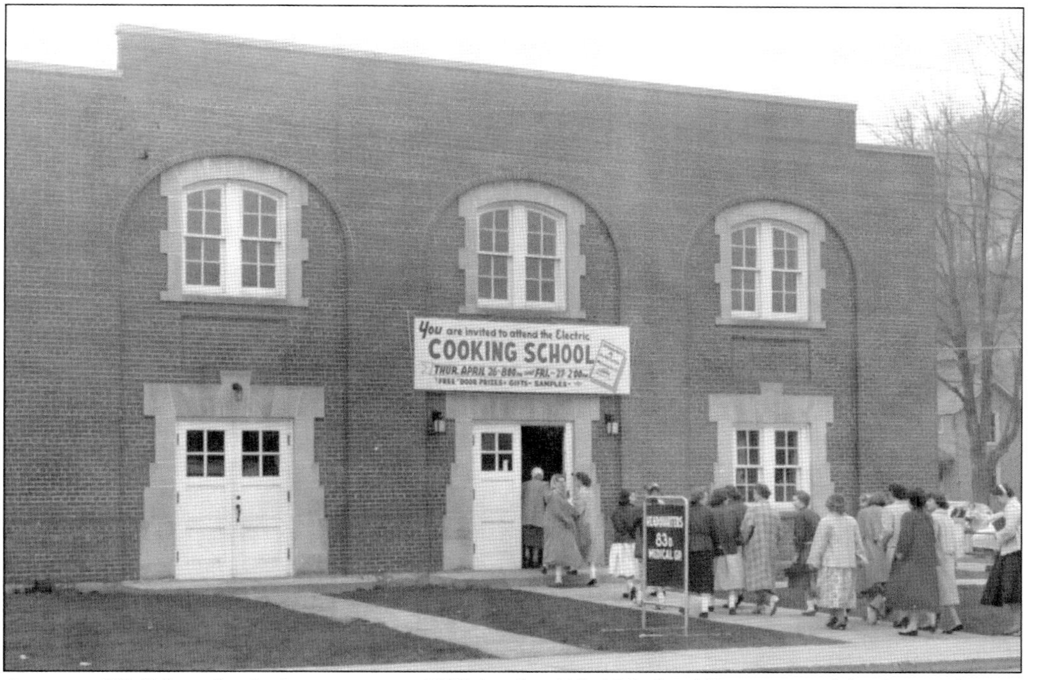

ARMORY. Wellsboro built the armory in 1932 for the 103rd Medical Regiment of the Pennsylvania National Guard. In 1957, Anne Coreney, a home economist, conducted an electric cooking school at the armory, sponsored by the Wellsboro Electric Company, at which gifts and prizes were given. The main door prize was a General Electric Spacemaker range. The armory, now part of the courthouse complex, was placed in the National Register of Historic Places in 1991. (Courtesy TCHS.)

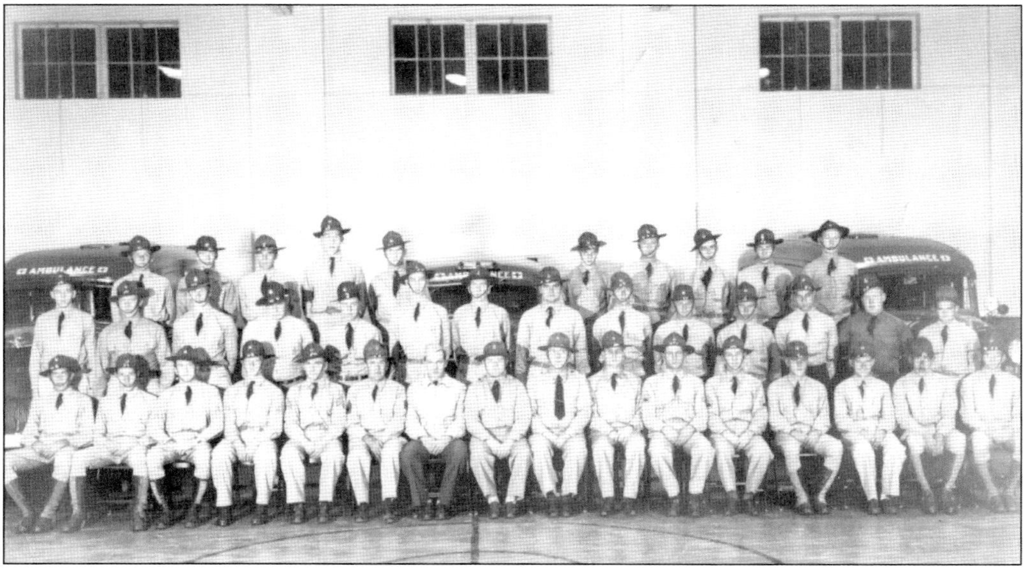

83RD MEDICAL GROUP. The 83rd Medical Group received authorization to organize in the National Guard effective June 15, 1949, with Col. Archibald Laird commanding. (Courtesy Victoria Pongrace.)

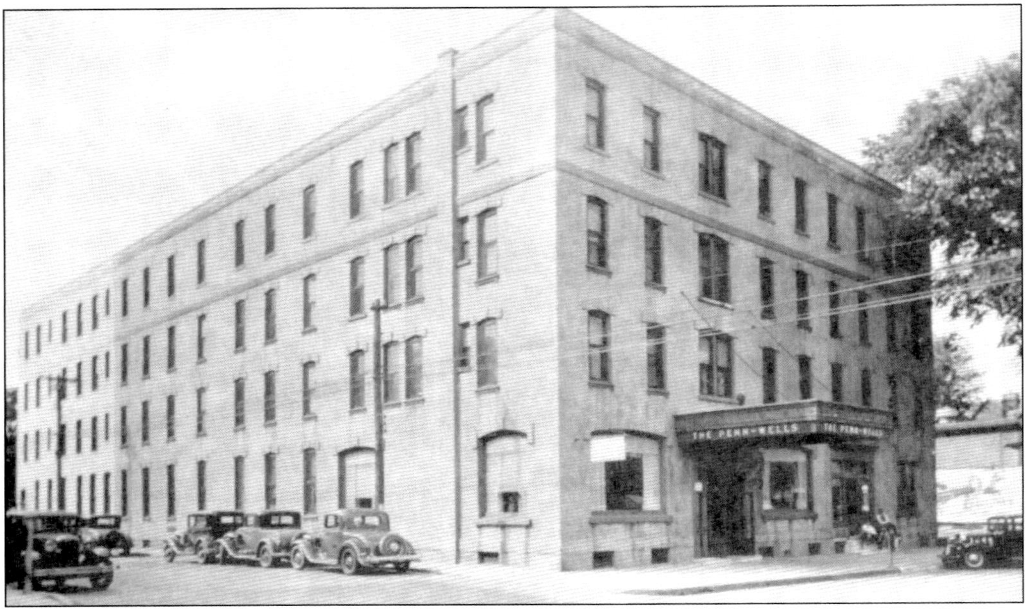

DINNER

Complete Meal Included in Price of Entree

SPECIAL from the COCKTAIL ROOM — MARTINI .20

CHOICE

Chilled Grapefruit and Orange Cup — Fresh Crab Flake Cocktail

Pear Nectar — Concord Grape Juice

Consomme Creole — Genuine Turtle Soup

Radish Roses — Hearts of Celery

Baked Fresh Lake Erie Trout, Lemon Points	.90
Fried Deep Sea Scallops, Tartar Sauce	.85
Fricassee of Chicken, Hot Biscuits	1.00
Broiled Choice Sirloin Steak	1.10
Baked Penn-Wells Ham, Fruit Sauce	.90
Pan Broiled Lamb Chops on Toast	1.00

CHOICE OF TWO

Whipped Potatoes — Baked Potatoes

Fresh Green Beans — Brussels Sprouts

Tomato and Cheese Salad

CHOICE

Green Apple Pie, Cheese — Pumpkin Pie

Bread and Butter Pudding — Cherry Sundae

Jello, Whipped Cream — Chilled Honey Dew Melon

Roquefort Cheese, Butter Crackers

French Vanilla or Chocolate Marshmallow Nut Ice Cream

Tea — Coffee — Milk — Buttermilk

SPECIALS

Turtle Soup, Fried Philadelphia Scrapple, Hot Apple Sauce	.70
Heinz Tomato Juice, Western Omelet	.70
Chilled Apple and Grape Cup, Chicken a la King	.70

Potato, Vegetable, Dessert and Beverage

PENN-WELLS HOTEL
Wellsboro, Penna

FRIDAY October 6, 1939
Served from Five-Thirty to Eight P.M

The Penn-Wells Hotel. On December 30, 1926, the Wellsboro Hotel stockholders met to discuss renaming the fire-damaged Coles House, which had reopened on July 28, 1926, following $95,000 in renovations, including a sprinkler system. The Honorable Horace B. Packer suggested the name Penn-Wells Hotel. Managers have included Hugh Dale (1926–1975), Frank Dunham (1972–1975), and Michael Goodreau (1975–1999).

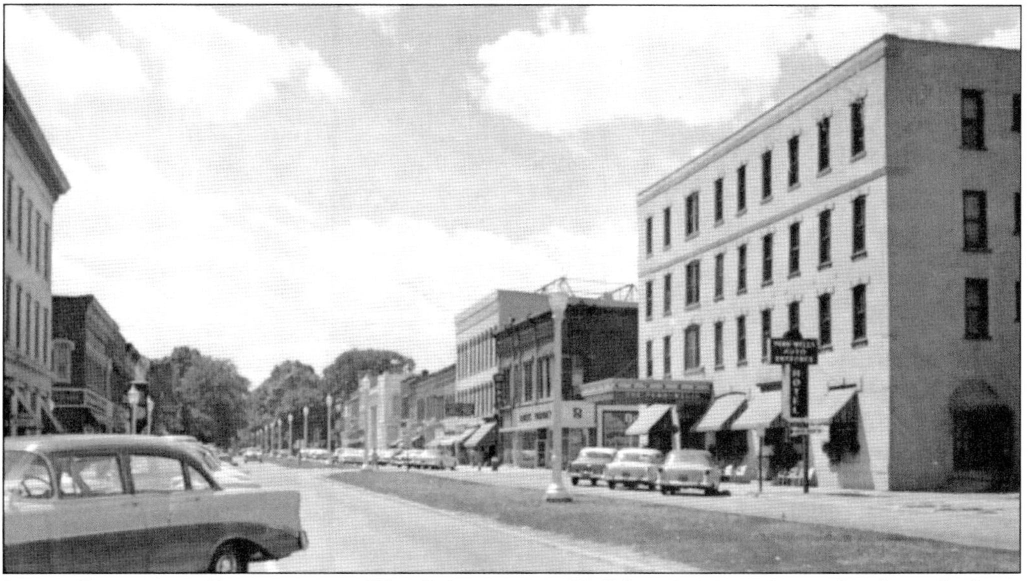

Light Poles and Boulevards. The fight to save Wellsboro's Main Street boulevards dates back to the 1930s but climaxed in 1963. The state wanted them removed, but Charles Webb and Frank Dunham proposed narrowing the islands and changing to parallel parking. The cast-iron light poles, installed about 1913, were replaced in 1968 by Wellsboro's signature gaslights. (Courtesy TCHS.)

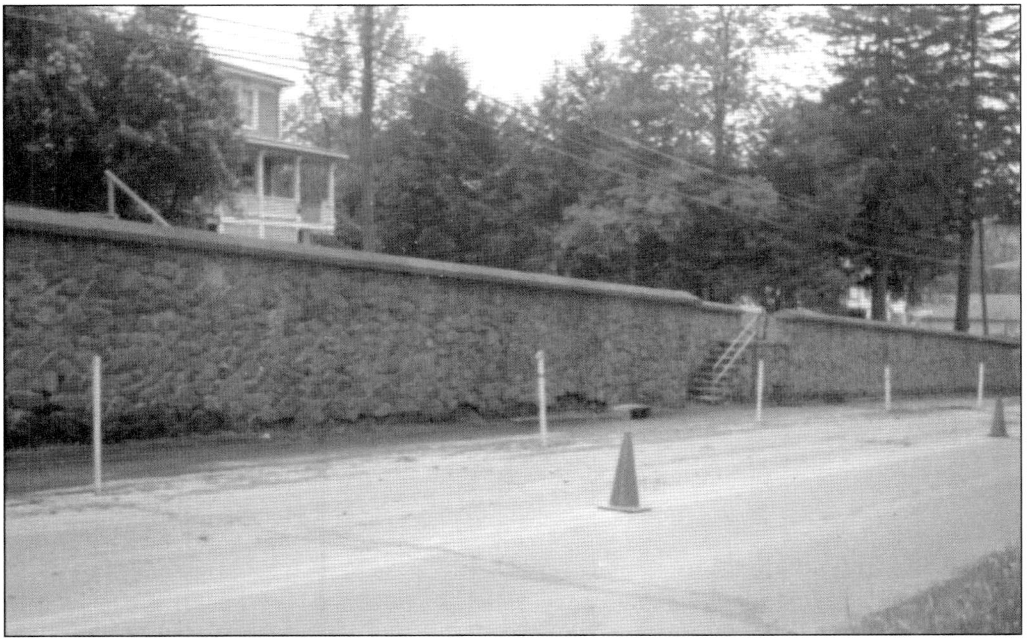

East Avenue Wall. The Work Projects Administration (WPA) built the old stone wall on East Avenue in 1939 for $19,000, embedding a horseshoe and a buckle in the structure. Local children enjoyed walking its distance or throwing snowballs at passing cars from behind the wall. A cracked section led to its demolition in the late 1980s. The wall was replaced in 1989 with a concrete retaining wall topped with a brown chain-link fence. (Courtesy Lorraine Nearing.)

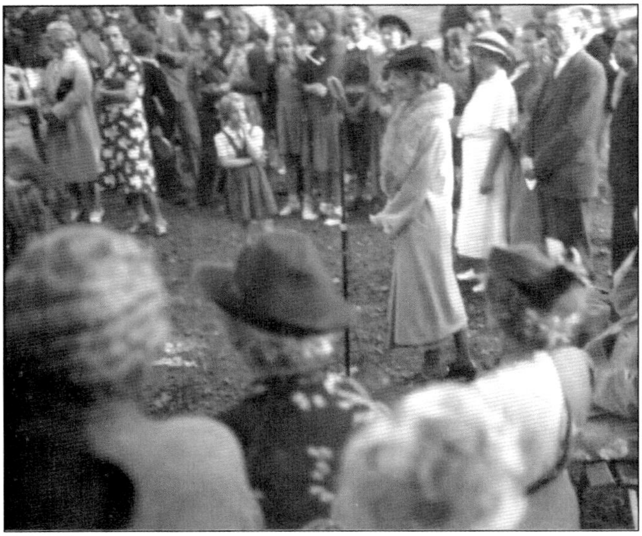

Fountain Dedication. On September 23, 1938, an audience of 2,000 people, including many schoolchildren, attended the unveiling of Wellsboro's beloved *Wynken, Blynken, and Nod* fountain on the Green. The Honorable Fred W. Bailey gave the bronze statue to Wellsboro's children in memory of his wife, Elizabeth Cameron Bailey, daughter of Judge David Cameron, who lived at 12 West Avenue. Eugene Field's 1889 poem "Dutch Lullaby" inspired the fountain's creator, Mabel Landrum Torrey, who attended the ceremony. (Courtesy TCHS.)

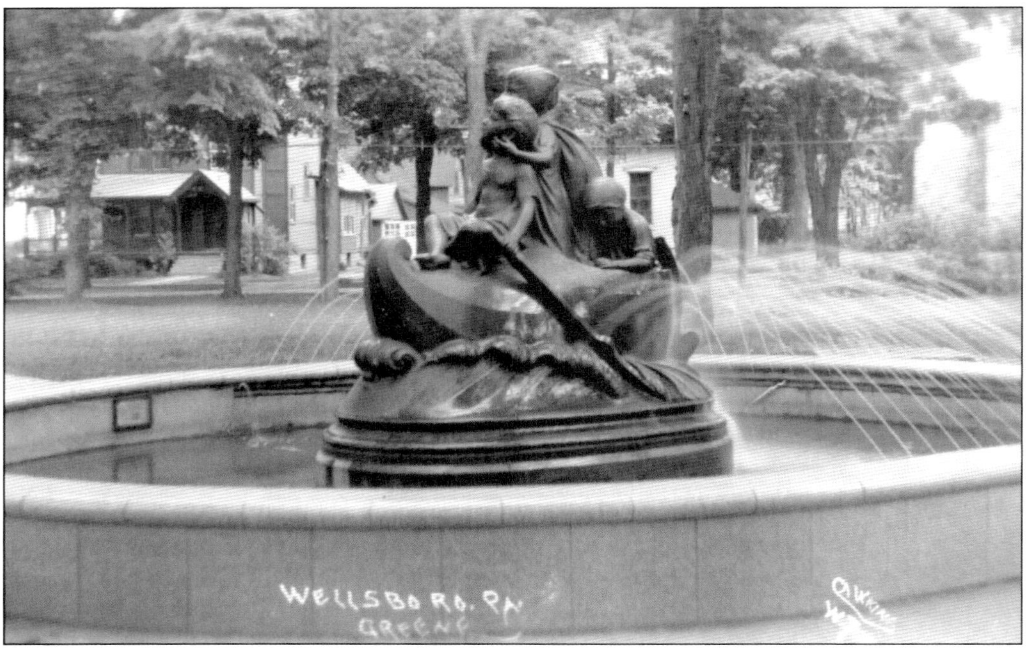

Wynken, Blynken, and Nod. The Wellsboro Lions Club financed the wrought-iron fence surrounding the fountain in 1950. Soldiers and Sailors Memorial Hospital contributed a plaque with the words of "Dutch Lullaby" in 1976. From time to time, soap bubbles appeared in the fountain, a mystery that remains unsolved.

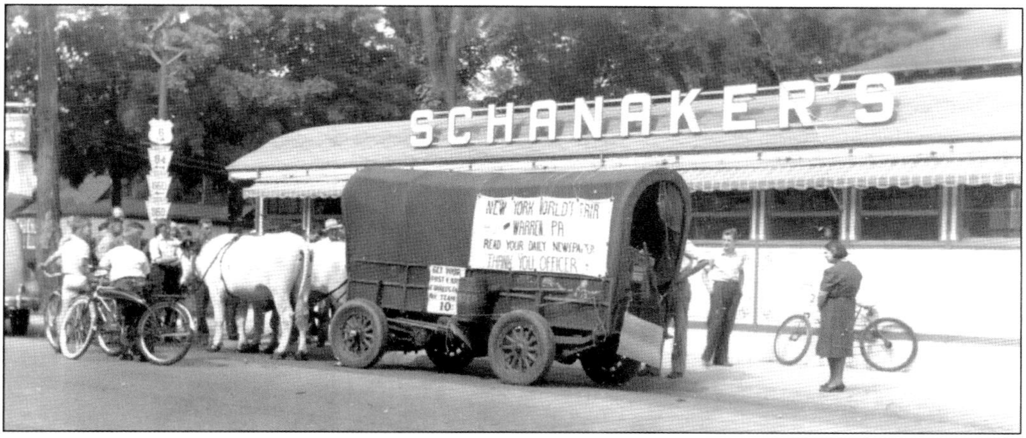

SCHANAKER'S DINER. In 1939, a Sterling diner arrived in two parts from Massachusetts. Louis Meier and his brother-in-law Walter Schanaker opened the diner, operating it as Schanaker's until the 1960s. Clem Sipe purchased the renamed Wellsboro Diner in 1968, followed by Dorothea Cummings in 1972. Juaneldn Rounsaville currently owns the landmark diner.

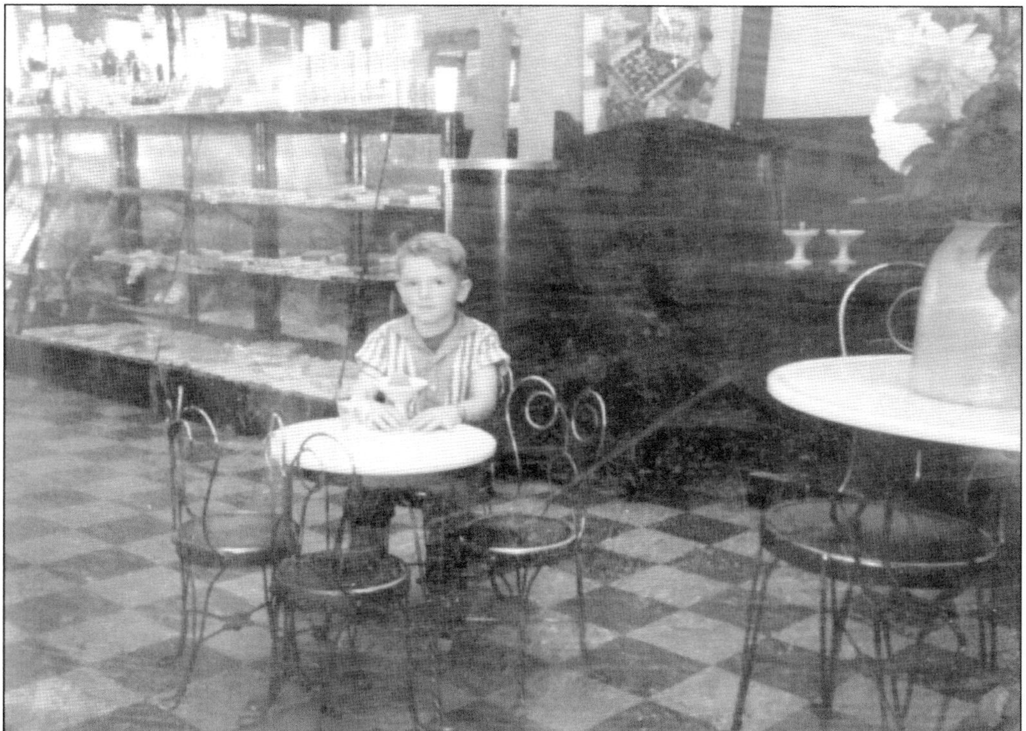

CANDY KITCHEN. A 1903 advertisement claimed, "Science has discovered that we all need a considerable amount of sugar as food." Numerous candy stores and ice-cream parlors operated in Wellsboro, including Owen Smith's Palace, which was sold to Mike Zarvis in 1915. Mike's brother Gus joined the business following World War II. Gus Zarvis invented the "Million Dollar Recipe" for hot fudge sauce. The Candy Kitchen closed in 1967; Zarvis gave the recipe to local restaurateur John Harris. In 1962, Shirley Weber photographed her son Ray at the marble-topped children's table in the Candy Kitchen. (Courtesy Ray Weber.)

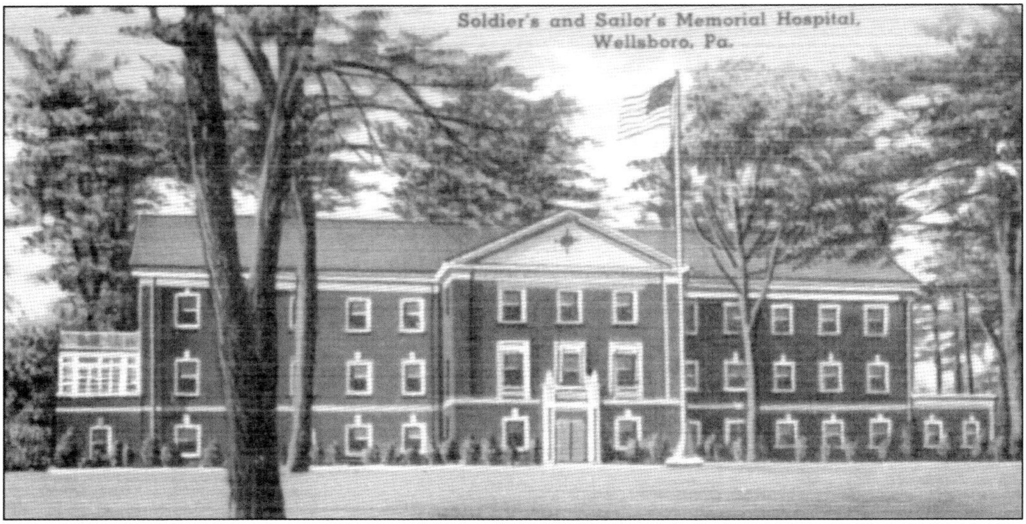

Soldiers and Sailors Memorial Hospital. Following World War I, prominent citizens, including Frank Watrous, Leonard Harrison, and Horace Packer, wished to honor veterans and their families with a hospital that provided free care. Time passed until legal action demanded that a hospital finally be built. By the time it opened on August 24, 1942, World War II was underway, making free care for veterans impossible. Soldiers and Sailors Memorial Hospital became a voluntary, nonprofit community hospital built on Simpson's Grove, so called because of pine trees on the property. Numerous historical buildings have been demolished, including the Catholic rectory in 2014, as the hospital has continued to expand up Central Avenue.

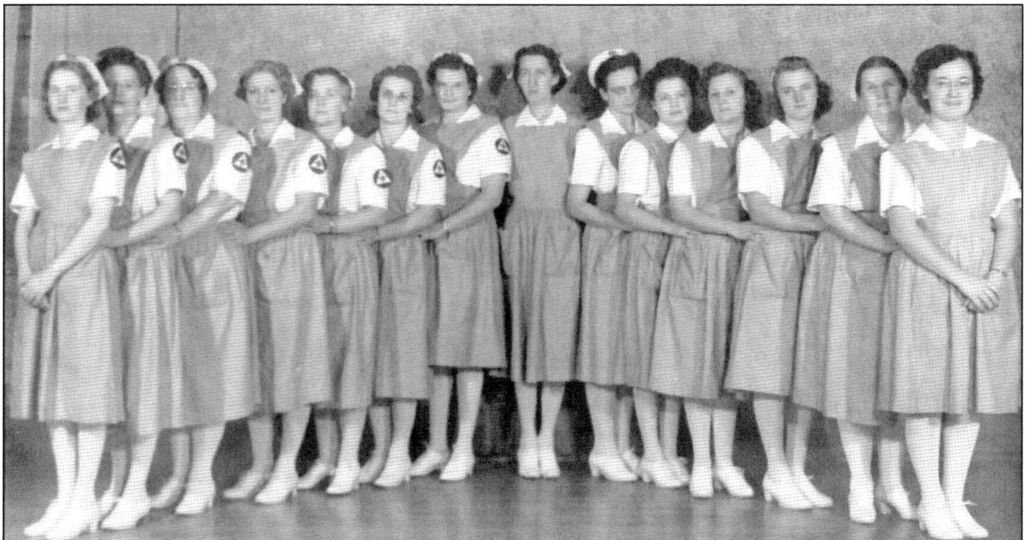

Red Cross Nurses' Aides. Soldiers and Sailors Memorial Hospital offered classes to train nurses' aides. The photograph shows the first Red Cross nurses' aide class of 1943. It includes, from left to right, Dorothy Scudder, Rema Boom, Mildred Geralds, Rachel Peake Suhr, Sally Webb, Winifred Williams, Martha Hastings, Laura Lawton, Josephine Bacon, Gertrude Vanderhoof, Florence Taynton, Lilian Petengill, Ethel Walker, and Geraldine Townsend. Not pictured is teacher Celeste Soderquist. (Courtesy TCHS.)

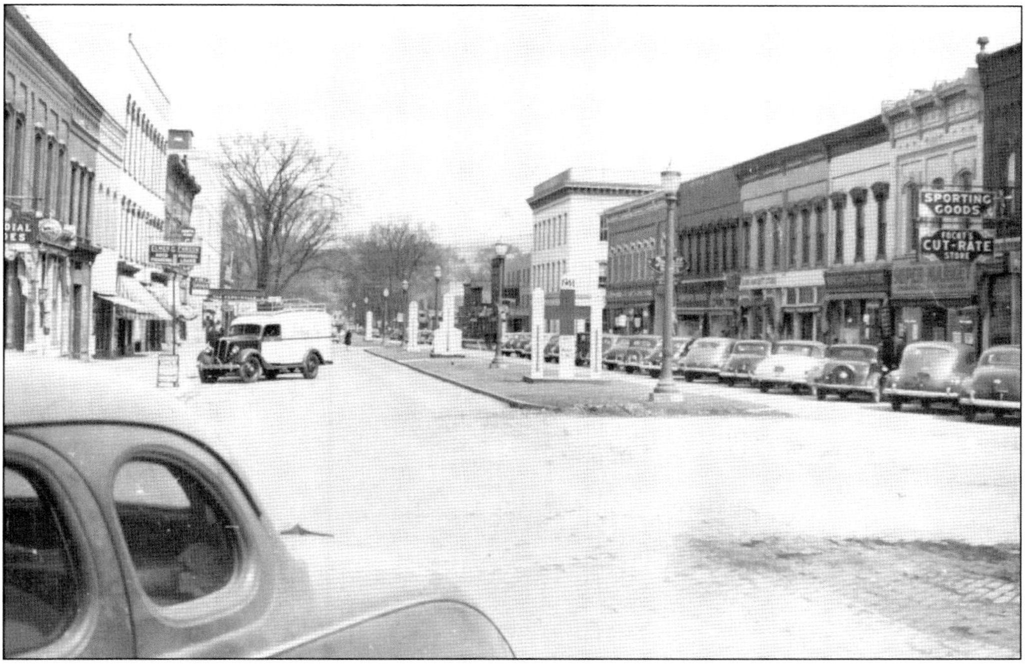

RED CROSS WAR LOAN DRIVE. The invasion of Normandy on June 6, 1944, launched the most ambitious war loan drive in American history, with a goal of $15 billion. The motto "Invest in Invasion" encouraged the people to buy "to the limit of their resources." Elwyn Lewis chaired the local effort. Larry Woodin offered free admission to bond buyers at a "Bond Premiere" of *The Kansan* to be shown at the Arcadia Theatre on June 22. Bonds were sold at banks, the post office, and Corning Glass Works. Wellsboro citizens far exceeded their quota, raising $758,568. (Courtesy Mia Anderson.)

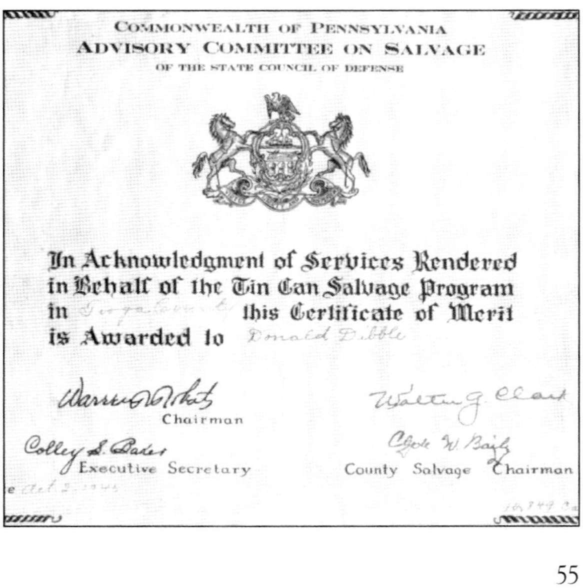
COMMONWEALTH OF PENNSYLVANIA
ADVISORY COMMITTEE ON SALVAGE
OF THE STATE COUNCIL OF DEFENSE

In Acknowledgment of Services Rendered in Behalf of the Tin Can Salvage Program in [illegible] this Certificate of Merit is Awarded to Donald Dibble

Chairman

Executive Secretary

County Salvage Chairman

TIN CAN SALVAGE. Wellsboro participated enthusiastically in salvage programs during World War II. A "key barrel" placed by the Trust Company clock on Main Street collected useless keys. Hunters deposited their empty shotgun shells at the nearest salvage center. Students collected salvage, especially tin cans, in order to advance from corporal to brigadier general, ranks denoted by service stripes and based on the number of cans they collected. The West Branch School's 15 pupils completed the highest per capita collection in April 1944, with Donald Dibble topping the list in 1945 with 10,849 cans. (Courtesy Donald Dibble.)

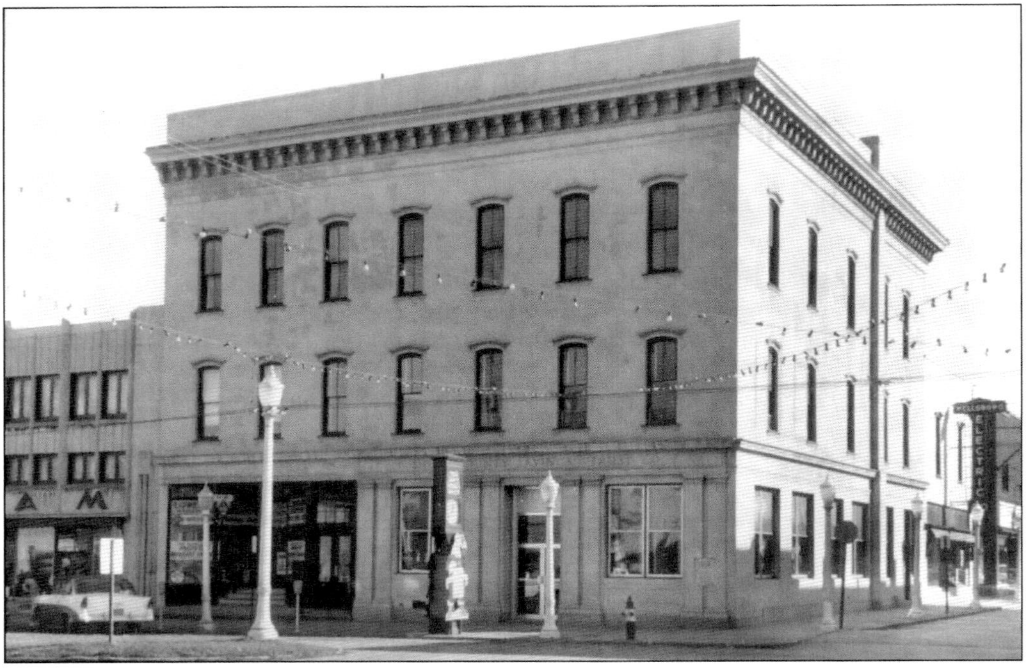

TIOGA COUNTY SAVINGS & TRUST COMPANY. In 1818, Jeremiah Brown built his home on the corner of Waln and Main Streets, later the site of Tioga County Savings & Trust. The bank purchased the Wilcox Hall building in 1910 and renovated it in 1923. Until the third floor was removed in 1964, the building was the largest in Tioga County. The town clock stood on the sidewalk between 1915 and 1965. Lowell's Hardware occupied the north corner of the building, remaining there until 1958. The corner of the building was enclosed in 1961. (Courtesy Northwest Bank.)

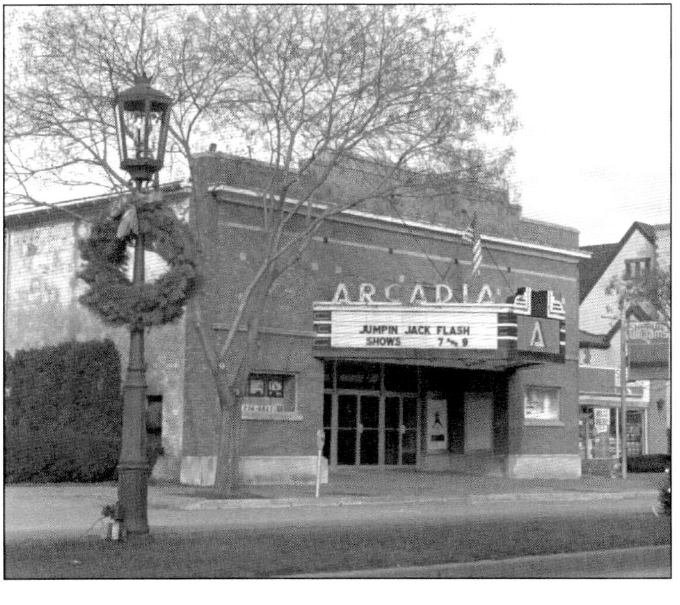

ARCADIA THEATRE. Irvin Focht and Leon Klock opened the Arcadia in December 1921. Equipped with an organ, a piano, and an orchestra, the theater showed a silent movie, *The Old Nest*, at its premiere. William Woodin and W.H. Seigel purchased the theater in 1929 and named Woodin's son Larry as the manager. The Arcadia achieved distinction by showing talkies in 1929, before most northern theaters. Frank Dunham purchased the Arcadia in 1958, followed by the Wellsboro Hotel Company in 1987. (Courtesy Elgin Sink.)

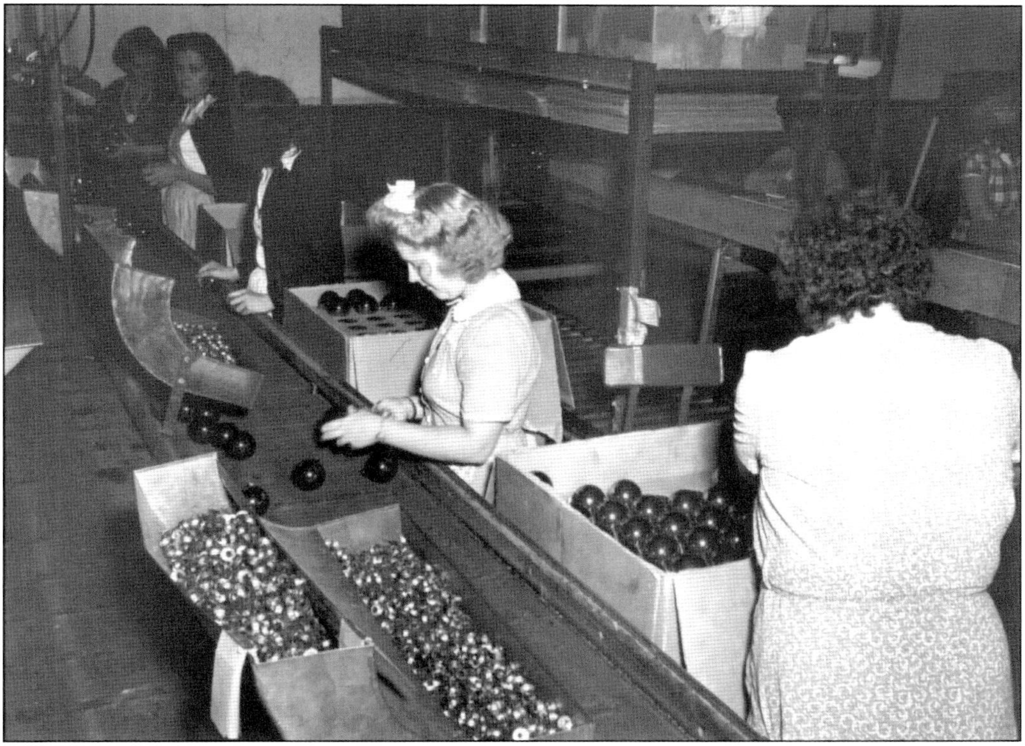

Christmas Ornaments. World War II impacted Corning Glass Works in unforeseen ways. The British blockade of Germany during World War II stopped shipments of Christmas ornaments from Germany and Czechoslovakia, creating an opportunity for Corning Glass Works (CGW) to begin producing Christmas bulbs in 1939. In 1940, astonishingly, CGW's 500 employees made more than 40 million ornaments. After December 7, 1941, Corning Glass became an E Defense Plant with regular inspections by Army personnel; tubes for radio transmitters also became a major product. (Courtesy Corning Incorporated Archives.)

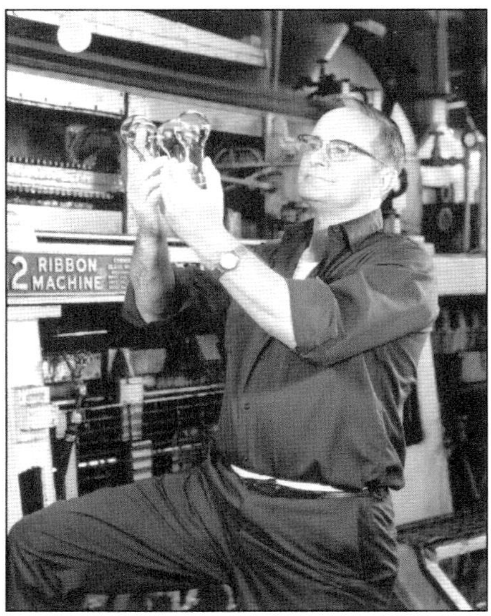

The Ribbon Machine. After the installation of inventor Billy Woods's world-famous ribbon machines at the Wellsboro plant in 1926, production of glass bulbs exploded. Wood's automatic glass-forming machines derived their name from the continuous ribbon of molten glass that fed through a series of mechanized steps, ultimately producing a lightbulb that was formed, frosted, packed, and shipped. The photograph shows Welford "Dreamer" Losinger checking bulbs for defects before packing. (Courtesy Corning Incorporated Archives.)

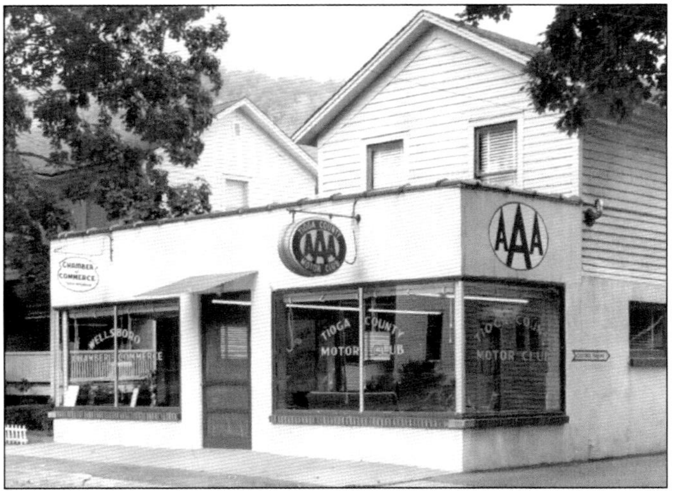

TIOGA COUNTY MOTOR CLUB. In 1926, Wellsboro organized the first Tioga County Motor Club, affiliated with the North Central Motor Club of AAA. In about 1950, the club moved to 13 Water Street, shown here. Leon Moshier managed the AAA from 1929 to 1960. The organization moved to Queen Street in August 1967. (Courtesy TCHS.)

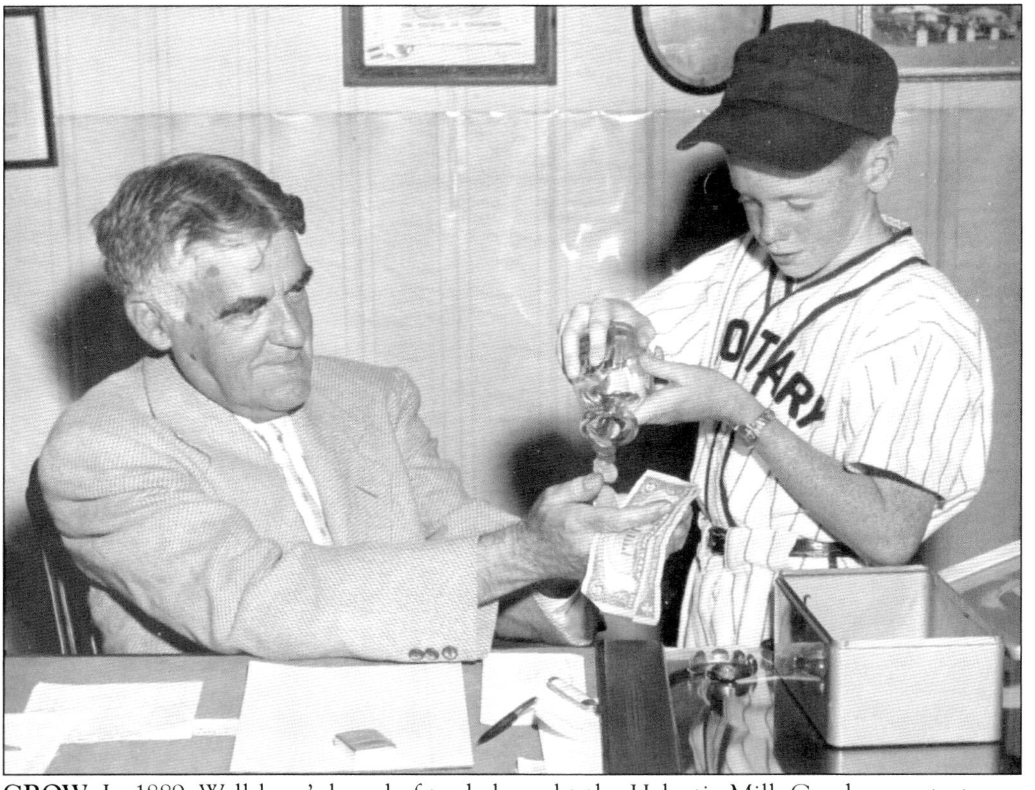

GROW. In 1889, Wellsboro's board of trade brought the Helvetia Milk Condensery to town. The chamber of commerce, previously the Community Club, attracted Corning Glass Works to Wellsboro in 1916. In 1956, the newly formed Growth Resources of Wellsboro (GROW) continued the tradition when it announced that Dresser Industries would settle in Delmar Township if the community could raise $180,000 in 10 days for site development. Clyde Bailey served as chairman of "Operation GROW." Elwyn Lewis was named GROW president in 1957. The photograph shows Bailey's grandson, Ed Osgood, contributing $9.84 to the community effort. (Courtesy Erin Webster.)

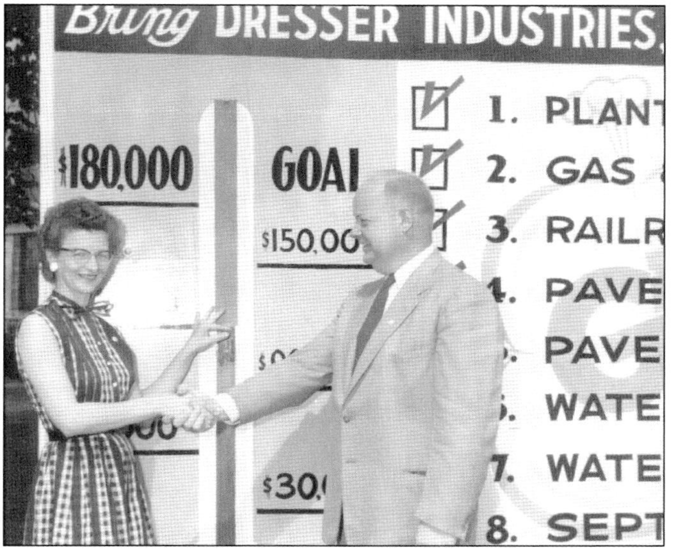

Dresser Industries. By July 1, 1956, through contributions and pledges made by banks, businesses, and individuals, Operation GROW raised $230,000 in 10 days, $50,000 above the goal of $180,000. In rapid-fire succession, ground breaking occurred on July 23; construction began on July 24; the plant opened on November 1; and the first part was produced on December 10. Steering committee member Bill Wilkinson is pictured in front of the fundraising thermometer with one of many participants. (Courtesy Teri Keck Carson.)

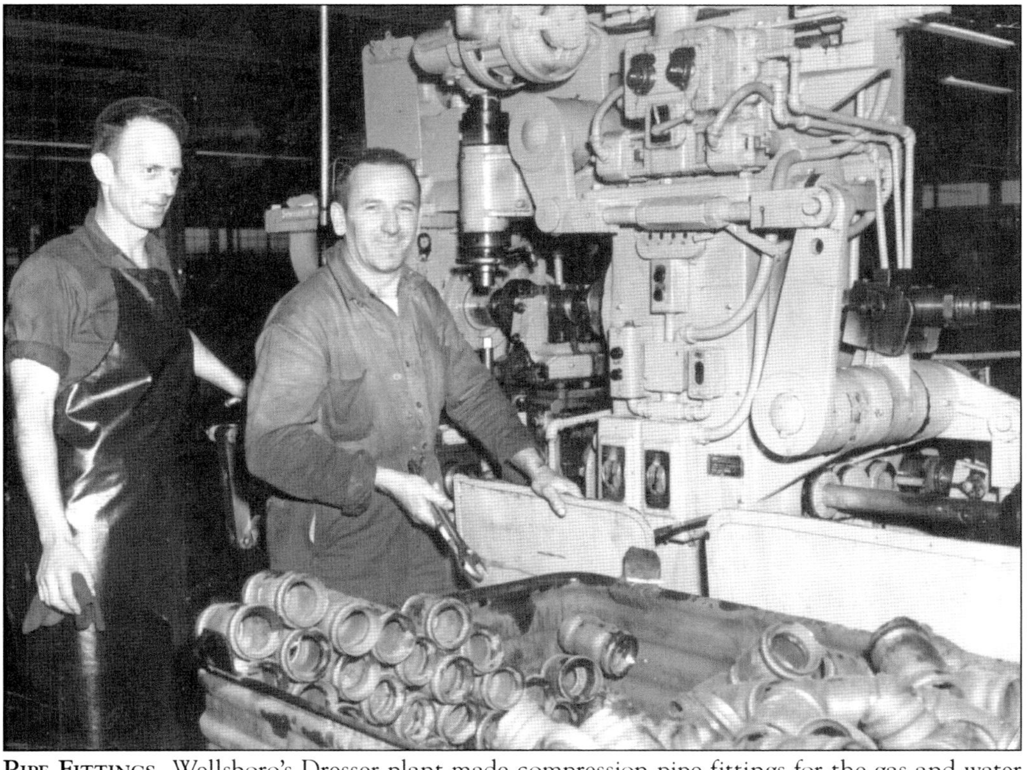

Pipe Fittings. Wellsboro's Dresser plant made compression pipe fittings for the gas and water industries. When interviewed by the *Wellsboro Gazette*, plant manager Robert V. Poling reported, "Dresser is particularly proud of its employees at Wellsboro. They are not only talented and skilled at their jobs but are also good citizens." The photograph shows Adam Kugla (right) and Waldo Smith working at the Dresser plant in 1957. (Courtesy Teri Keck Carson.)

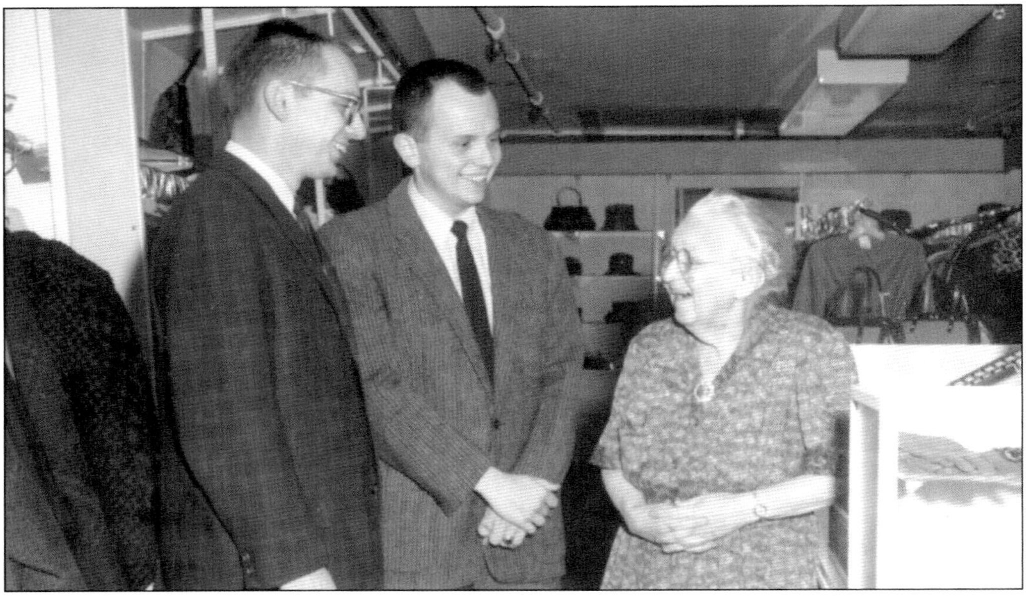

Dunham's Department Store. Roy J. and Fannie Treat Dunham purchased an interest in an existing grocery store on Main Street in March 1905. For over 100 years, the Dunham family operated innumerable businesses and participated in countless civic activities in Wellsboro. Roy Dunham and son Frank built the three-story department store on Main Street in 1932, in the middle of the Depression, in part to generate jobs. When Roy died in 1937, Frank took over the family business. Frank's son James signed on in 1955; John joined the business in 1961. Youngest brother Bob followed in 1966 and now operates Dunham's Furniture. John's daughter Ann carries on the family tradition as vice president of merchandising. Fannie, pictured in 1964 with grandsons James (left) and John (right), managed the upstairs office until she became ill at work in May 1970. She died the following day. (Courtesy Ann Dunham Rawson.)

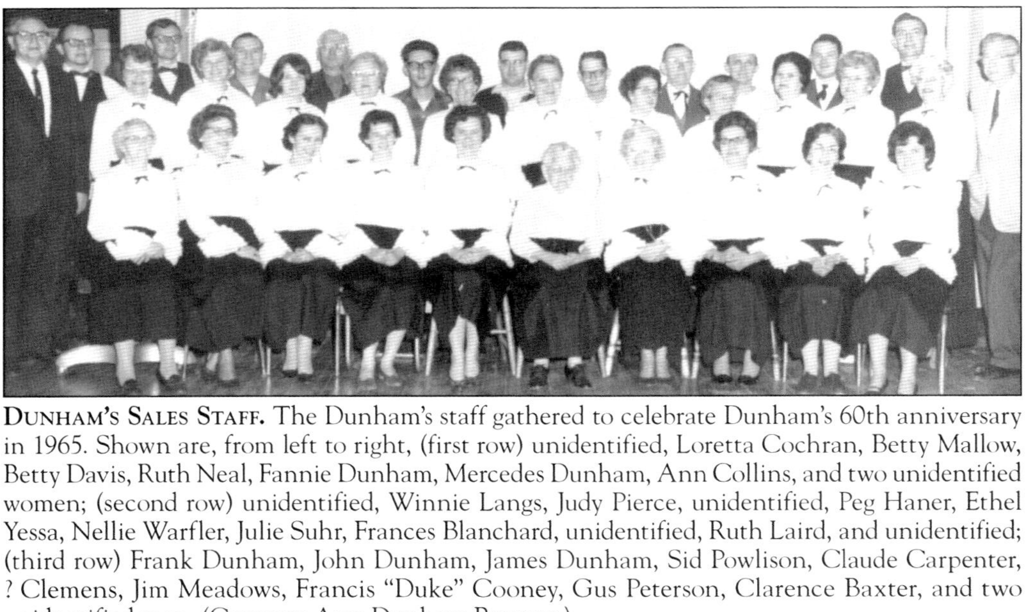

Dunham's Sales Staff. The Dunham's staff gathered to celebrate Dunham's 60th anniversary in 1965. Shown are, from left to right, (first row) unidentified, Loretta Cochran, Betty Mallow, Betty Davis, Ruth Neal, Fannie Dunham, Mercedes Dunham, Ann Collins, and two unidentified women; (second row) unidentified, Winnie Langs, Judy Pierce, unidentified, Peg Haner, Ethel Yessa, Nellie Warfler, Julie Suhr, Frances Blanchard, unidentified, Ruth Laird, and unidentified; (third row) Frank Dunham, John Dunham, James Dunham, Sid Powlison, Claude Carpenter, ? Clemens, Jim Meadows, Francis "Duke" Cooney, Gus Peterson, Clarence Baxter, and two unidentified men. (Courtesy Ann Dunham Rawson.)

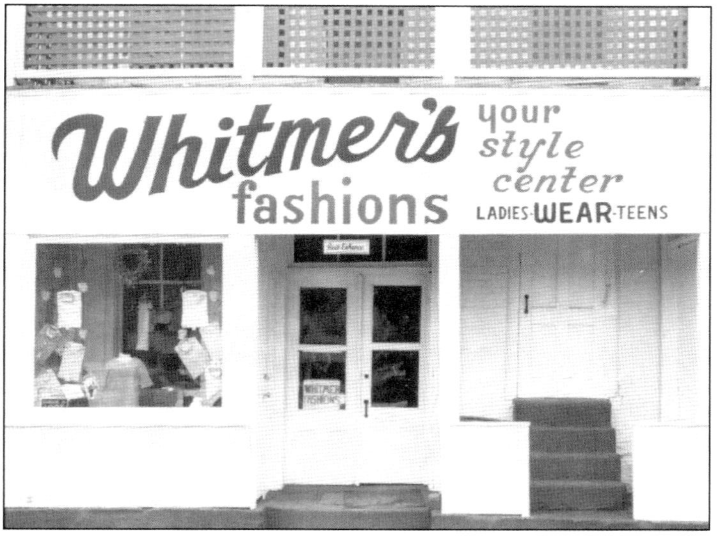

WHITMER'S FASHIONS. Joanna and Paul Whitmer purchased the Mildred Shoppe from Mildred Moran in 1961. Whitmer's motto, "We Help You Dress Your Best for Less," guided the business until 1987, when Silvina and Ronald Smith purchased the motto and the building. Whitmer's is remembered for its artful window displays, which made window-shopping on Main Street such a pleasure. (Courtesy TCHS.)

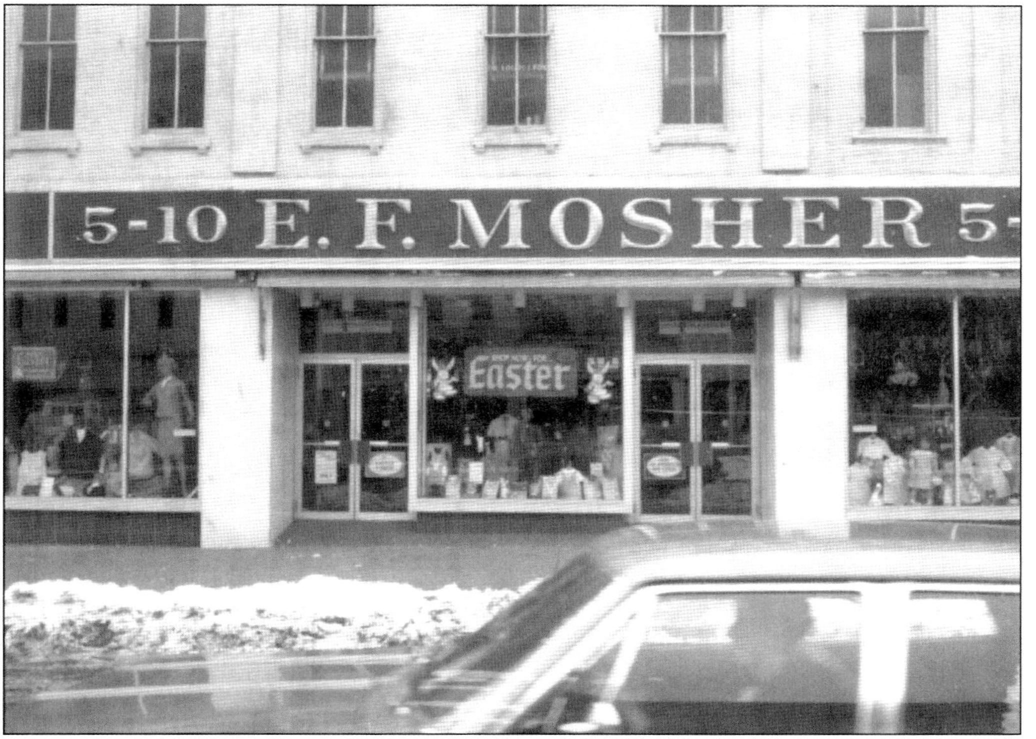

MOSHER 5 & 10 CENT STORE. Robert F. Mosher established his dime store at 77 Main Street in 1907. Elbert F. Mosher followed in 1923. The store was enlarged, with James G. Paxson as manager, in 1953 when Market Basket moved out of the Mosher Building on Main Street and into a cinder-block building that later became the Acme Supermarket. When the Candy Kitchen closed in 1967, Mosher purchased the property and expanded in the opposite direction. Paxson purchased the business in 1963, renaming it Paxson's Ben Franklin. James J. Paxson operated the store from 1974 until it closed on February 29, 2000. Timeless Destination, an upscale restaurant, opened at that location later that year. (Courtesy James Paxson.)

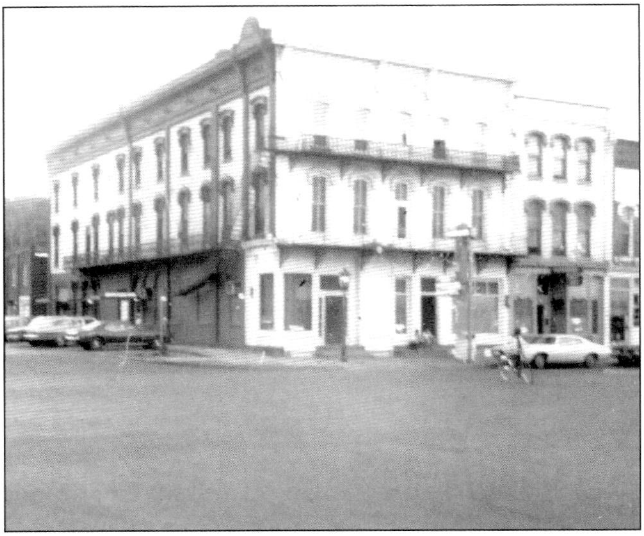

PARKVIEW HOTEL. This historic building located at the corner of Central Avenue and Main Street changed occupants numerous times between 1875 and 1953, the year that the Parkview Hotel opened under the management of Daniel Jamison, with his mother, Alice Newell, as cook. In 1965, Morrell "Smokey" Spencer purchased the edifice, managed by Ambrose "Om" Bogaczyk. Raymond Finizio bought the building in 1974, renaming the business the Lamplighter Inn. (Courtesy of James and Joann Spencer.)

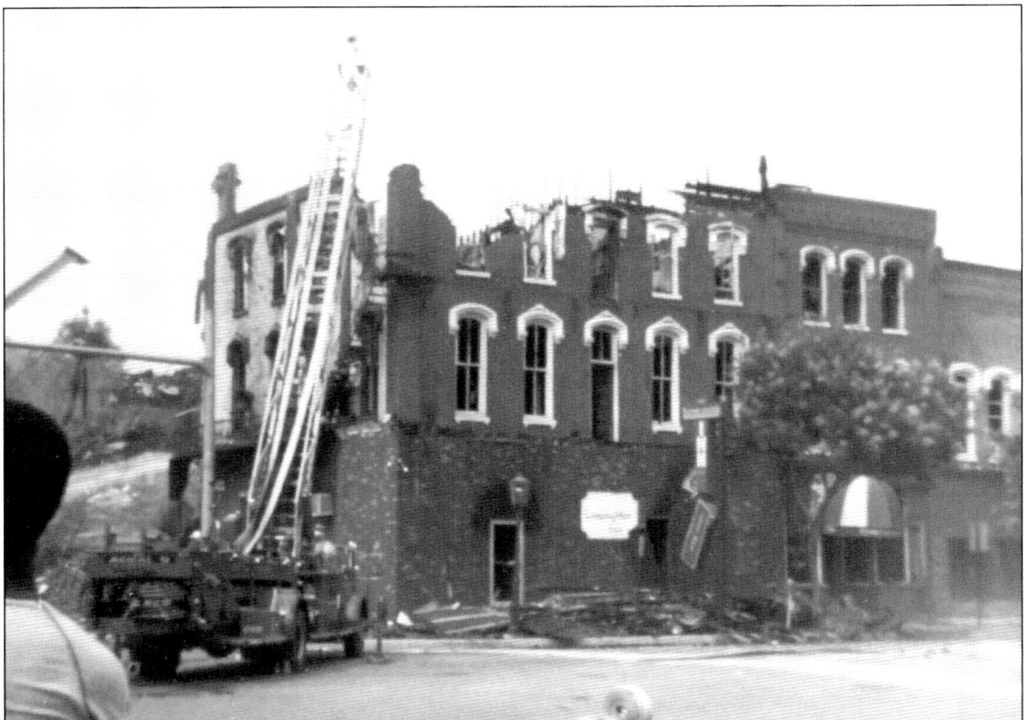

LAMPLIGHTER FIRE. On August 29, 1980, the 105-year-old building that housed the Wilcox House (1875), the A.C. Evans Apartment House (1920s), the Parkview Hotel (1953–1969), and the Lamplighter (1974–1980) burned in a devastating fire that claimed the lives of three men—Jeffrey Kropp (age 28), Harold Smith (age 42), and Roland Davis (age 30). Investigation revealed that the fire had been intentionally set. The court case that followed in 1987 produced a disappointing verdict, holding nobody fully accountable for the loss of life or for the destruction of one of Wellsboro's remaining historic buildings. District attorney James E. Carlson proclaimed that the Lamplighter case was over. (Courtesy WFD.)

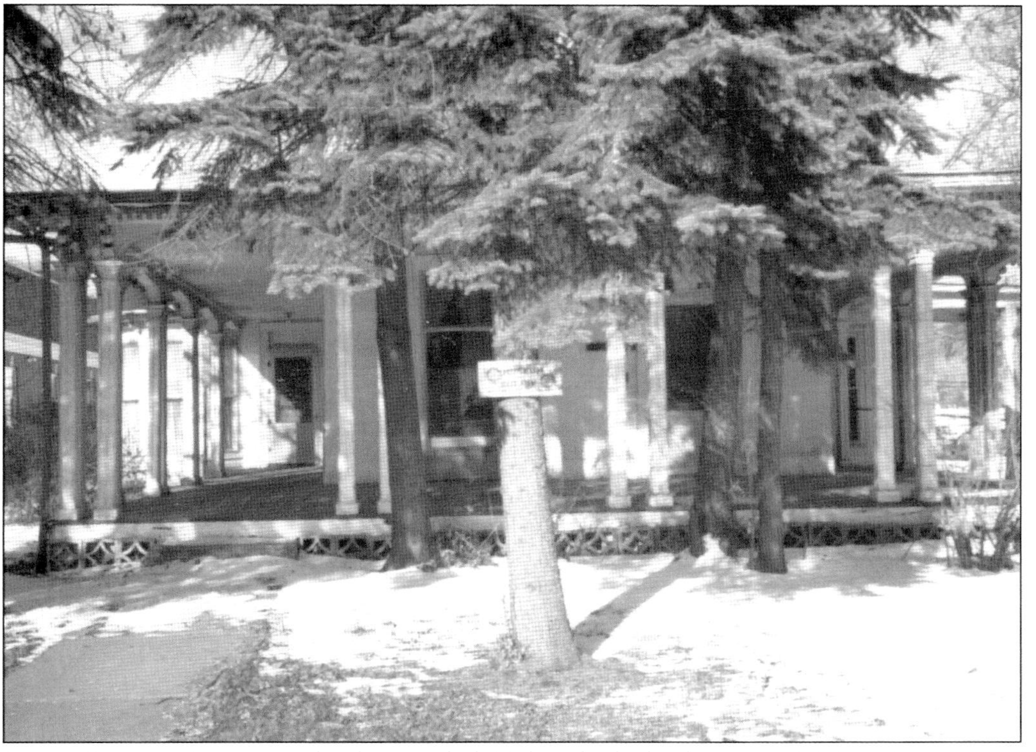

Clark Wilcox House. Lumber baron Clark Wilcox built this house at 12 Main Street; it was later occupied by Charles F. Miller, a 20th-century descendent of pioneer Mary Wells Morris. Dr. Archibald Laird located his ophthalmology practice in this building; in May 1984, he also opened the Museum of Rotary, the first museum of its kind in the United States. The Wellsboro Hotel Company purchased the property in 1989 and razed the buildings. The Penn Wells Motel currently occupies the site. (Above, courtesy Victoria Pongrace; below, courtesy Archibald Laird II.)

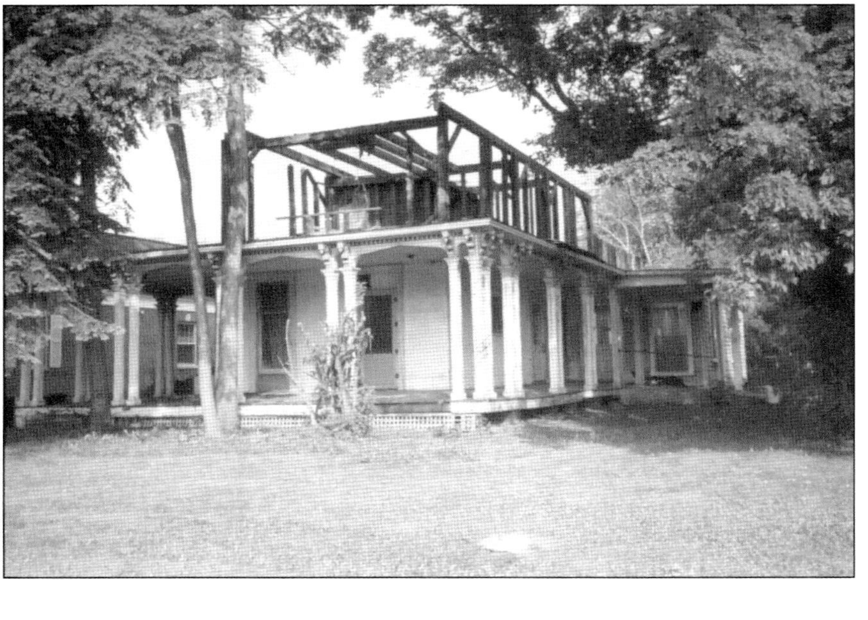

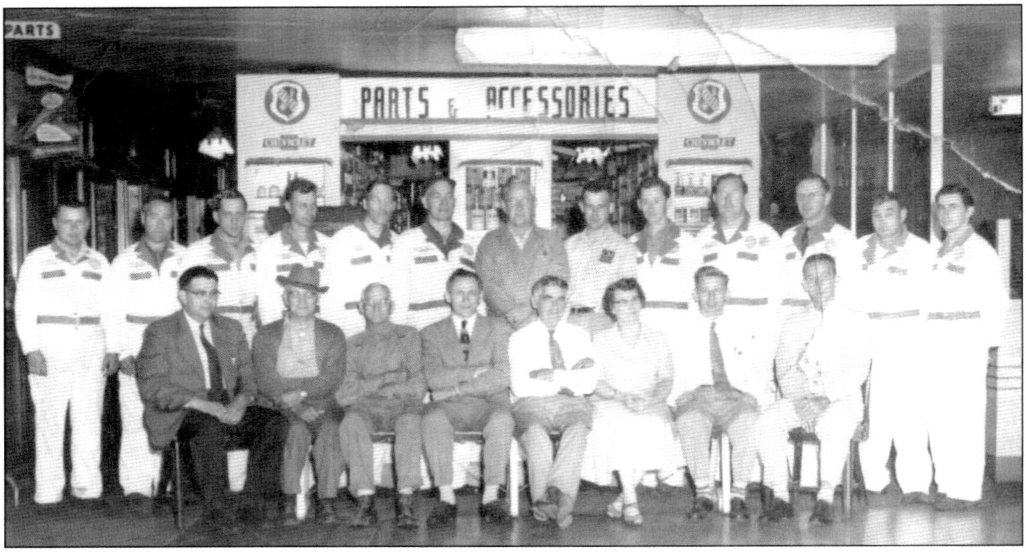

Evans Auto Company. Evans Auto, located on the corner of Pearl and Waln Streets, began as the firm of Evans and Snyder in 1914. Evans bought out his partner in 1915 and changed the name to the Otis H. Evans Auto Company. In 1933, the name changed again, to Evans Auto Company; Evans served as president until his death in 1941. In 1917, the business sold Buicks, and in 1930, Chevrolets. The Evans Auto Garage opened in 1923. Pictured are, from left to right, (seated) John Harris, Willard Bryant, Steve Yessa, Ted Osgood, Clyde Bailey, Wanda Austin, Don Smithgall, and Ben Powers; (standing) Frank Dominski, Marina Summers, Burton Briggs, Max Gillespie, Hugh Champaign, Frank Brooks, Albert Soderquist, Wallace Bailey, Jesse Bryant, Charles Hollenbeck, Glenn Blair, Harold Davis, Elwood Austin. (Courtesy Cheri Hollenbeck Bartolotti.)

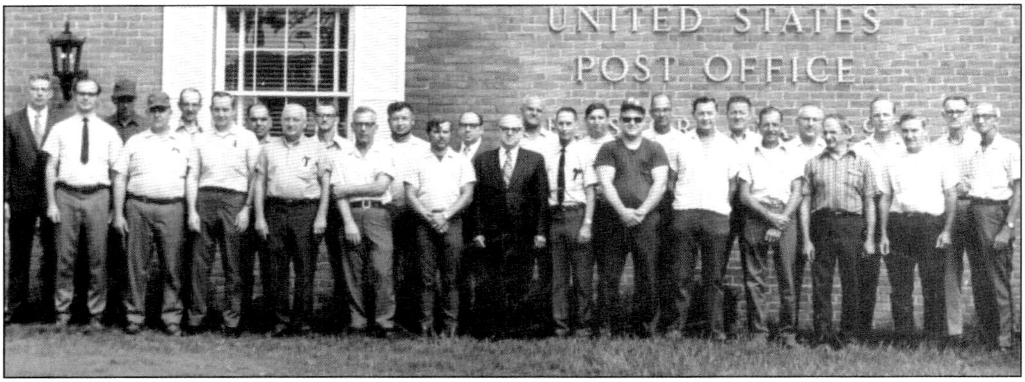

Main Street Post Office. In 1970, the Wellsboro Post Office was selected to serve as the Sectional Center Post Office for 35 other offices in handling mail. Having outgrown its home on Waln Street, the post office moved to a new facility on lower Main Street on January 1, 1971. This photograph, taken at that time, includes, from left to right (first row) Raymond Strykowski, Buster Gerow, Donald Boyce, Daniel Jones, Quay Brocious, Peter Losinger, postmaster Bud Fullwood, John Shumway, Gary Mahonski, Sam Linton, Norton Benjamin, Gordon Erway, Bill Obourn, and James Jackson; (second row) assistant postmaster John Frazier, George Baker, Mac Wetmore, James Saturn, Loren Losey, Dean Hall, Larue Goodreau, Robert Ward, Theodore Zuchowski, Vince Calhoun, Benjamin Hall, James Anderson, Thomas Stager, and John E. Wilcox. (Courtesy Mia Anderson.)

Four

Community Life

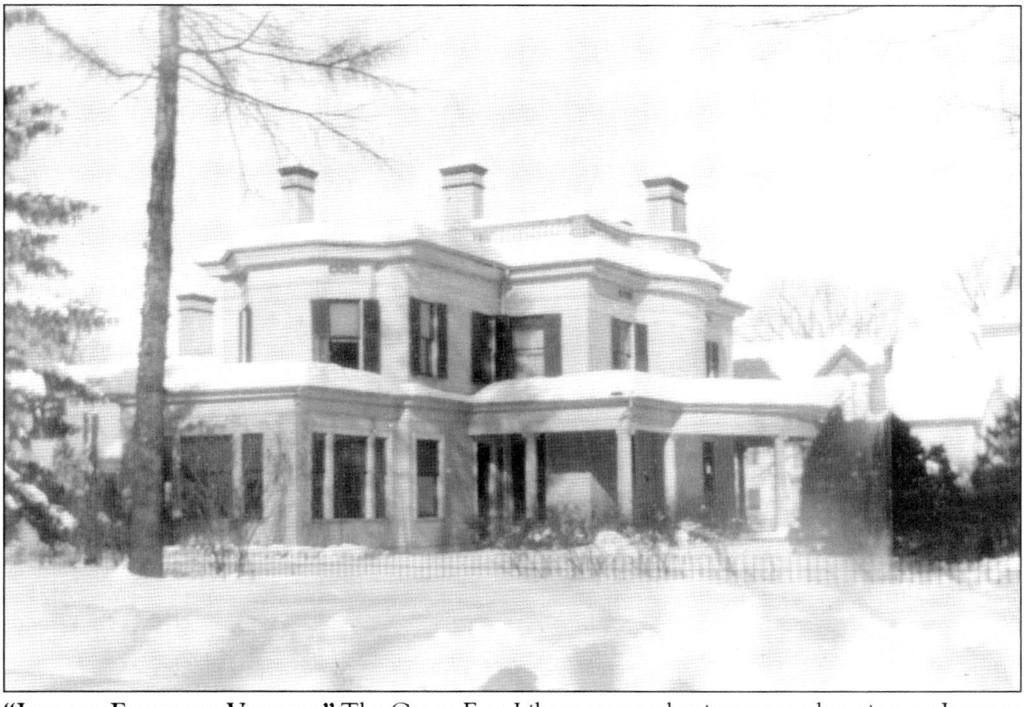

"LIBRARY FENCE FOR VICTORY." The Green Free Library opened at its present location on January 26, 1917. The town donated the 5,190-pound fence to the war scrap effort in 1943. The fence traveled by truck to Painted Post, where it was cut up for immediate shipment to a steel mill. Clyde Bailey, county salvage chairman, reported that $40 had been added to the Rehabilitation Fund. (Courtesy Mike Spencer.)

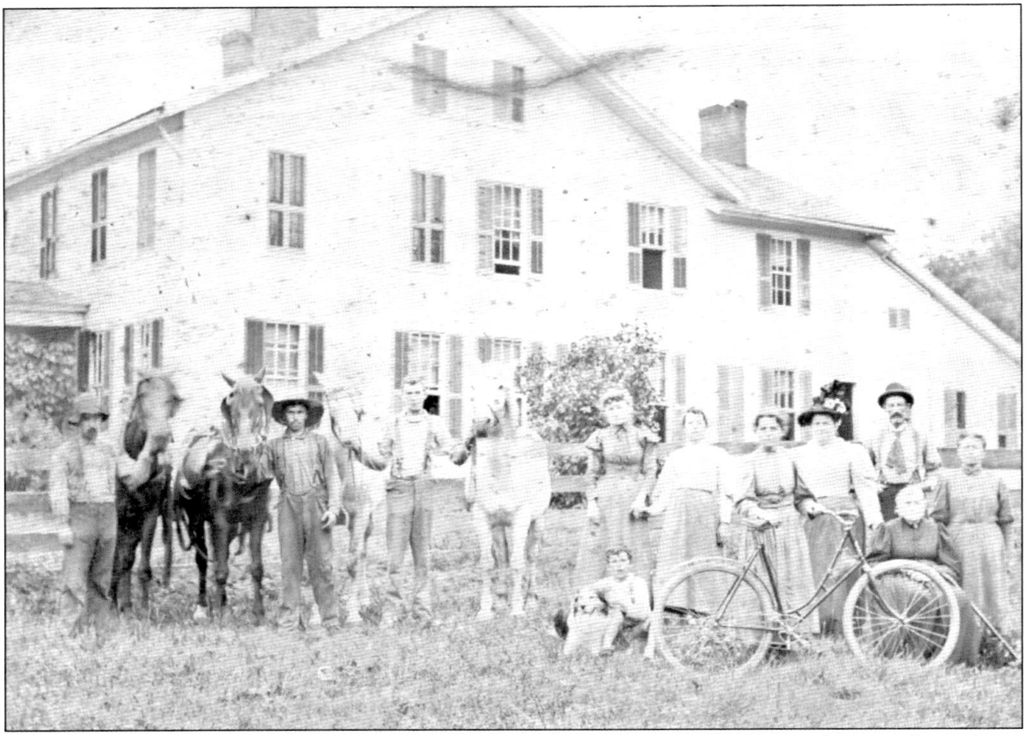

TYOGA COUNTY COUNTRY CLUB. Storms that caused the flood of 1919 also destroyed two large barns and 20 tons of hay at the Edwin Matson farm, two miles west of Wellsboro. This loss may have motivated the family to sell their 206-acre farm and large farmhouse to the Tyoga County Country Club. Organized by a group of young, enthusiastic people, the club officially opened on July 4, 1923. (Courtesy Dean Andrews.)

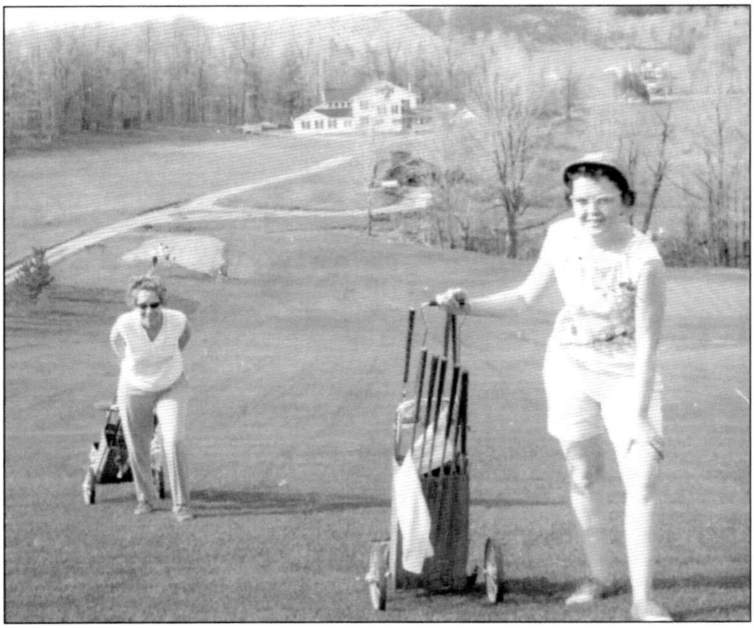

GOLF COURSE. The topography of the Matson farm lent itself to sports, especially golf. Situated on a rolling hillside, rich in natural hazards, the original four-hole course was expanded to eighteen holes in 1979. Here, members Janet Wilkinson (right) and Mary Maynard enjoy a round of golf. (Courtesy Elgin Sink.)

ALLEN LEWIS. Golfers identified in this image are Wellsboro High School principal Allen Lewis (center) and Harold Keck Sr. (right). Note the 1957 Cadillac parked nearby. (Courtesy Elgin Sink.)

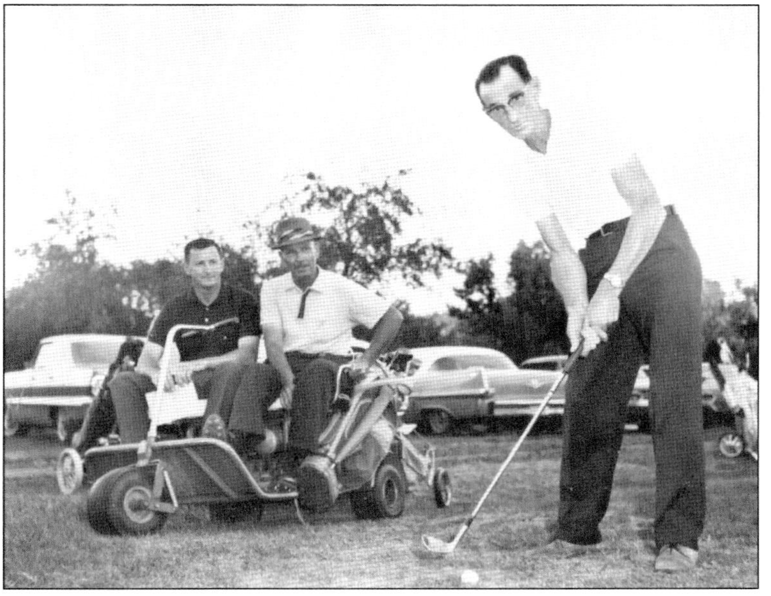

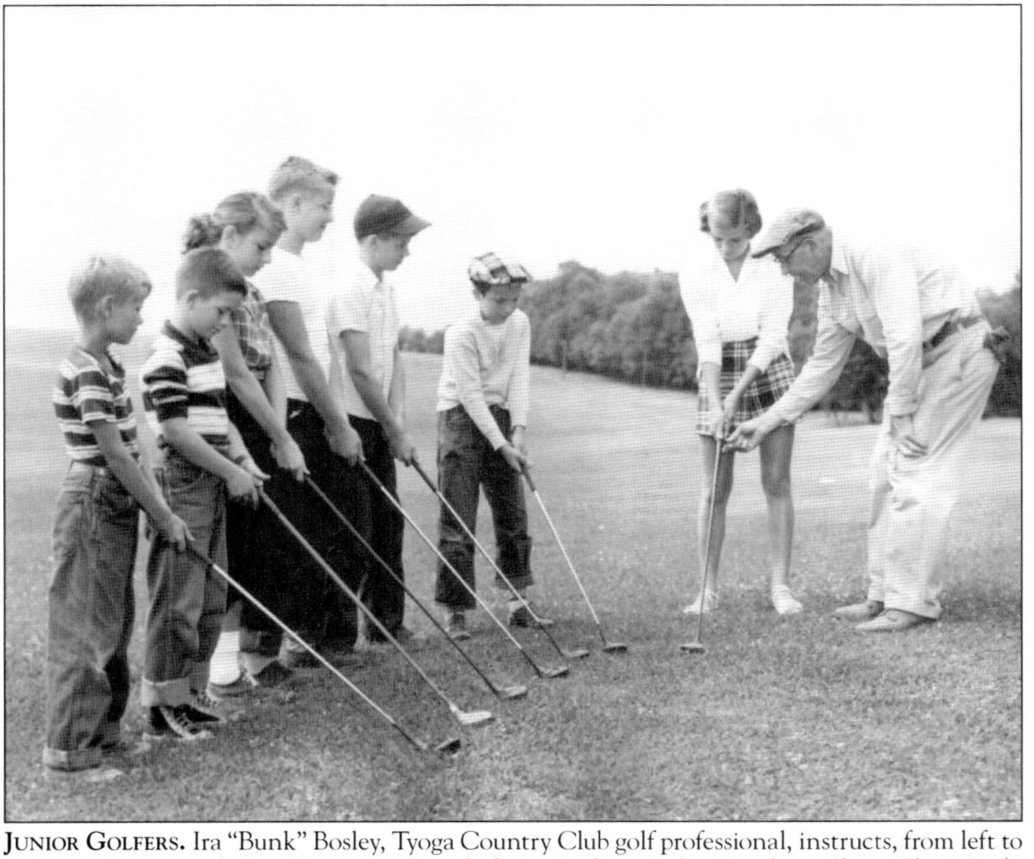

JUNIOR GOLFERS. Ira "Bunk" Bosley, Tyoga Country Club golf professional, instructs, from left to right, Dick Maynard, Tim Kerns, unidentified, Art Lofgren, John Knudsen, Elgin "Skip" Sink, and Margie Doumaux in 1953. (Courtesy Elgin Sink.)

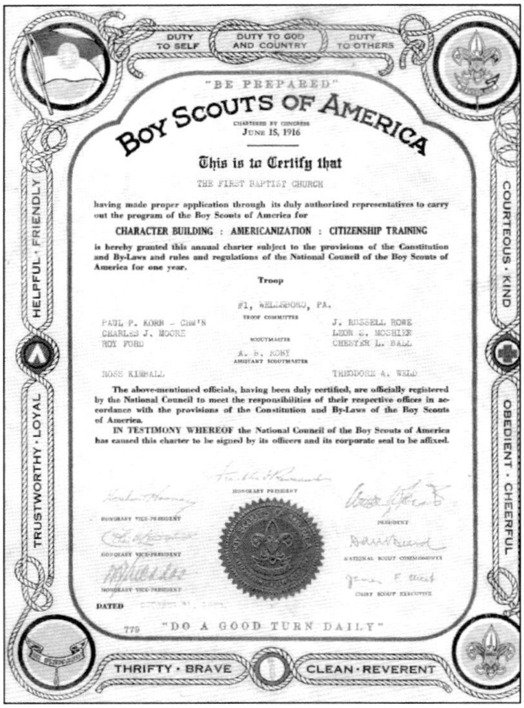

DUTY TO SELF
DUTY TO GOD AND COUNTRY
DUTY TO OTHERS

"BE PREPARED"

BOY SCOUTS OF AMERICA

CHARTERED BY CONGRESS
JUNE 15, 1916

This is to Certify that

THE FIRST BAPTIST CHURCH

having made proper application through its duly authorized representatives to carry out the program of the Boy Scouts of America for

CHARACTER BUILDING : AMERICANIZATION : CITIZENSHIP TRAINING

is hereby granted this annual charter subject to the provisions of the Constitution and By-Laws and rules and regulations of the National Council of the Boy Scouts of America for one year.

Troop

#1, WELLSBORO, PA.

TROOP COMMITTEE

PAUL P. KORB – CHM'N
CHARLES J. MOORE
ROY FORD
J. RUSSELL ROWE
LEON S. MOSHIER
CHESTER L. BALL

SCOUTMASTER
A. B. ROBY
ASSISTANT SCOUTMASTER

ROSS KIMBALL
THEODORE A. WELD

The above-mentioned officials, having been duly certified, are officially registered by the National Council to meet the responsibilities of their respective offices in accordance with the provisions of the Constitution and By-Laws of the Boy Scouts of America.

IN TESTIMONY WHEREOF the National Council of the Boy Scouts of America has caused this charter to be signed by its officers and its corporate seal to be affixed.

HONORARY PRESIDENT
HONORARY VICE-PRESIDENT
PRESIDENT
HONORARY VICE-PRESIDENT
NATIONAL SCOUT COMMISSIONER
HONORARY VICE-PRESIDENT
CHIEF SCOUT EXECUTIVE

DATED

779 "DO A GOOD TURN DAILY"

HELPFUL · FRIENDLY
TRUSTWORTHY · LOYAL
COURTEOUS · KIND
OBEDIENT · CHEERFUL
THRIFTY · BRAVE
CLEAN · REVERENT

Boy Scouts of America Certificate. Representatives of the First Baptist Church received this certificate, dated October 31, 1933, founding Wellsboro's first Boy Scout troop. Committee members included Roy Ford, Wellsboro Candy Company; J. Russell Rowe, Rowe's Bookstore; Leon S. Moshier, Tioga County Motor Club; and Theodore A. Weld, Wellsboro Telephone Company.

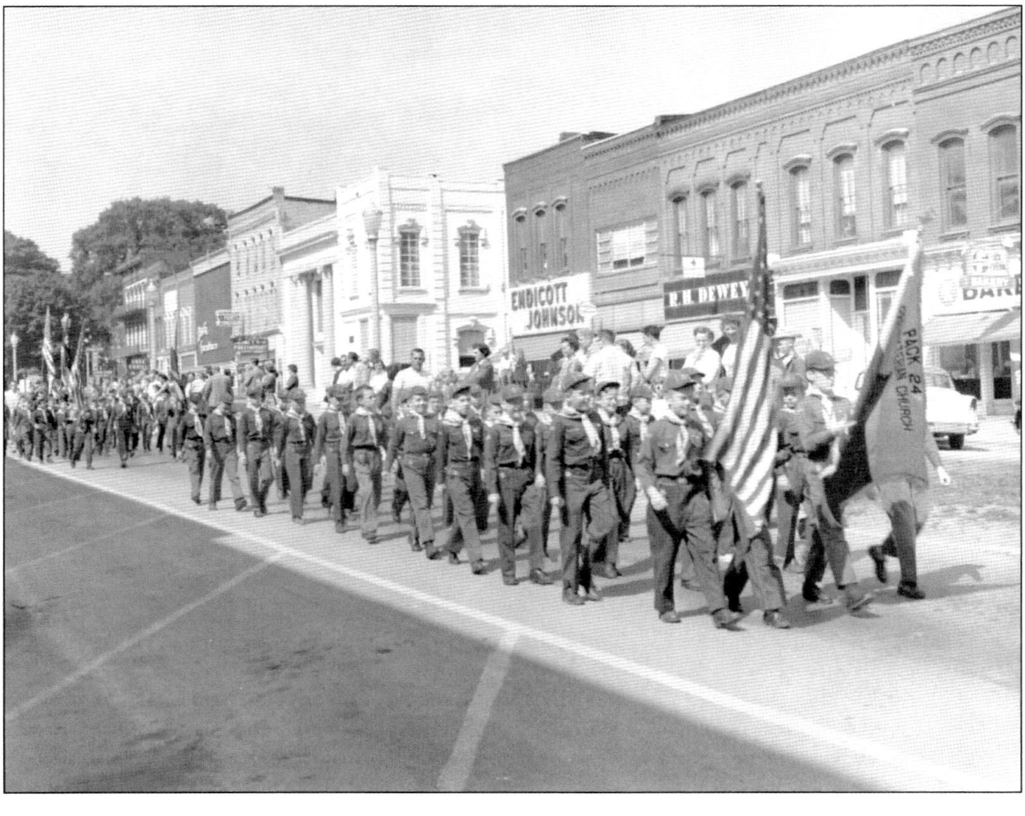

Cub Scout Parade. Cub Scouts, led by Pack 24 of the Presbyterian church, march down Main Street between Crafton and Waln Streets in the mid-1950s. (Courtesy Dennis Bliss.)

Troop 32 of the First Methodist Church. Reorganized in 1961 under the direction of Dr. Archibald Laird, Troop 32 watches as Laird's son Archie performs on the bar in his Meade Street backyard. Members of this Boy Scout troop include, from left to right, Carlo Bennett, Dennis Brucklacher, Barry Brucklacher, James Dale, Terry Goff, Jerry French, Russell Jackson, Alba Monks, and Archie Laird. (Courtesy Archibald Laird II.)

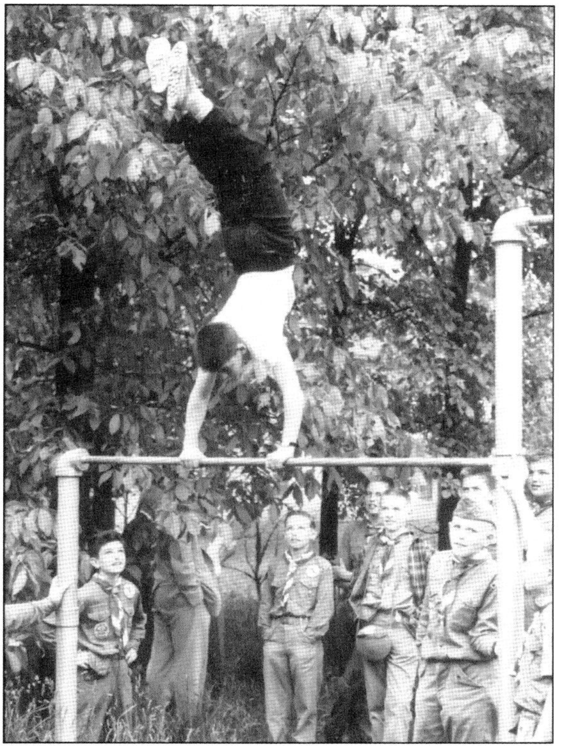

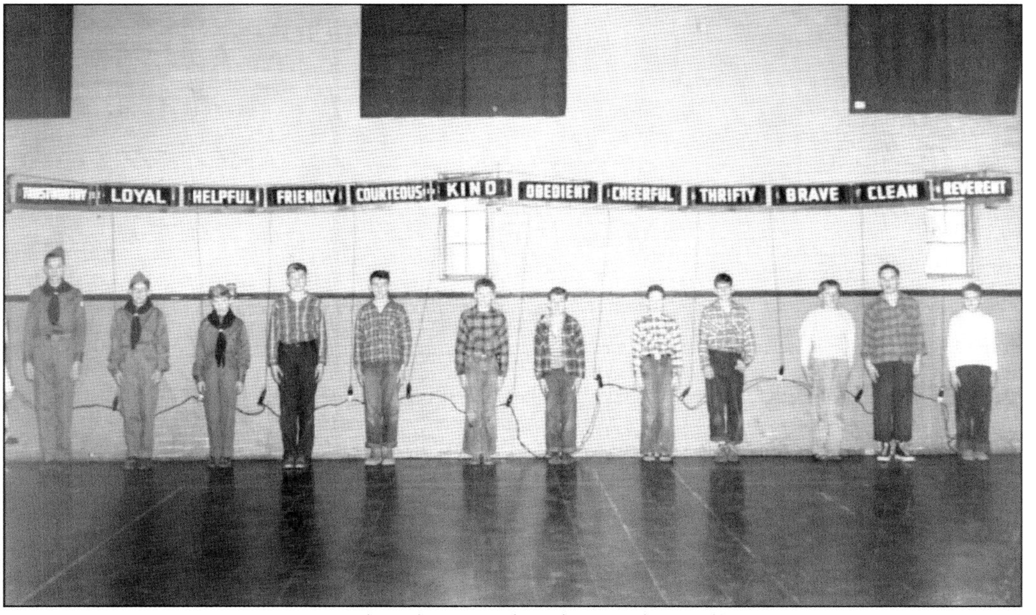

Twelve Points of Scout Law. This photograph, taken at the Wellsboro Armory on January 2, 1950, emphasizes the character traits valued by the Boy Scouts of America. The boys pictured include, from left to right, David Patterson, Washburn Laird, Robert Laird, Donald LeVan, Arden Sears, William Robertson, William Sticklin, Dick Cruttenden, John Sticklin, Billy Rouse, James Hinder, and Fred Simons. (Courtesy Victoria Pongrace.)

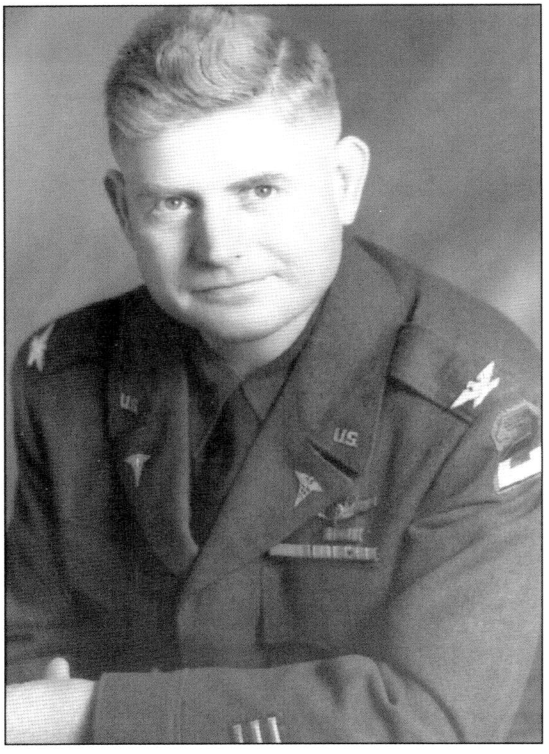

Brig. Gen. Archibald Laird. Author of *Twentieth Century Wildcats: A History of the Pennsylvania National Guard Medical Units in Tioga County 1920–1963*, Laird achieved literary, civic, professional, and military accomplishments that testify to his intelligence, energy, and character. He served in the US Army during World War II; practiced ophthalmology from 1931 to 1987; and founded the Rotary Museum at 12 Main Street. (Courtesy Archibald Laird II.)

The National Guard. The National Guard marches in the 1966 Laurel Parade with Ellsworth Rumsey leading at far right. (Courtesy Dennis Rumsey.)

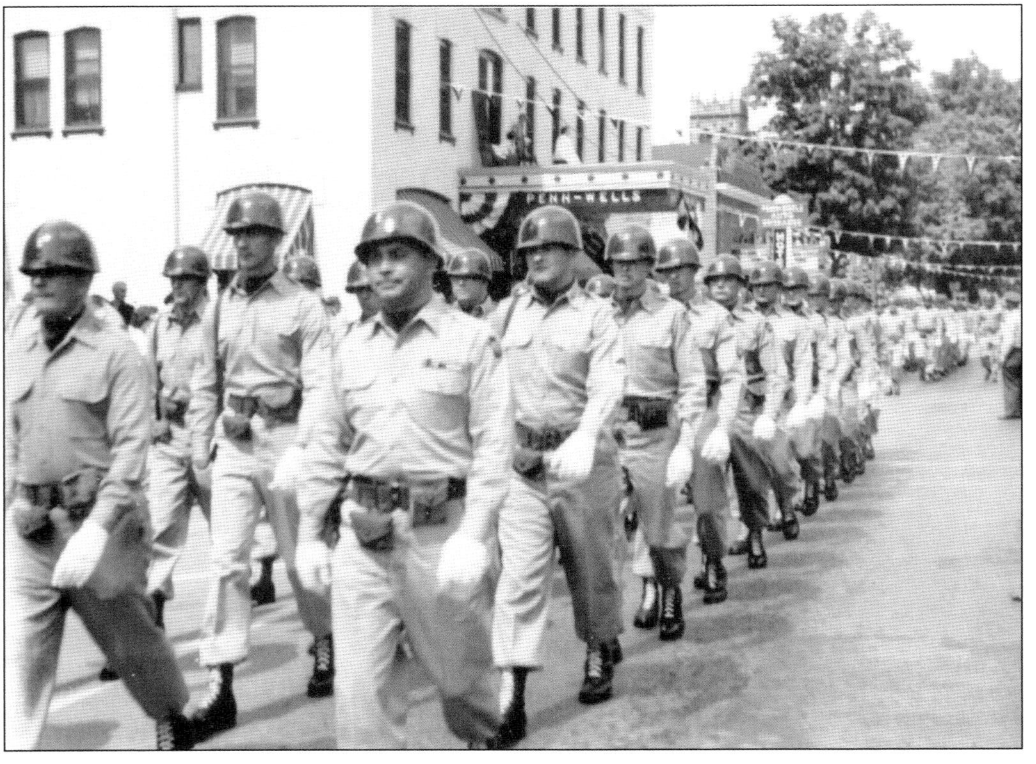

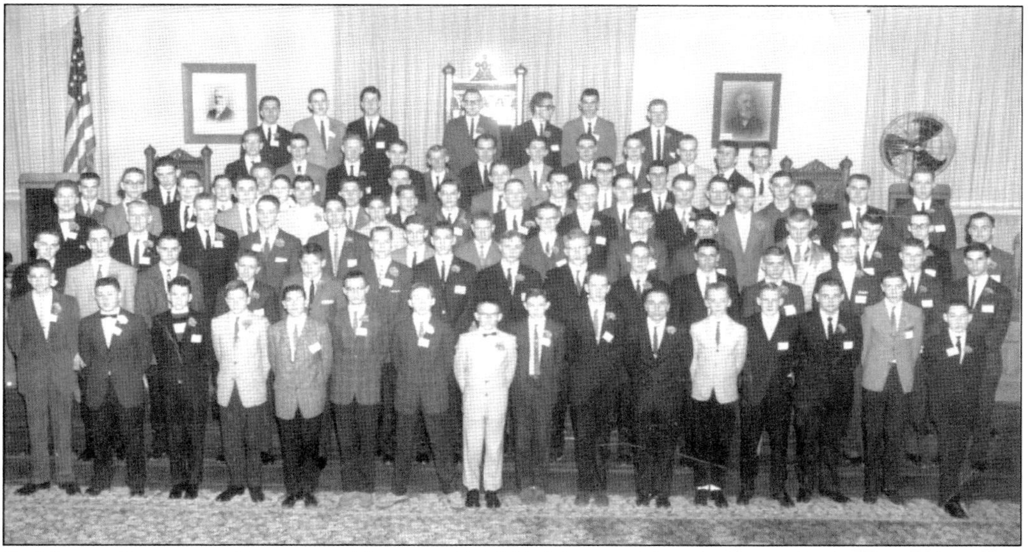

DEMOLAY CHARTER. Constituted January 11, 1858, Masonic Temple, Ossea Lodge No. 317 met in Masonic Hall, Williams Block, until 1894. Thereafter, the Masons leased Annandale Hall in the Simpson Block. The DeMolay Charter was issued in 1962. Charter members, pictured here, include graduates of Wellsboro High School classes from 1963 to 1967. (Courtesy Archibald Laird II.)

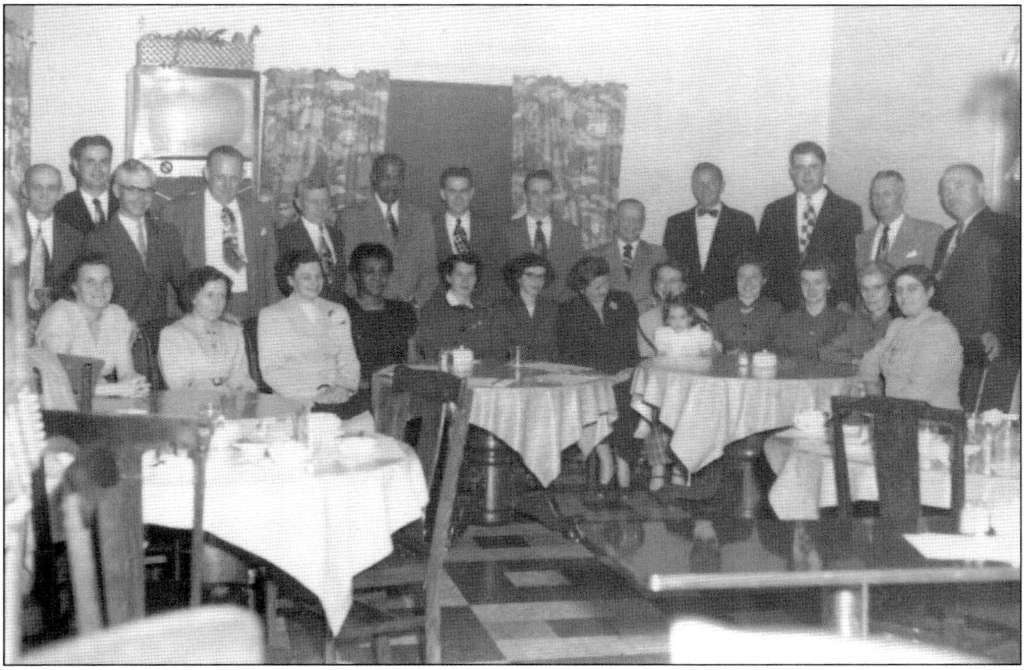

VOLUNTEER AMBULANCE ASSOCIATION BANQUET. The first ambulance in Wellsboro was a 1938 LaSalle hearse driven by undertaker Austin Johnson. Johnson promised firefighters that they could keep the hearse if they found personnel to drive it. The Firemen's Volunteer Ambulance Association was created in November 1942. Fire chief John Dugan congratulated ambulance personnel in 1984, saying that they had "done a tremendous job . . . at the scene and enroute to the hospital . . . they have saved a great many lives."

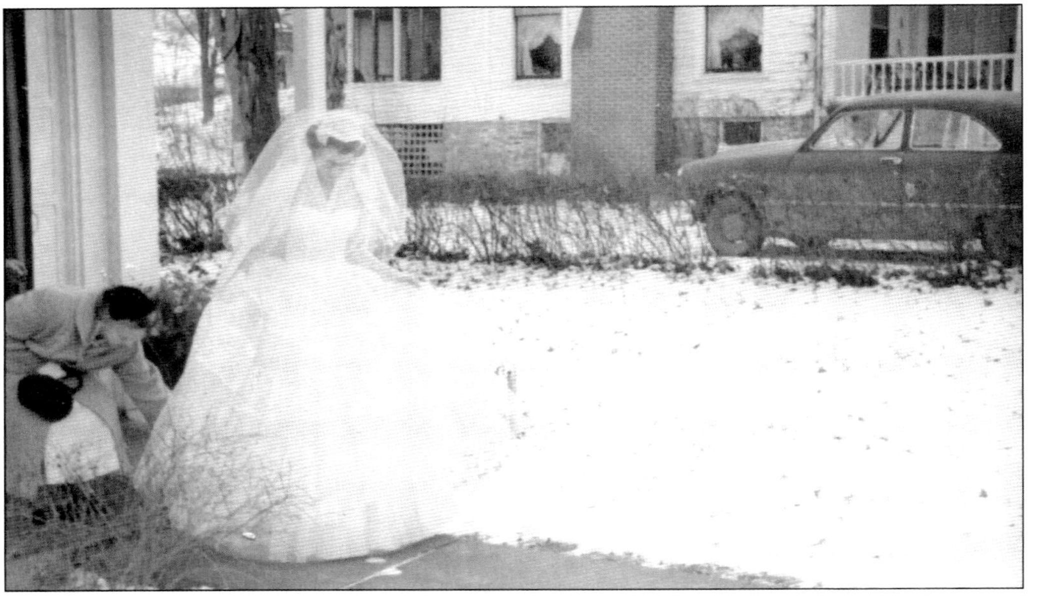

Jane Elizabeth Phelps Gustafson. On December 11, 1955, Jane Phelps, daughter of Ransom and Thelma Phelps of Thumptown, married Robert Gustafson of Colton, Oregon, at the Baptist church, located at the intersection of Pearl Street and Central Avenue. Rev. David Burrows officiated. (Courtesy David Gustafson.)

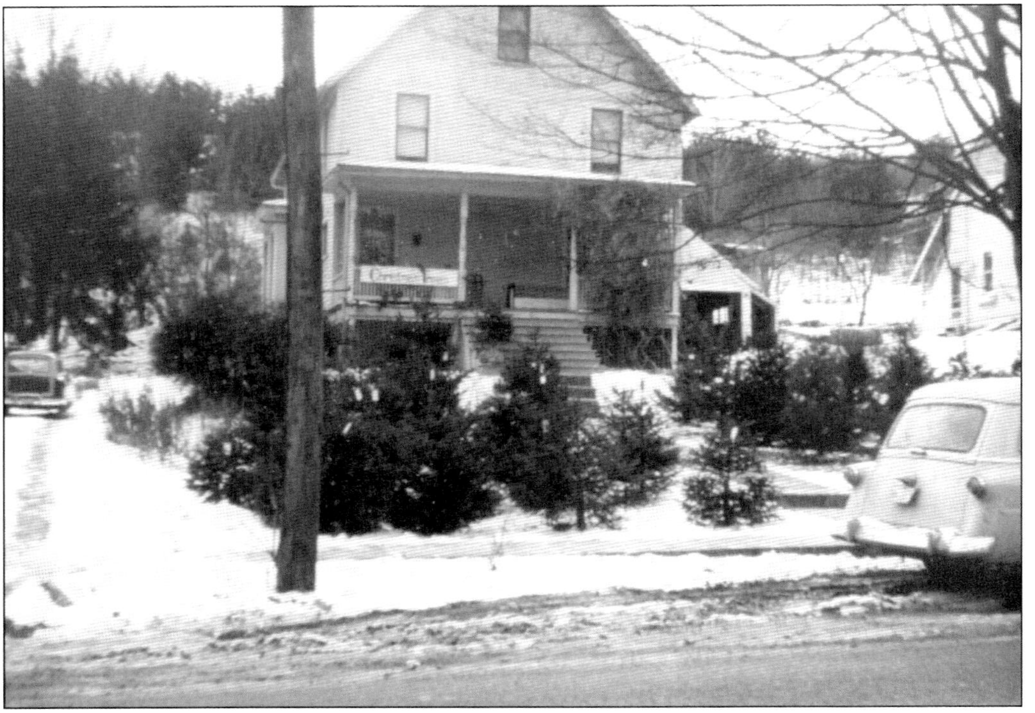

Christmas Trees. From 1953 to the early 1960s, Curt Lytle sold Christmas trees at 11 Bacon Street. Cathy, his daughter, recalls that her father's front-yard business was great fun for his children. (Courtesy Cathy Lytle DeLuca.)

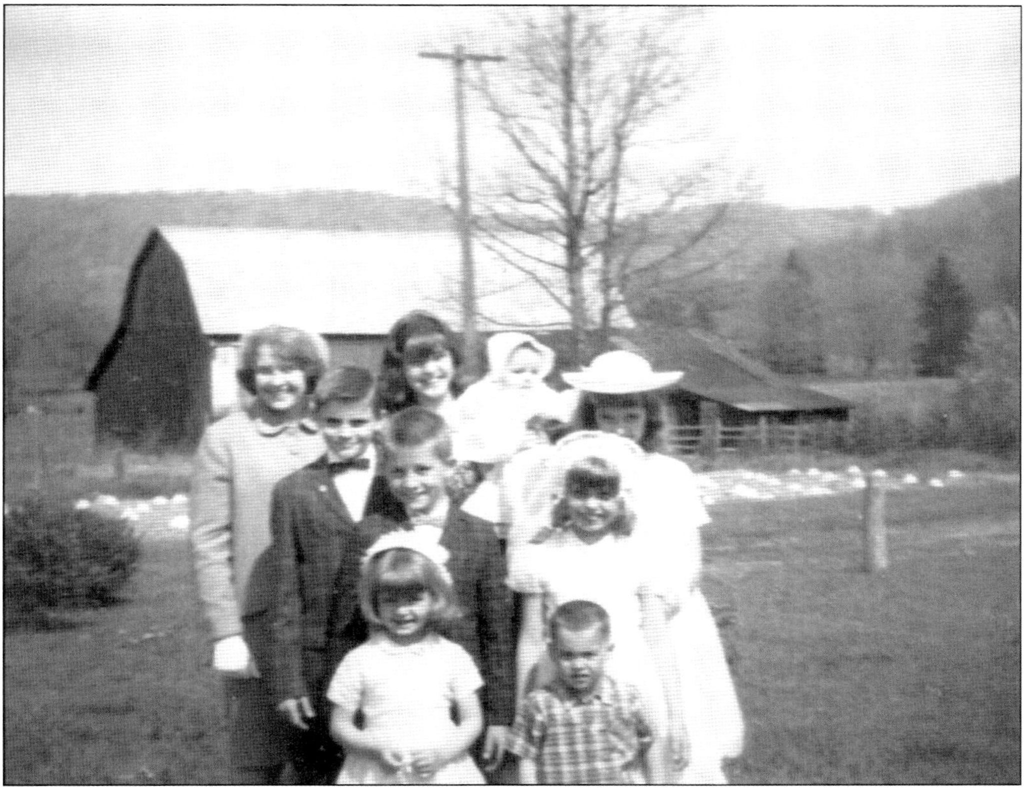

St. Peter's Roman Catholic Church. Wellsboro's Catholic church was founded in 1879, with Father McDermott appointed pastor. On November 12, 1880, St. Peter's Catholic Church purchased the academy building erected in 1820 on Pearl Street. In 1890, the church bell was consecrated and named "Joseph." Above, the Webster children pose for a First Communion photograph. Below, Fr. Arthur McAndrews stands with Sister Marceil's class of First Communicants, many of whom attended Wellsboro High School between the years 1963 and 1965. (Above, courtesy Webster family; below, courtesy Patricia Benjamin Schwab.)

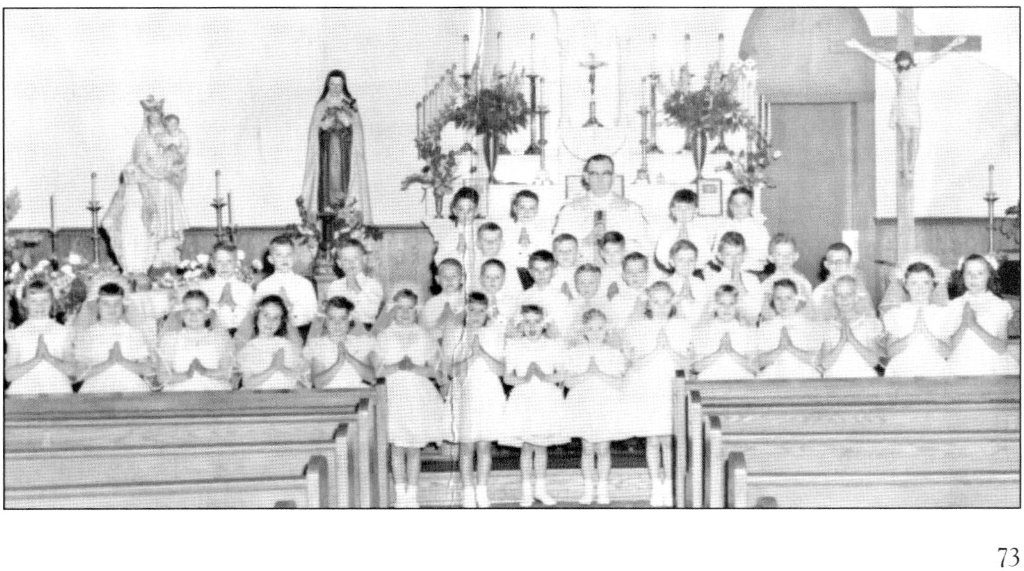

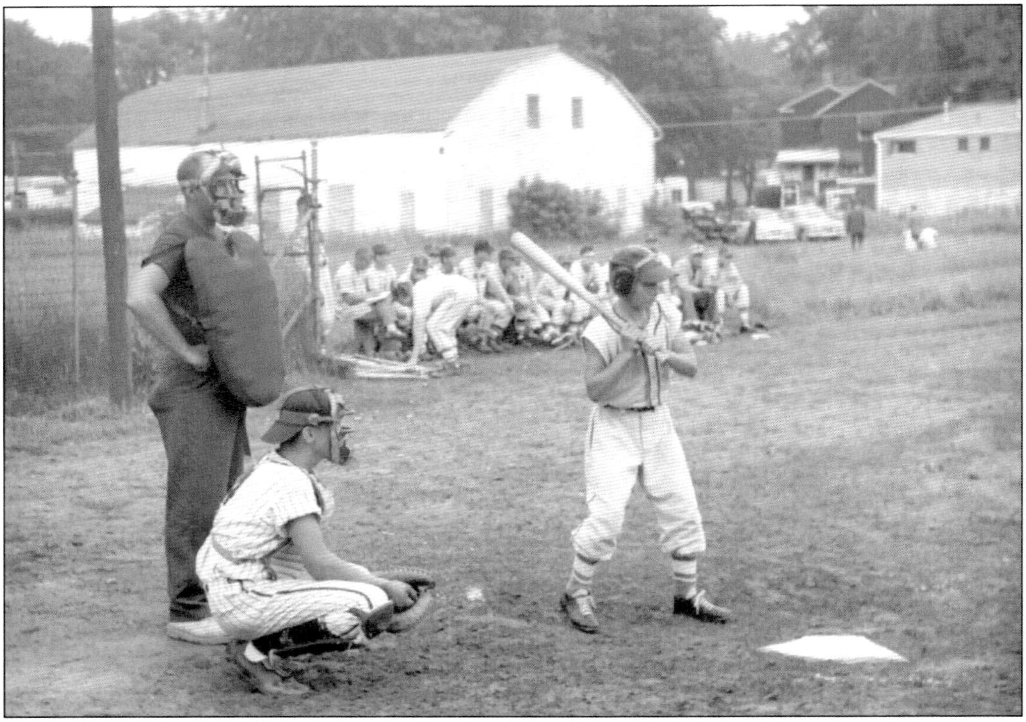

Little League. In 1950, Willard "Dud" Smith started a midget league in Wellsboro. Assisted by Frederick Husted and Art Doumaux, Smith launched the league with four teams in July 1950, joining the Little League program in 1951. Approximately 800 people watched the first game at a new field, which was acquired in 1952 and located on Charleston Street, today the location of a McDonald's restaurant. The league later moved to Packer Park on Queen Street, but, because batters kept hitting balls into the park swimming pool, it moved again in 1981 to the present location on upper Charleston Street. (Both, courtesy Dennis Bliss.)

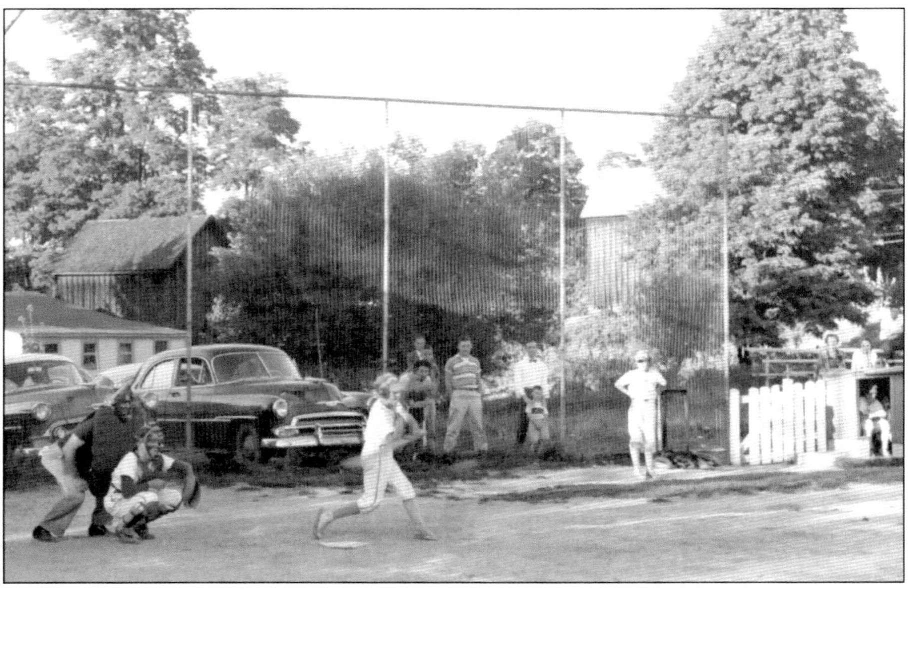

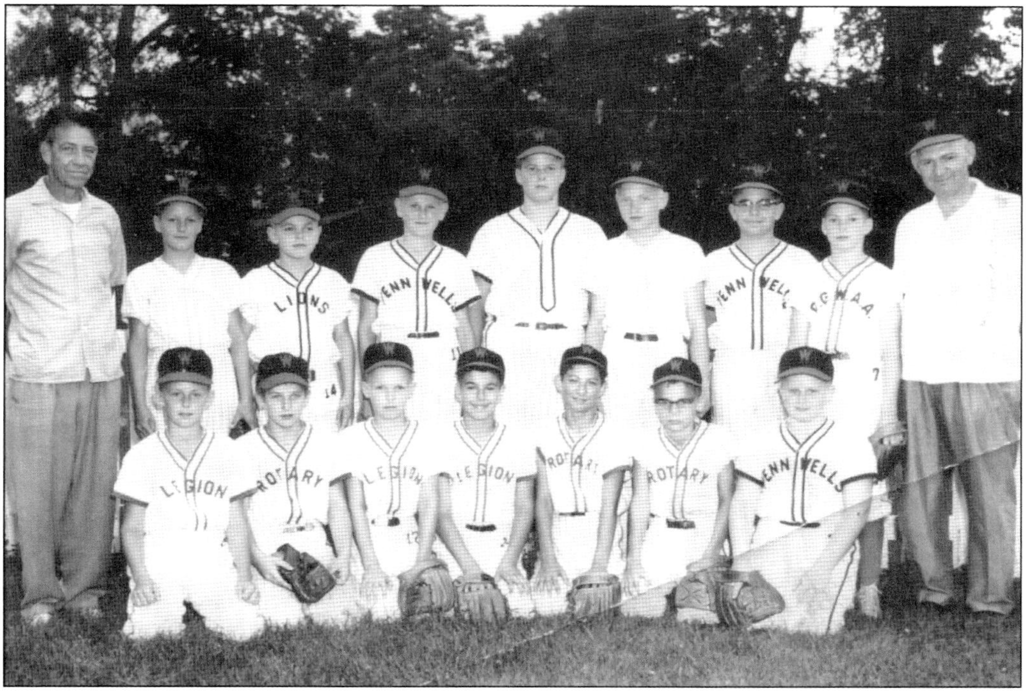

Little League All-Stars. The 1960 Little League all-star team picture includes, from left to right, (first row) Robert Erway, John Perry, Skip Meyers, William Cook, Theodore "Ted" Zuchowski, Timothy Burns, and Robert Blair; (second row) coach James McMullen, Michael Cooney, Edward McHenry, Scott Wilcox, Clifford Cole, Charles Colony, John Wilcox, Ronald Boyce, and coach James Stevens.

Corning Glass Works Little League Team. Pictured are, from left to right, (first row) Terry Learn, David Smith, James Williamee, Scott Dean, Dennis Bliss, Barry Smith, and Harold Tombs (coach); (second row) Thomas Hubba, Dale Tombs, Joseph Strykowski, Vern Campbell, Timothy Smith, David Howey, and Douglas Zuchowski. (Courtesy Dennis Bliss.)

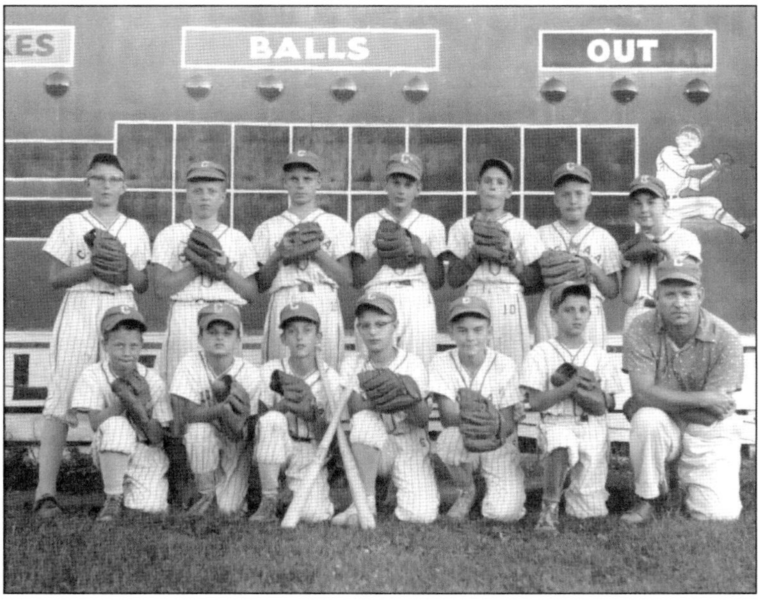

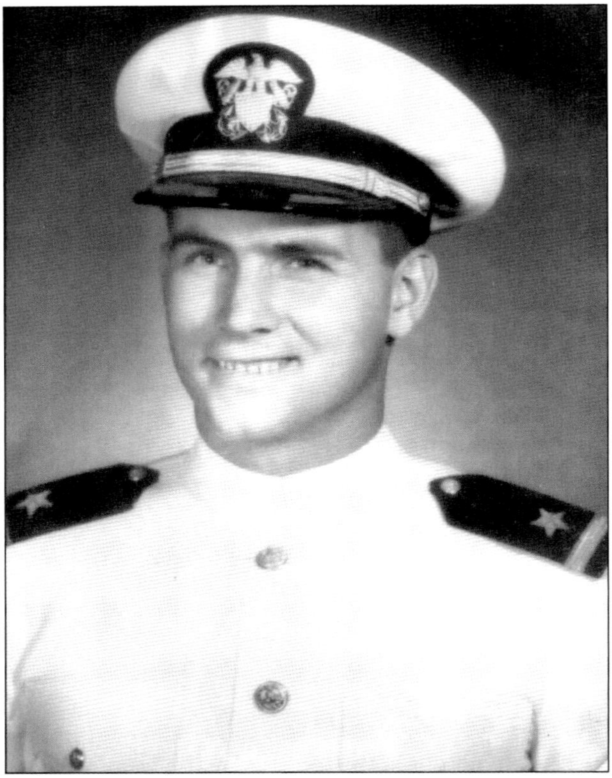

JOHN PREVOST MEMORIAL SMALL FRY FOOTBALL. Ensign John Antoine Prevost died on August 20, 1960, in a tragic accident over the Pacific Ocean. The airplane in which Ensign Prevost served as navigator was returning from Manila to the carrier USS *Oriskany* and crashed because of engine failure. Born on May 9, 1935, Prevost is remembered as an exceptional student leader and athlete. Max Mickey, the commissioner of small fry football, and his assistants Dr. Robert Bair and James Stevens, established a memorial fund in Prevost's name. (Both, courtesy Louis Prevost.)

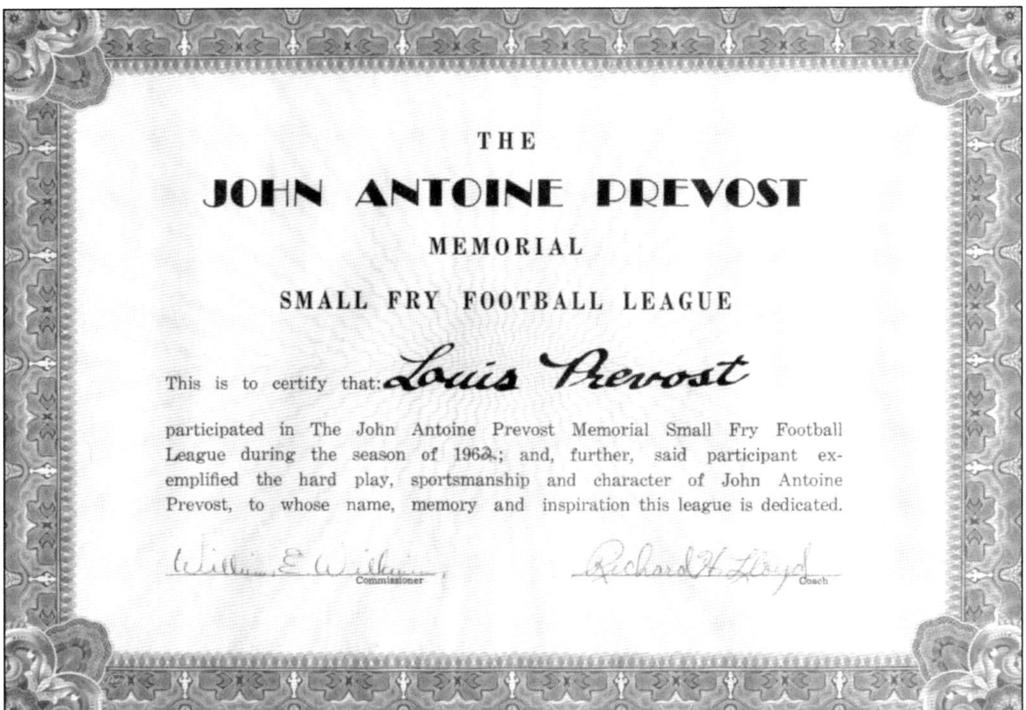

THE

JOHN ANTOINE PREVOST

MEMORIAL

SMALL FRY FOOTBALL LEAGUE

This is to certify that: Louis Prevost

participated in The John Antoine Prevost Memorial Small Fry Football League during the season of 1962; and, further, said participant exemplified the hard play, sportsmanship and character of John Antoine Prevost, to whose name, memory and inspiration this league is dedicated.

Commissioner

Richard H. Lloyd, Coach

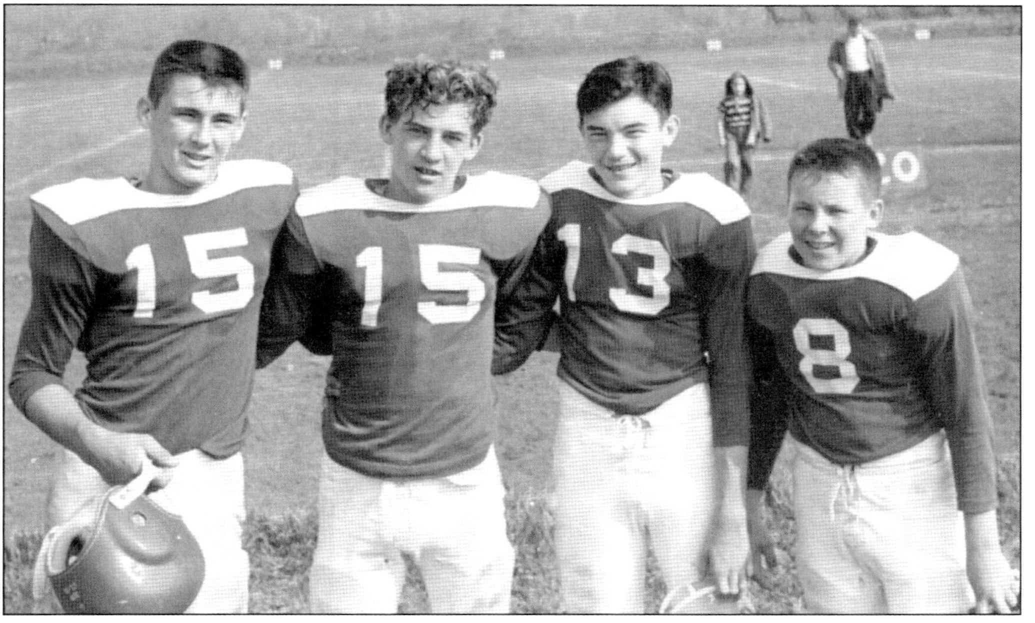

SMALL FRY ALL-STARS. The John Prevost Memorial Small Fry football teams completed their first season on the Wellsboro High School field in October 1960. The photograph shows, from left to right, Roger Dibble, Gary Cowles, Dennis Bliss, and Kevin Maynard. The 1960 team coaches were Harold Tombs (Blue Devils), Bill Wilkinson (Golden Bears), Ray Storti (Green Demons), and Don Horton and Lyle Harmon (Redmen). (Courtesy Dennis Bliss.)

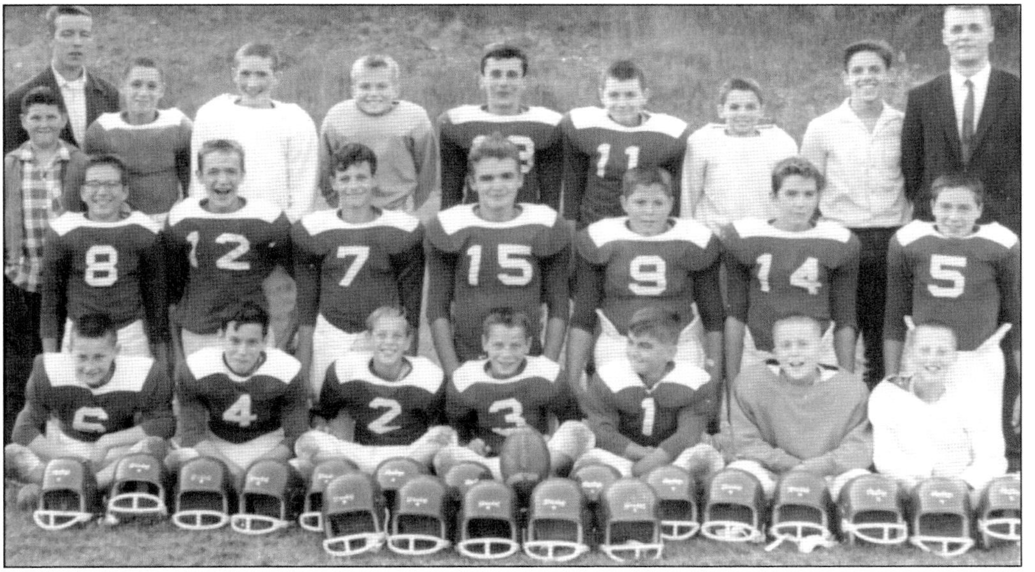

THE 1961 REDMEN. Pictured are, from left to right, (first row) Marvin Focht, Mark Storti, Dennis Brucklacher, Timothy Burns, John "Jack" Mosher, Ronald Dexter, and Thomas Ward; (second row) Barry Kirkpatrick, Roger Hallock, John "Jack" Cooney, Ronald Windel, John Davis, Bradley Windel, and Harold "Bud" Eichorn; (third row) manager William "Billy" Myers, coach James Kelley, Peter Stevens, David Winter, Robert Anderson, Richard Orsini, Louis Prevost, Thomas Callahan, William Briggs, and coach Richard "Dick" Lloyd. (Courtesy Louis Prevost.)

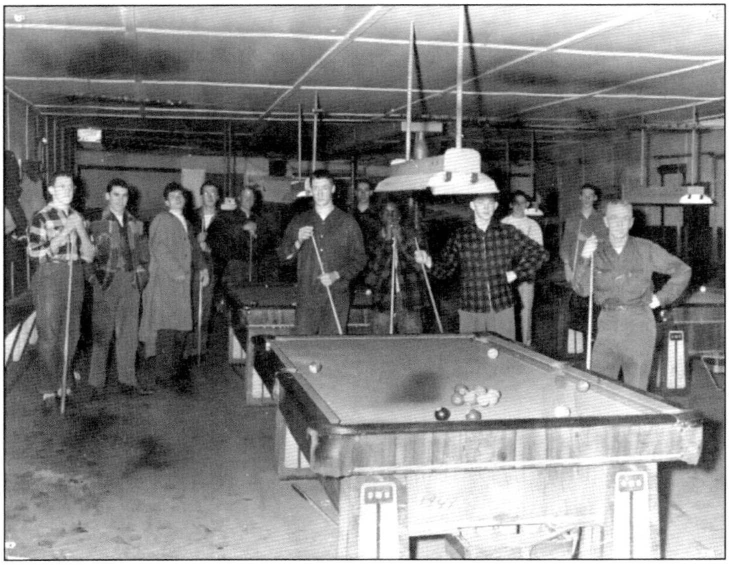

Edward's Recreational Billiard Parlor. Arthur C. "Tunk" Edwards operated the pool hall on Pearl Street for more than 40 years. He died on January 4, 1978. One of Tunk's pool tables can be found today at Jane and Tom Kerr's home in Tiadaghton. Harland's Family Style Restaurant currently occupies the former site of Tunk's pool hall. (Courtesy Elgin Sink.)

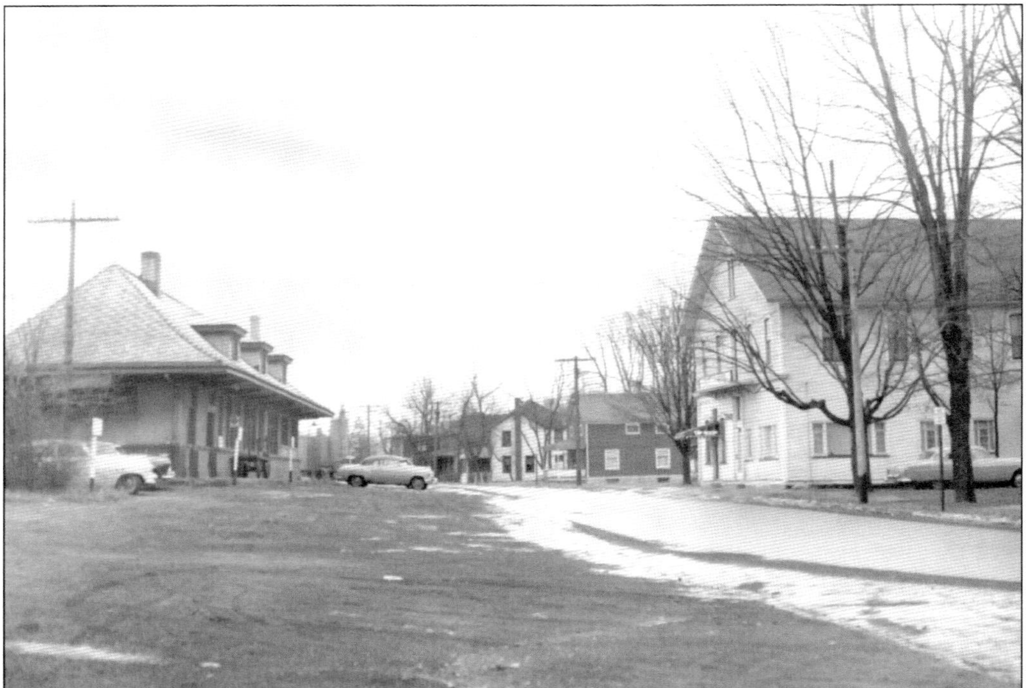

Spencer's Hotel. Joseph Riberolle built Spencer's Hotel (right), now the Wellsboro House, on Charleston Street in 1872. It has been operated over the years as a hotel and tavern, and owners have included Seth Daggett, the Honorable Stephen F. Wilson, Mayne English (1920s), Fred Boom (1930s), Cecil and Dorothy Day (1940s), and Morrell "Smokey" Spencer, who operated the hotel beginning in 1954. Pres. Theodore Roosevelt patronized the tavern during Judge Wilson's tenure. Recent owners have included Ronald Johnston, Steven Banik and William Boroch (the Backstreet Bar), and, since 2006, Chris Kozuhowski (the Wellsboro House). (Courtesy James and Joann Spencer.)

Five

WELLSBORO'S PRIDE

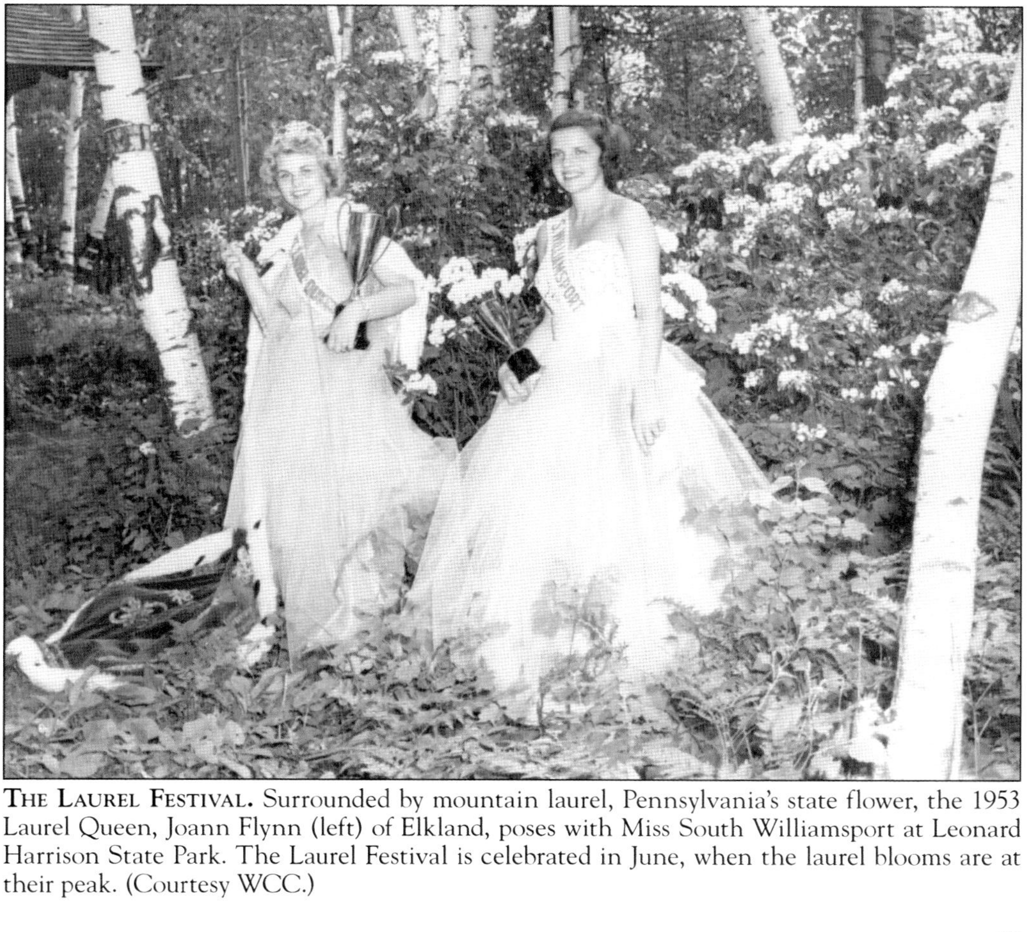

THE LAUREL FESTIVAL. Surrounded by mountain laurel, Pennsylvania's state flower, the 1953 Laurel Queen, Joann Flynn (left) of Elkland, poses with Miss South Williamsport at Leonard Harrison State Park. The Laurel Festival is celebrated in June, when the laurel blooms are at their peak. (Courtesy WCC.)

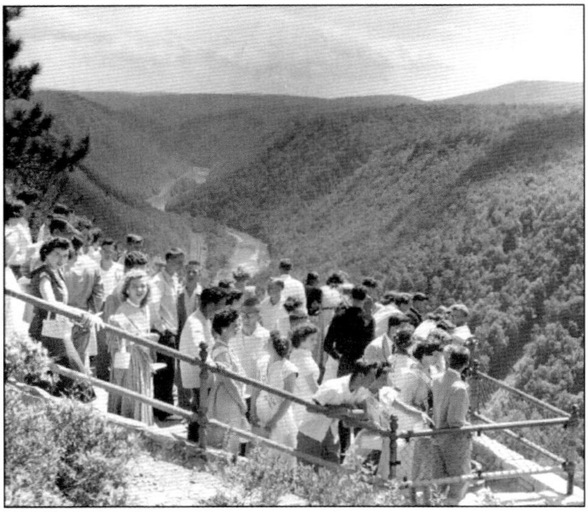

Harrison Park Lookout. In 1922, Harrison donated over 100 acres of land, including the site known as "the Lookout," to the Commonwealth of Pennsylvania to establish a park. During the 1930s, the Civilian Conservation Corps (CCC) improved Harrison Park, making it more attractive to tourists. In 1936, Larry Woodin initiated a national publication campaign to promote "Pennsylvania's Grand Canyon." The first Laurel Festival, sponsored by the Lions Club, took place in 1938. By 1941, almost 100,000 people had visited Leonard Harrison State Park. (Courtesy Teri Keck Carson.)

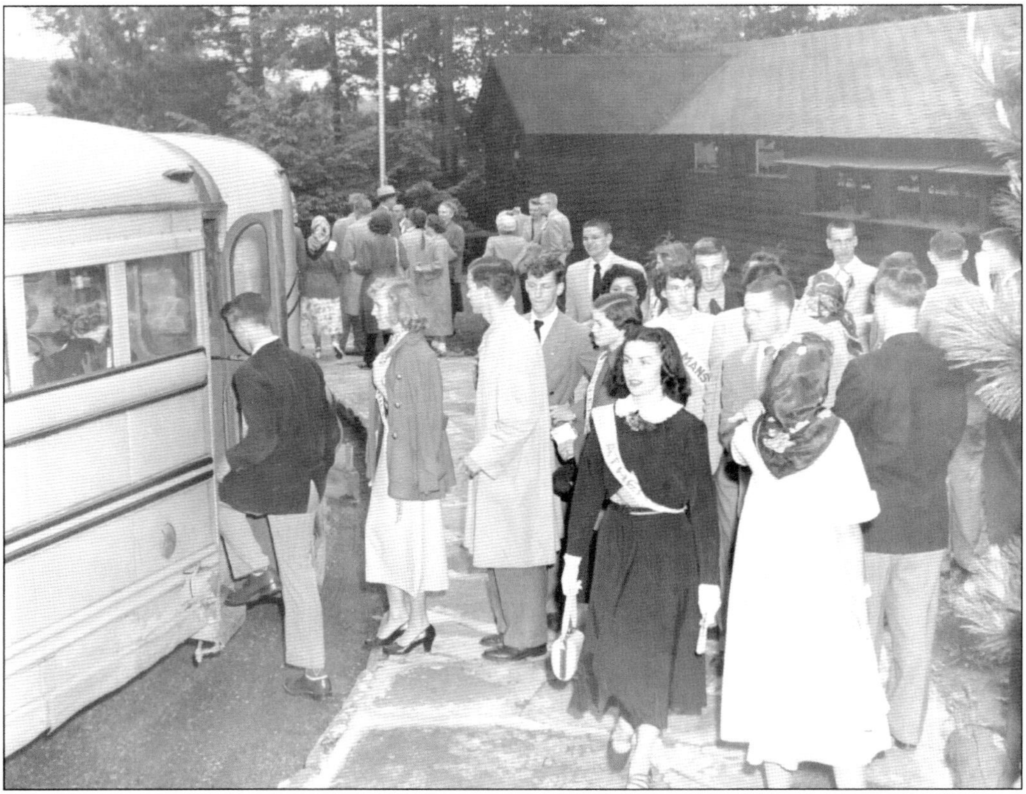

The Queen Candidates. Initially, the Lions Club, organized in 1929, contacted other clubs in the region, asking them to send a candidate for Laurel Queen. Later, high schools across the state were invited to participate. Individual photographs of the young women appeared in the store windows on Main Street a week before the candidates arrived to stay at the Penn-Wells Hotel. A full calendar of events, including a motorcade to the canyon, was planned for the candidates. Escorts arrived with the candidates beginning in 1950; the young men stayed with local families. (Courtesy WCC.)

Woodland Park Pool. Several candidates for Laurel Queen are pictured visiting the Woodland Park Pool, constructed by the Works Progress Administration in 1938. The deteriorating pool was replaced by the Packer Park pool in 1970. (Courtesy WCC.)

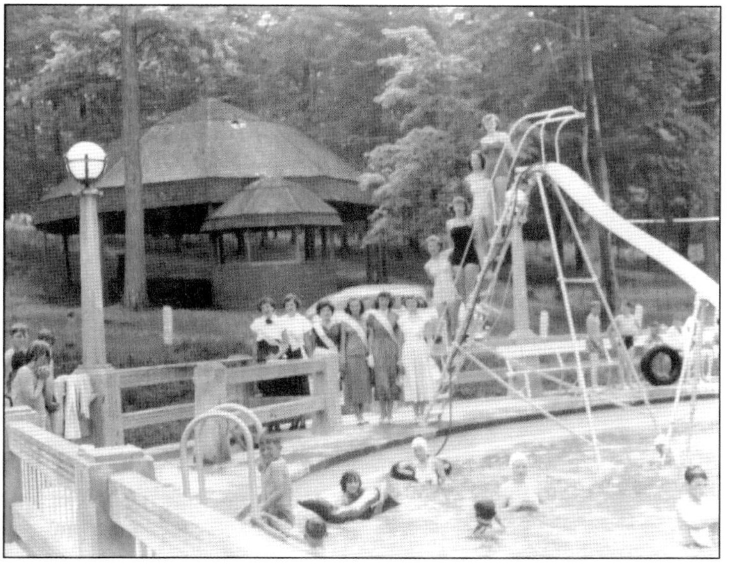

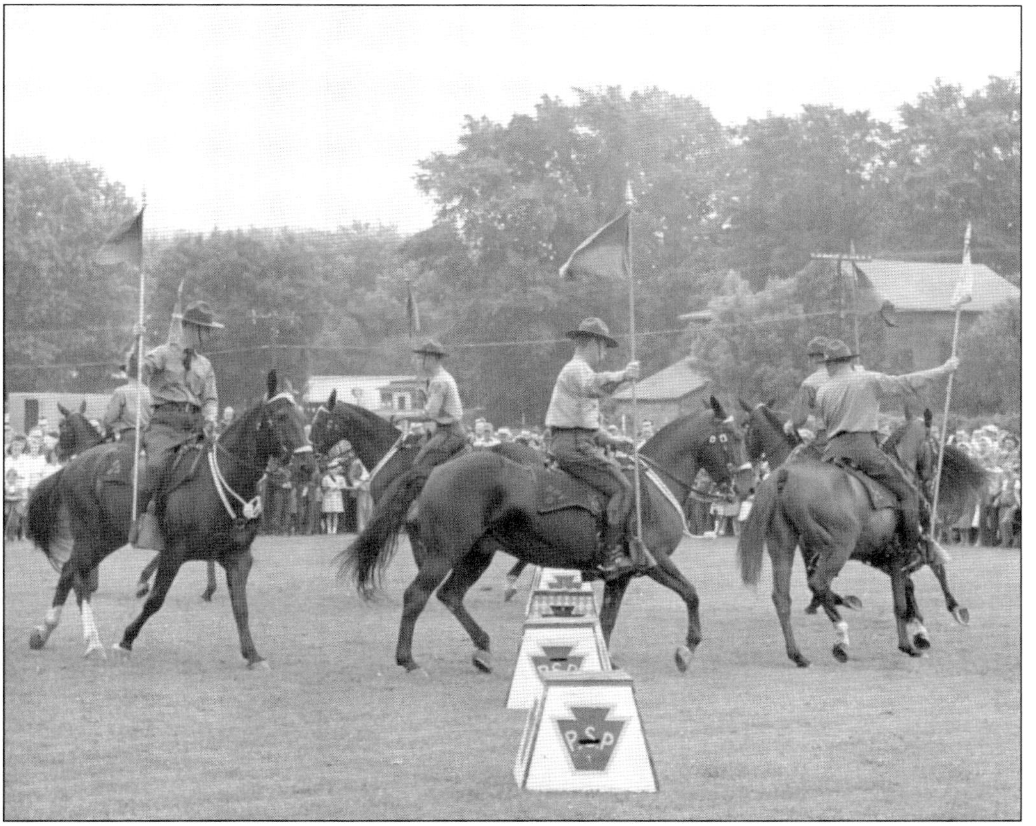

Pennsylvania State Police Maneuvers. The Pennsylvania State Police often performed at the Laurel Festival. Their performances began in 1949 at Packer Field on Queen Street. In this photograph, "Take Time to Be Safe" guided horseback maneuvers at the Laurel Festival State Police Rodeo. (Courtesy WCC.)

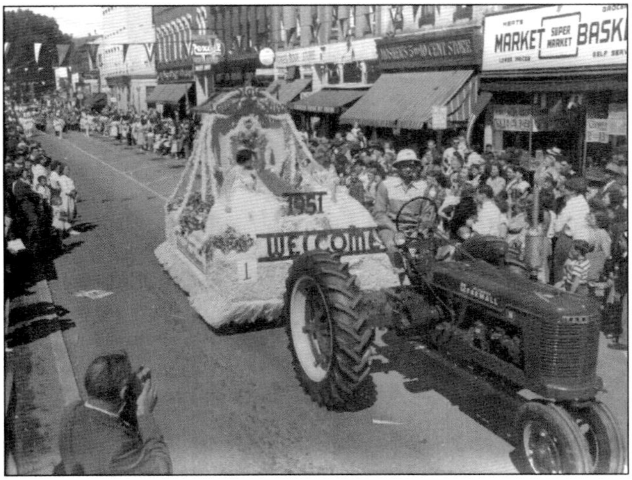

Laurel Festival Parade Route. The length and the route of the Laurel Parade varied over the years. This photograph shows Kelts Dillman's McCormick Farmall tractor pulling the chamber of commerce float the "wrong way" up Main Street in 1951. Miss Wellsboro, Patricia Jane White, and Miss Suburban Wellsboro, Joan Phillips, rode the float with the 1950 Laurel Queen, Phoebe Erickson, who won a four-year tuition scholarship to a state-sponsored university. (Courtesy Deborah Dillman Kear.)

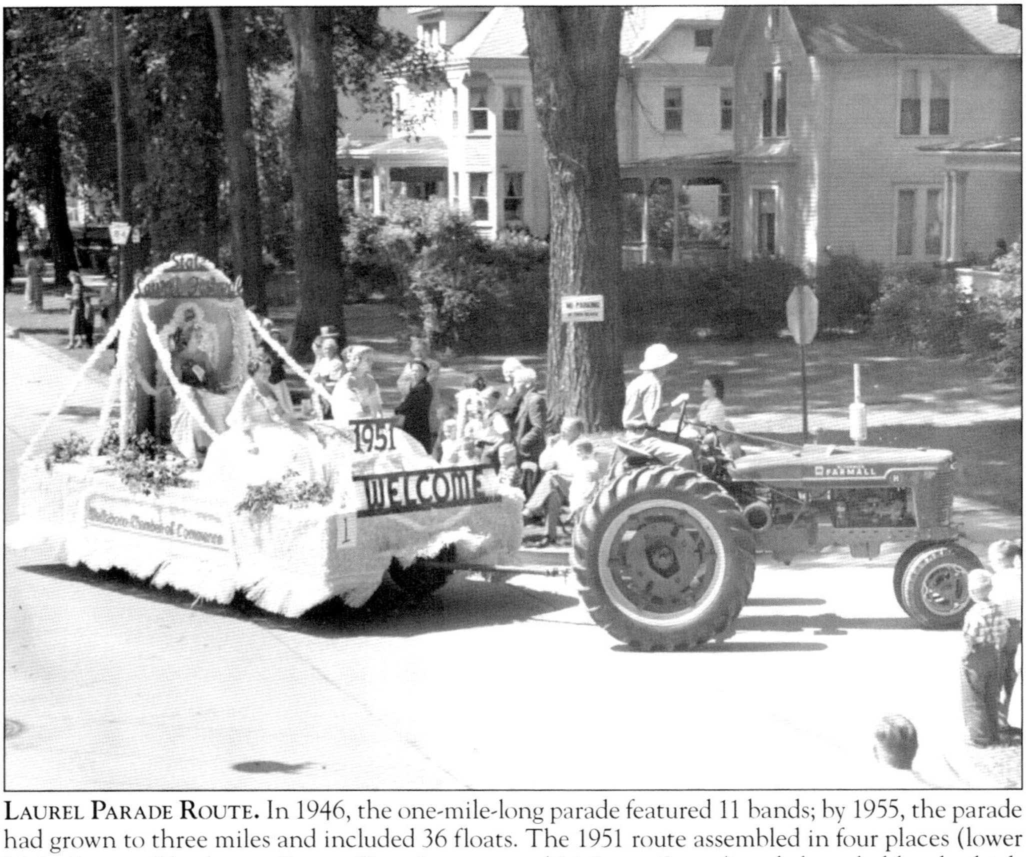

Laurel Parade Route. In 1946, the one-mile-long parade featured 11 bands; by 1955, the parade had grown to three miles and included 36 floats. The 1951 route assembled in four places (lower Main Street, Charleston Street, East Avenue, and McInroy Street) and then, led by the high school band, traveled up the right side of Main Street to King, Pearl, Central, Walnut, Waln, Grant, East, McInroy, and Charleston Streets, and then, finally, back up the left side of Main Street, ending above Norris Street, where it dispersed. The photograph shows the 1951 parade turning onto Walnut Street and going toward East Avenue, the corner where the medical offices of Erway, Wilson, and Bachman were later located. (Courtesy Deborah Dillman Kear.)

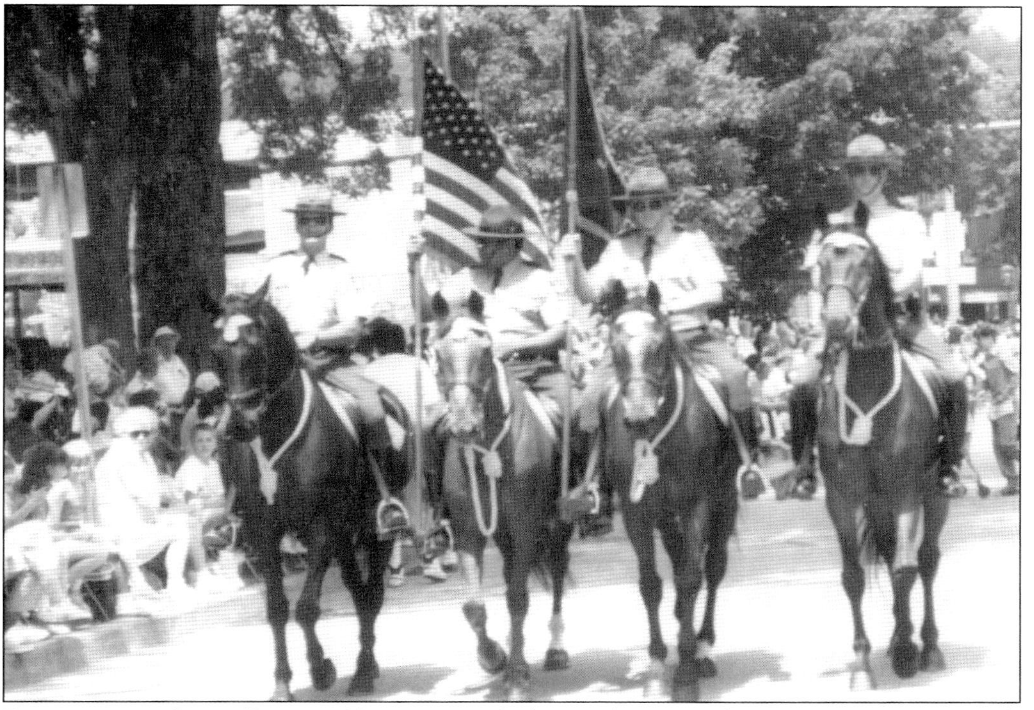

Pennsylvania State Police. Always a crowd-pleaser, the Pennsylvania Mounted Police ride proudly through the borough on parade day. (Courtesy WCC.)

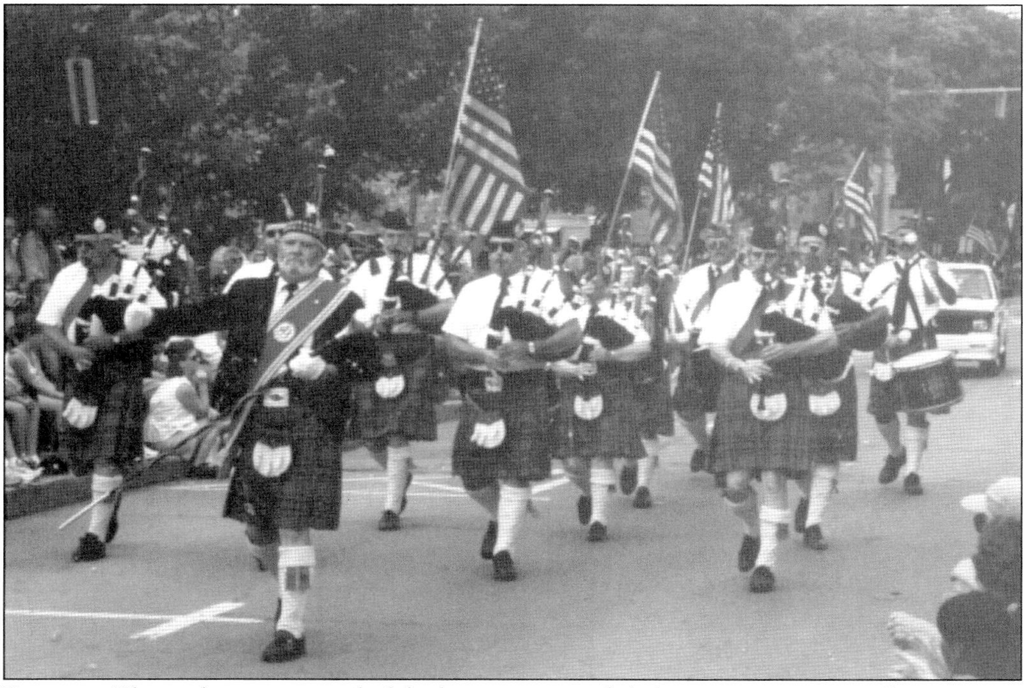

Bagpipes. The soul-stirring sound of the bagpipes never failed to excite spectators. Pipers were a perennial favorite at the Laurel Festival Parade. (Courtesy WCC.)

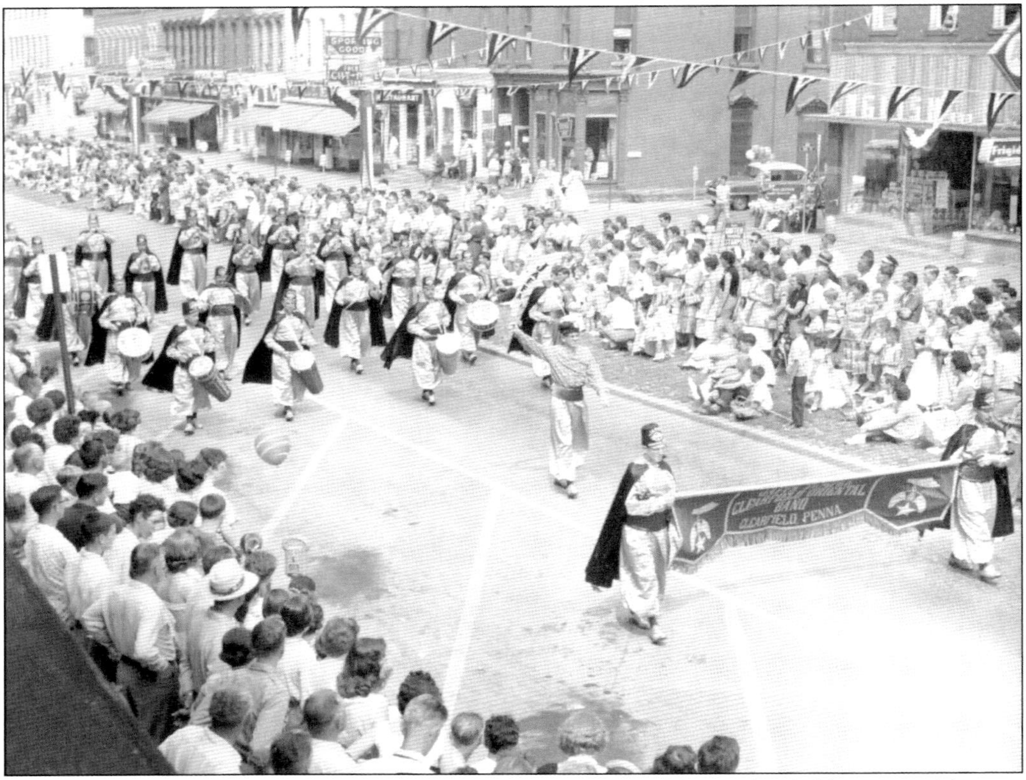

JAFFA TEMPLE ORIENTAL BAND. The Jaffa Temple Oriental Band from Clearfield County, Altoona, Pennsylvania—home of the Jaffa Shrine Center—was noted for its lively performances and colorful costumes. (Courtesy WCC.)

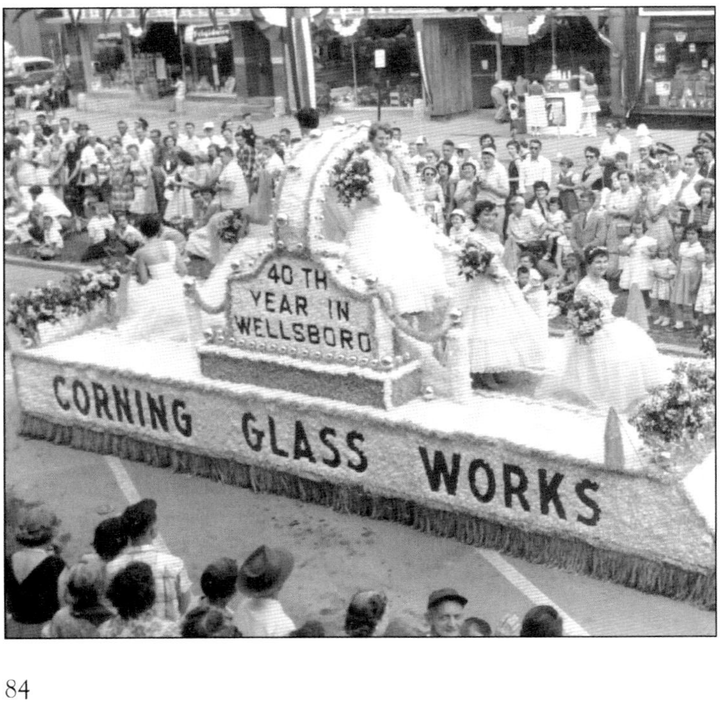

CORNING GLASS WORKS FLOAT. The floats produced by Corning Glass Works were predictably spectacular. Prizes were given to the best floats beginning in 1951, and CGW often won. This 1956 float celebrated CGW's 40th year in Wellsboro. Note the Christmas-ornament embellishments on the float. (Courtesy WCC.)

The Falcons Baton and Drum Corps. Led by the indomitable Mary Ann Cleveland from Stony Fork, the Falcons, also known as FORCE, included baton-twirling girls and boy drummers. Beginning in 1972, Cleveland and her husband, Kenneth, won praise for the Falcons and also for the generous ways in which they reached out to those in need.

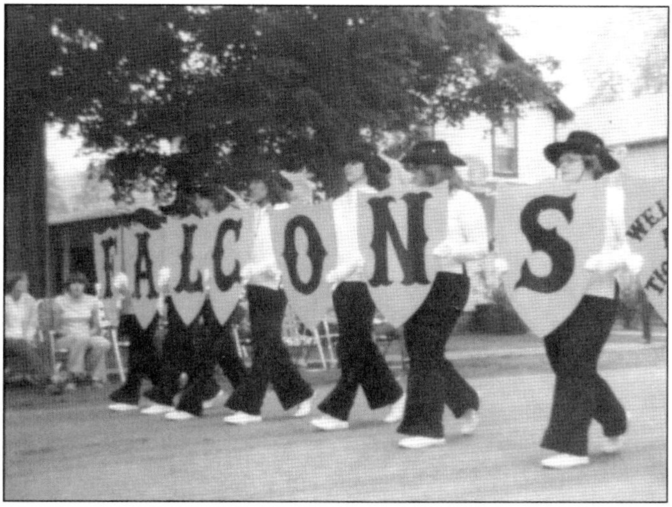

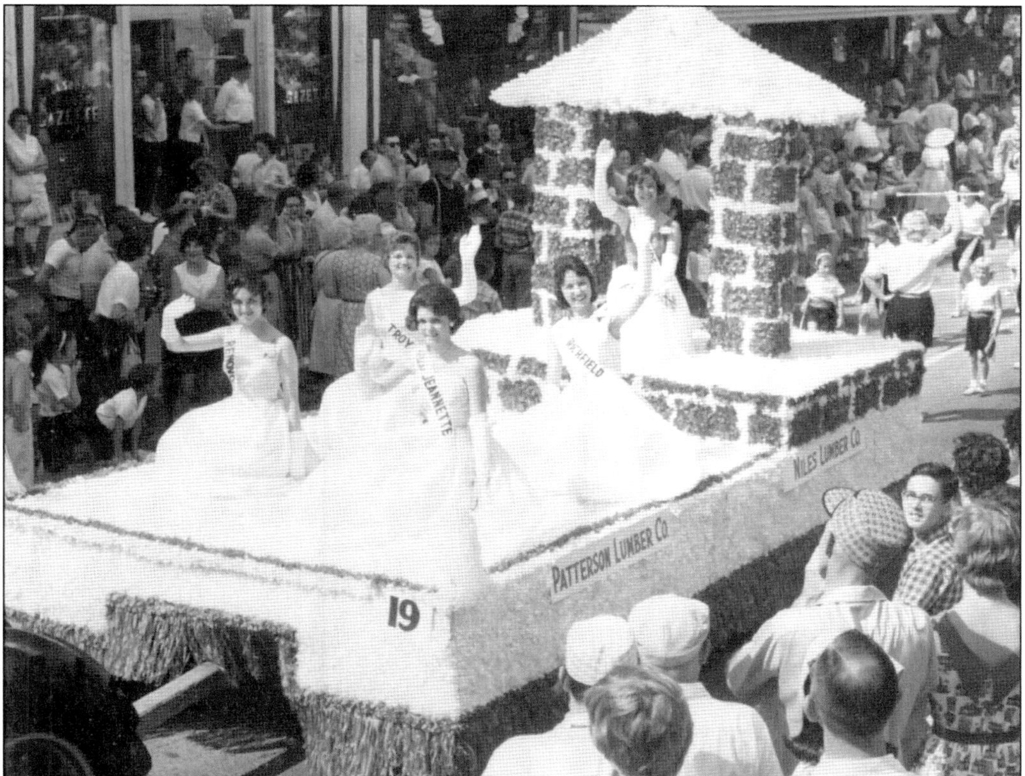

Lumber Companies Float. Patterson Lumber Company (Charleston Street) and Niles Lumber Company (West Avenue/Route 660) date back to the days when the local economy depended heavily on the lumber industry. Niles Lumber Company burned in 1952, but Wellsboro firefighters saved the main building. The Patterson mill eventually moved to Galeton, but the company maintains an office in Wellsboro. This fourth-generation business, describing itself as a steward of the nation's natural resources, practices forest-renewable and responsible land management. (Courtesy WCC.)

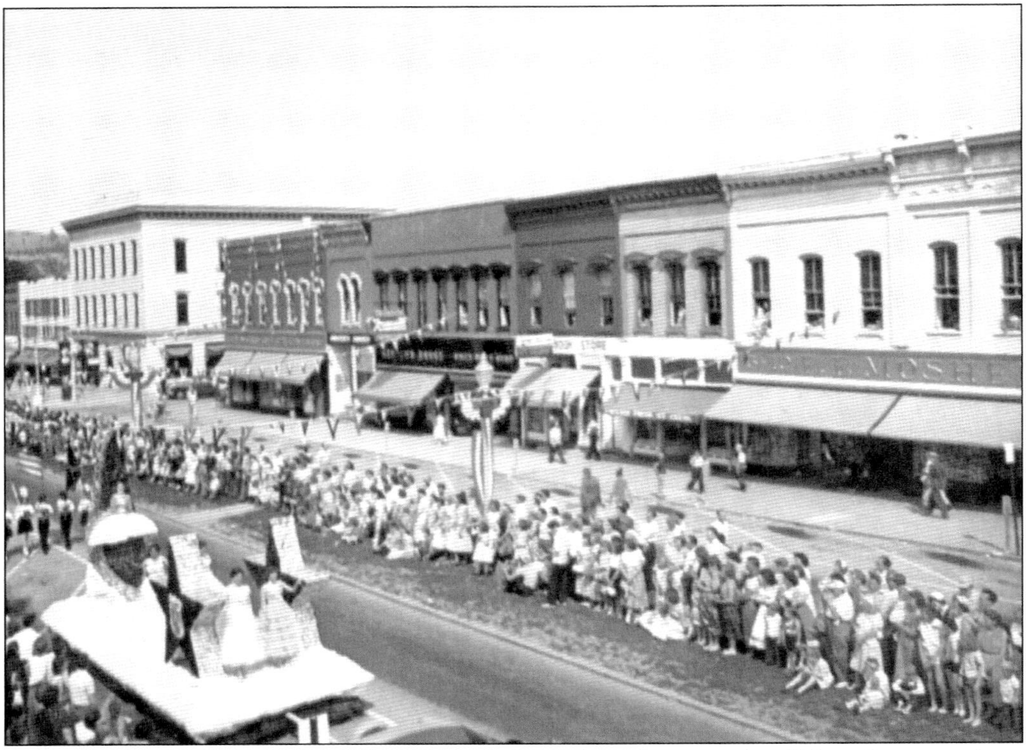

MAIN STREET. This postcard recalls businesses located on the east side of Main Street in about 1950. Visible stores along the route are, from right to left, the Market Basket (eventually absorbed by Moshers 5 & 10, located next door); the Candy Kitchen (also absorbed by Mosher's); the Rowe Book Store; Kentch's Drug Store; and Newberry's Five and Dime, located on the corner of Main and Waln Streets. Note that Tioga Savings & Trust, located on the opposite corner of Main and Waln Streets, was still a three-story building at the time.

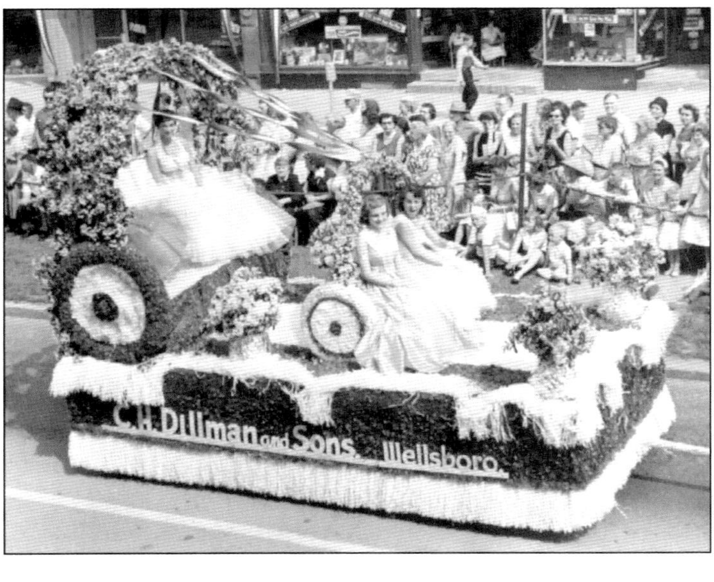

C.H. DILLMAN AND SONS FLOAT. C.H. Dillman and Sons International Harvester dealership was at the former site of the Honorable Jerome B. Niles estate. The Niles lot turned the corner from Walnut Street to Central Avenue and included Judge Niles's home at 31 Central Avenue and his son Aaron's home at 33 Central Avenue. The Baptist church and parking lot currently occupy this site. (Courtesy WCC.)

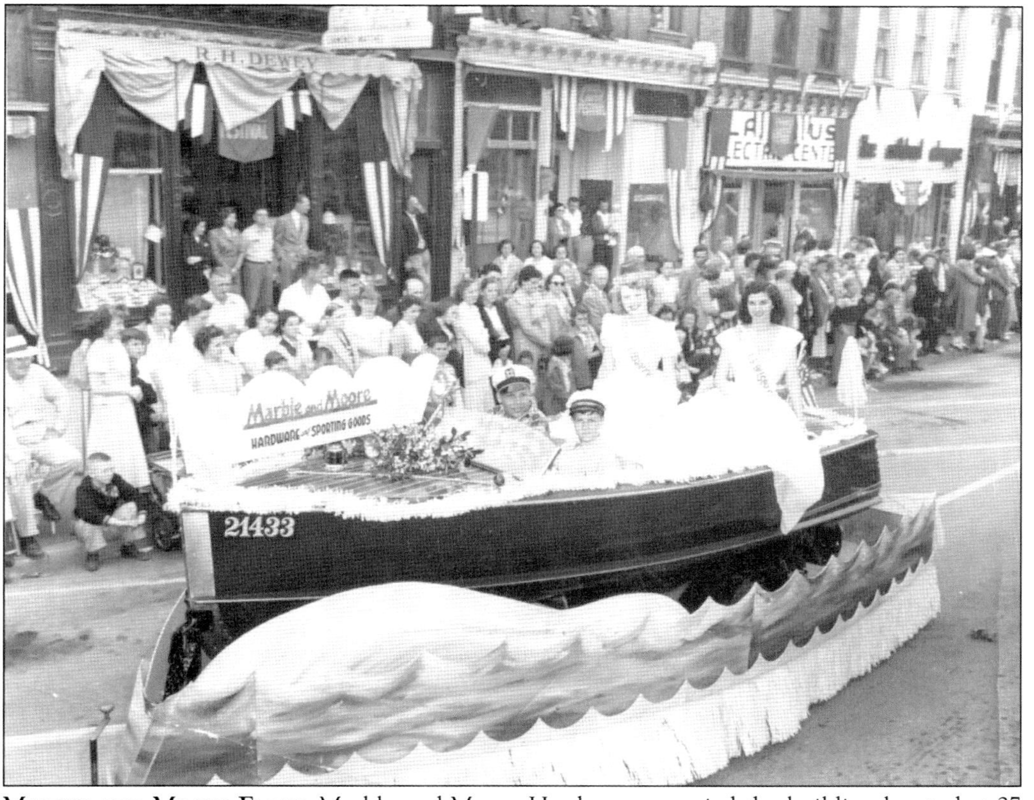

MARBLE AND MOORE FLOAT. Marble and Moore Hardware occupied the building located at 27 Main Street on the corner of East Avenue. Glenn and Evelyn Bliss later operated Bliss's True Value Hardware at the same location, followed by Main Street Antiques, the Fifth Season, and From My Shelf Bookstore and Gifts. For many years, the building's East Avenue wall featured a gigantic mural of Pennsylvania's Grand Canyon. The popular image was painted over in 2005. (Courtesy WCC.)

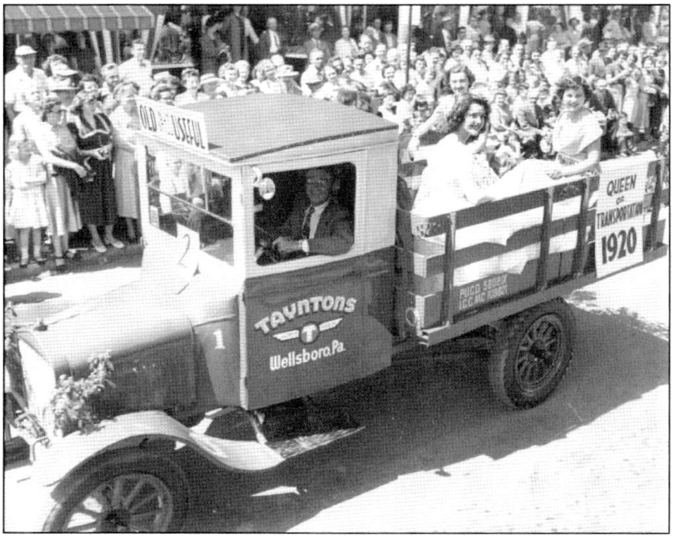

TAYNTON'S TRUCKING COMPANY. Horace W. Taynton created his trucking company with a team of horses in 1913. He acquired his first used truck in 1917, and his first new truck, a Ford Model T, in 1923. The Model T delivered raw silk from Japanese silkworms to Wellsboro's silk mill during the early 20th century. Taynton's Trucking Company operated in Wellsboro for over 70 years. (Courtesy WCC.)

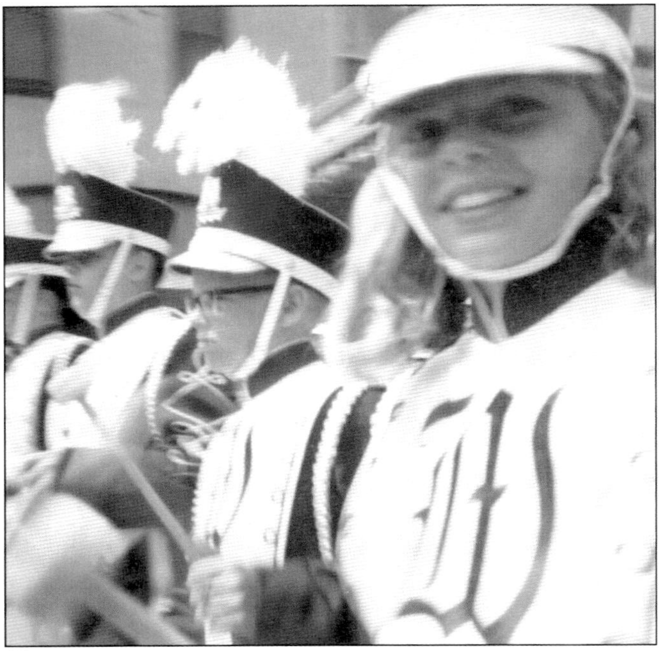

Wellsboro Junior High Marching Band. Sue Ellen Benjamin's "million dollar smile" lights up this 1966 photograph of the Wellsboro Junior High School Marching Band, directed by Lenore "Nodie" Johnson Bujno. One of the band's most memorable tunes was "The Green Berets," to which the band slow marched up Main Street for a portion of its Laurel Parade performance. (Courtesy Sue Benjamin.)

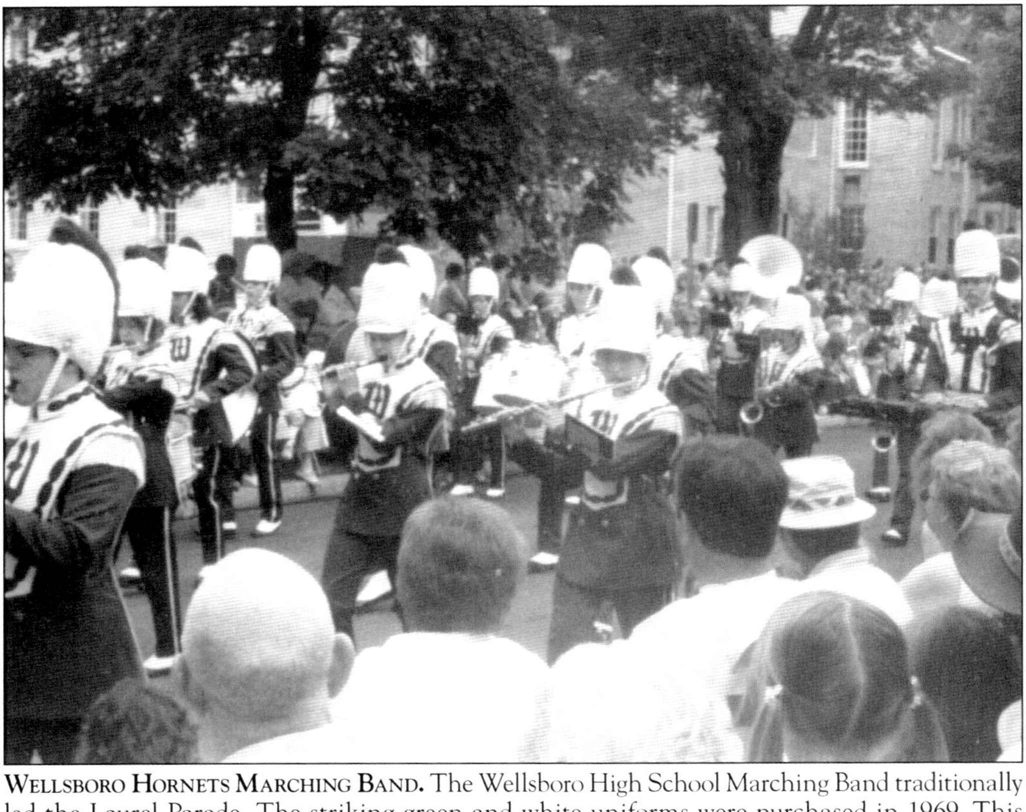

Wellsboro Hornets Marching Band. The Wellsboro High School Marching Band traditionally led the Laurel Parade. The striking green and white uniforms were purchased in 1969. This photograph was taken in 1981 from the Green, just above the courthouse.

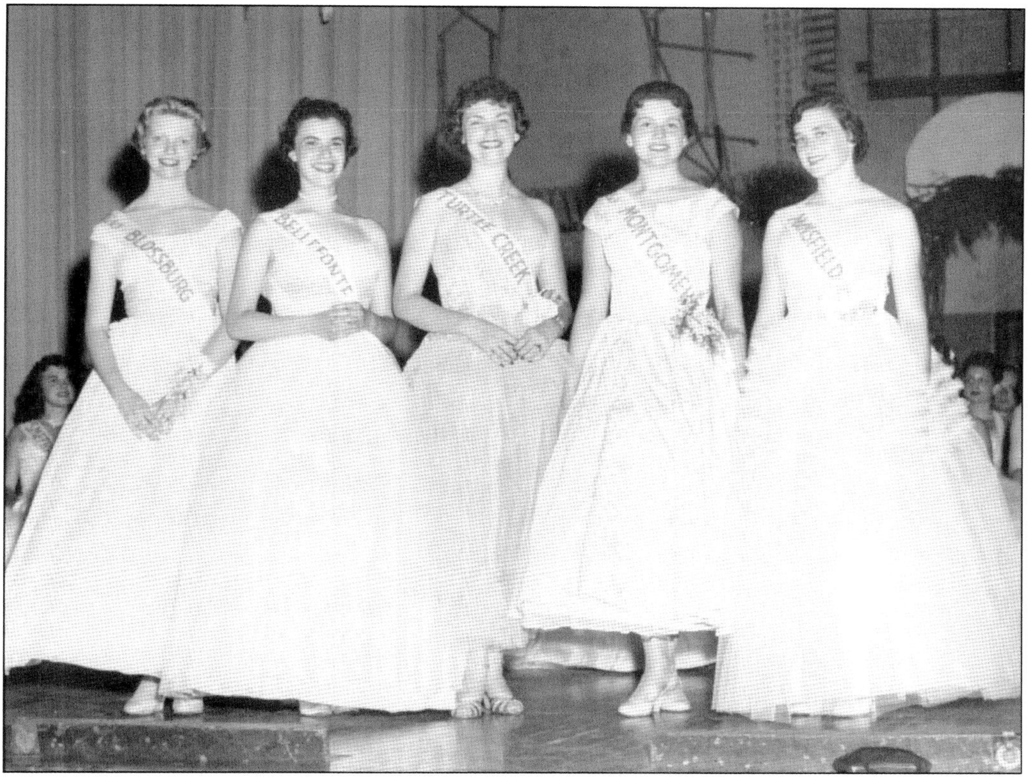

LAUREL QUEEN FINALISTS. The location of the Laurel Queen coronation varied over the years, from the Arcadia Theatre to the high school to the Green. In 1956, Janet Krause of Bellefonte was selected from 68 candidates as Laurel Queen; Miss Montgomery was runner-up. The coronation ceremony was held at the high school. (Courtesy WCC.)

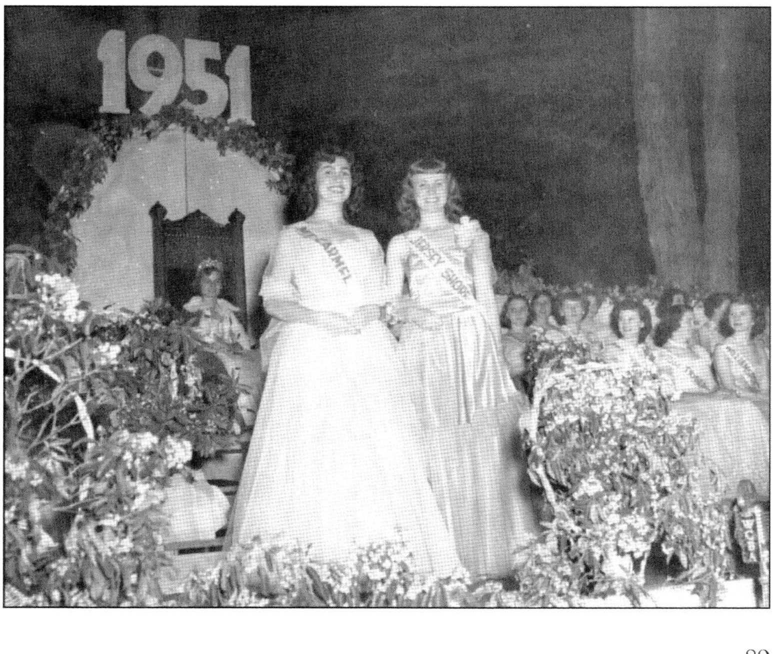

CORONATION ON THE GREEN. The judges selected Miss Jersey Shore, Sherill Verna Hiller, as the 1951 Laurel Queen. The coronation took place in the evening on the Green. (Courtesy WCC.)

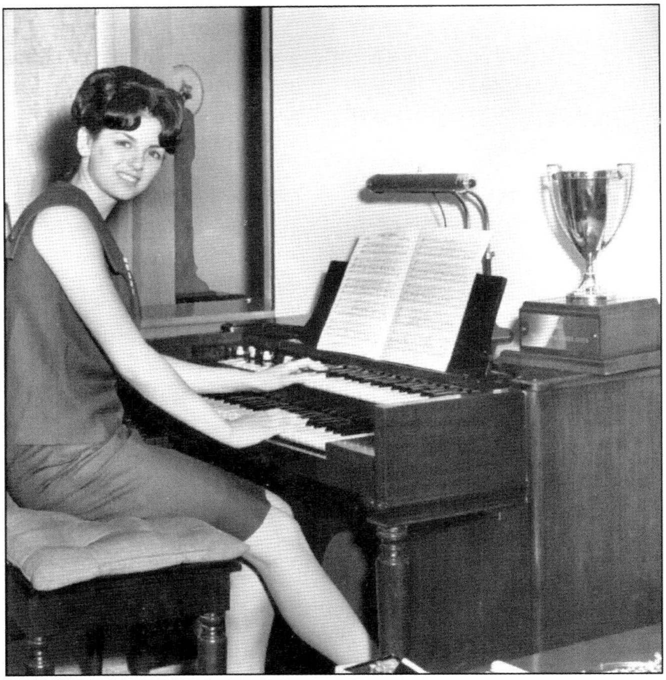

1964 Laurel Queen. This photograph shows Jeanne Brague, the 1964 Laurel Queen, seated at the organ. Although Miss Blossburg displayed musical talent, contestants for Laurel Queen were judged primarily on poise, charm, personality, and beauty. (Courtesy WCC.)

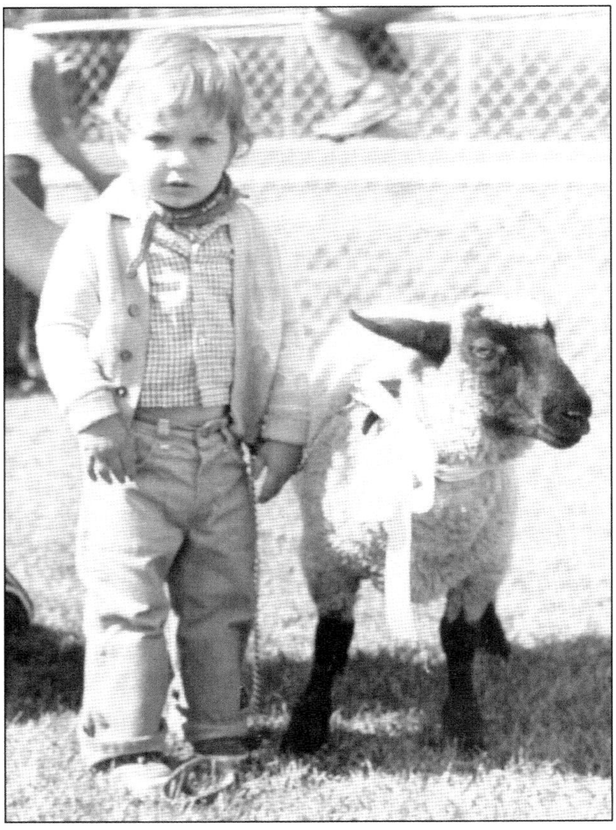

The Pet Parade. The children's Pet Parade occurred for the first time in 1959. Winners that year included Donna Whipple's pony and colt. Linda Day's dog Dennis won "Best Tail-Wagger"; Rebecca Ralph's toad won "Most Odd-Looking." Mark and Ellen Wilcox showed basset hound puppies that won "Most Sad-Looking." Mike Burton won first prize with a Shetland sheepdog. (Courtesy Bill Bachman.)

Six

SCHOOL DAYS

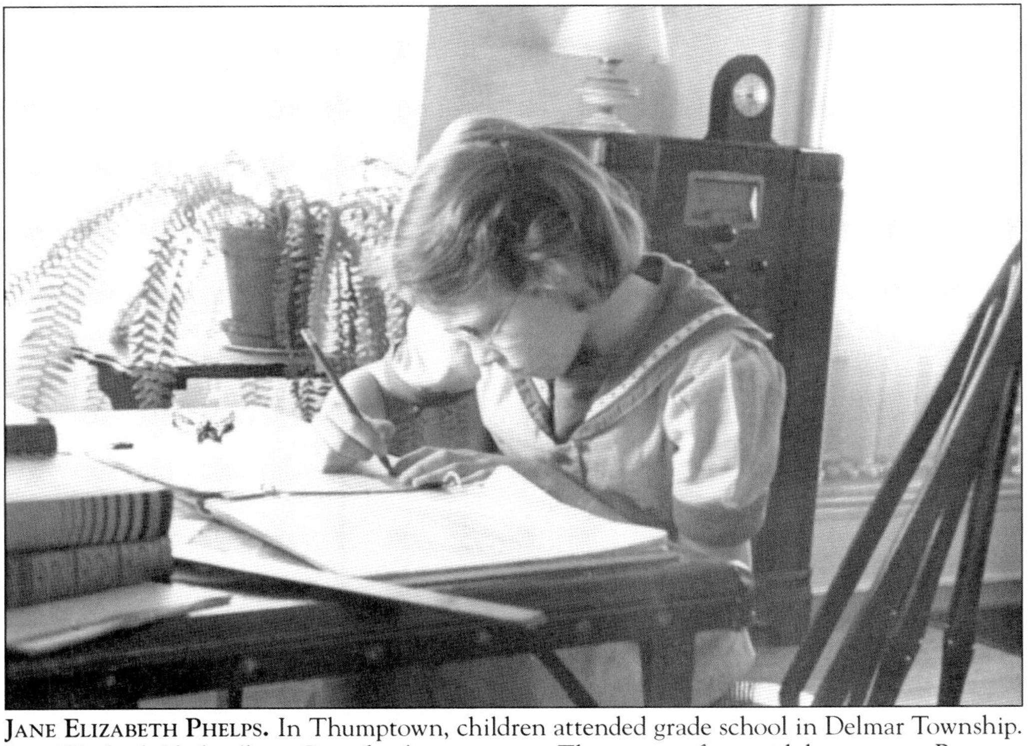

JANE ELIZABETH PHELPS. In Thumptown, children attended grade school in Delmar Township. Jane Elizabeth Phelps (later Gustafson) grew up on a Thumptown farm with her parents, Ransom and Thelma Phelps. This glimpse of young Jane Elizabeth doing her homework in 1945 reveals the importance of education to the Phelps family. (Courtesy David Gustafson.)

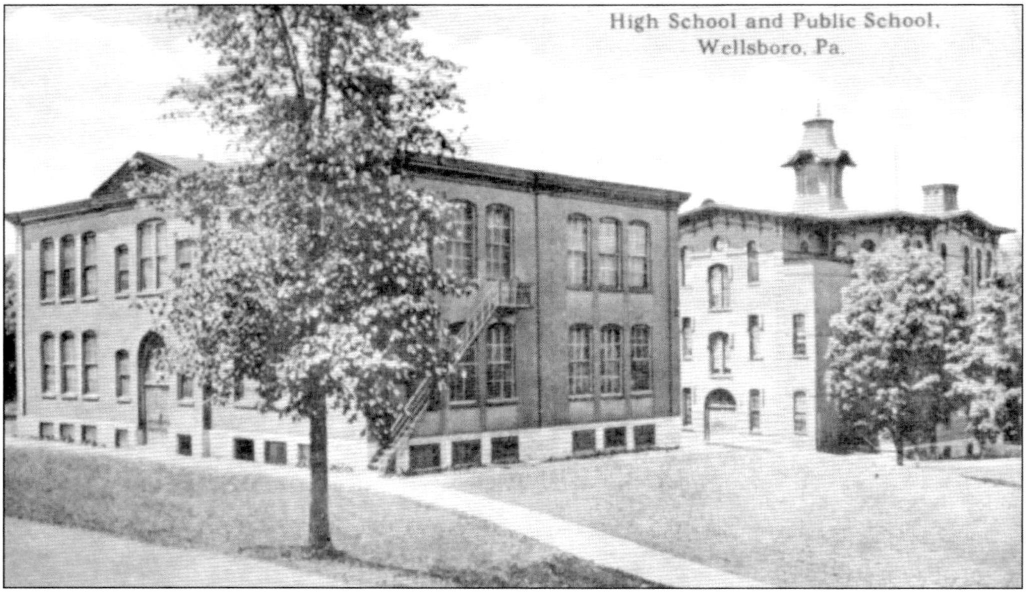

GRANT STREET SCHOOLS. In the background stands the Wellsboro High School that was dedicated August 20, 1875. The grade school in the foreground opened January 1, 1897. Both schools were located on a lot bounded by Bacon, Waln, and Grant Streets. In 1897, the school employed 12 teachers: 2 men and 10 women. The men's monthly salary averaged $96.78; the women's average pay was $43.30. A new high school on lower Nichols Street replaced the Grant Street High School in 1933, and the building was demolished. The site became the play yard for the younger students.

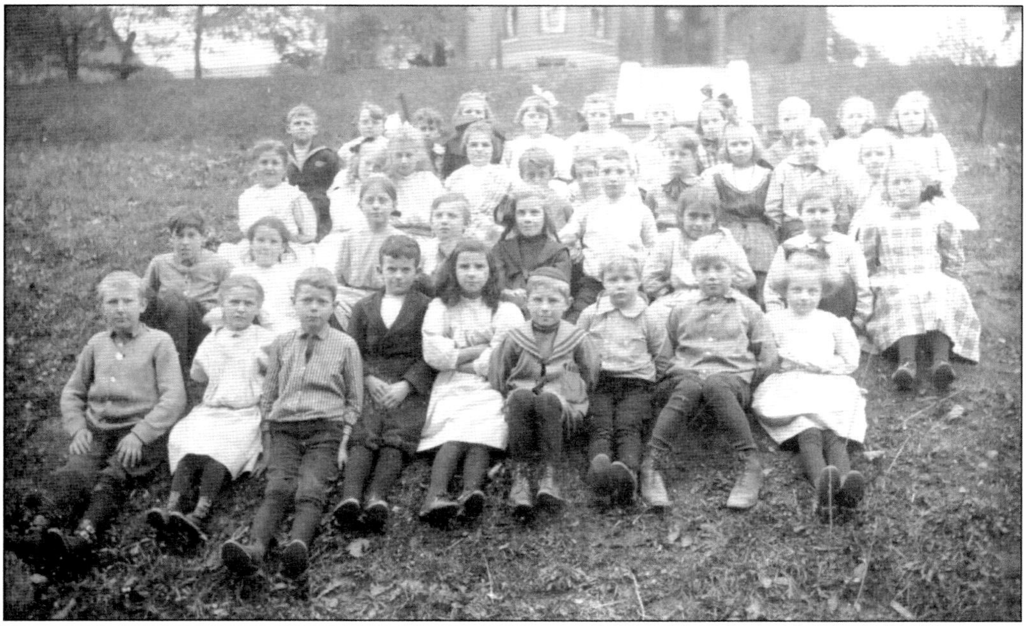

GRANT STREET STUDENTS. The 1909 Grant Street grade school students, taught by Florence Kiefer and Esther Butler, includes Charles Webb, pictured in the first row, fourth child from the right, wearing the jaunty sailor outfit. Young Charles later became the Honorable Charles G. Webb, who presided from 1951 to 1972. (Courtesy Mike Spencer.)

Florence J. Wheeler (1897–1992). A lifelong resident of Wellsboro, Florence Wheeler taught many generations of elementary and junior high school students. Diagramming sentences seemed to be her specialty, an acquired skill for which her students remain grateful. Wheeler was born March 5, 1897, the daughter of Harry D. and Orva M. Dobbs Wheeler. She graduated in 1915 and attended West Chester Normal School. She died at the Green Home on November 19, 1992, and was buried in the Wellsboro Cemetery.

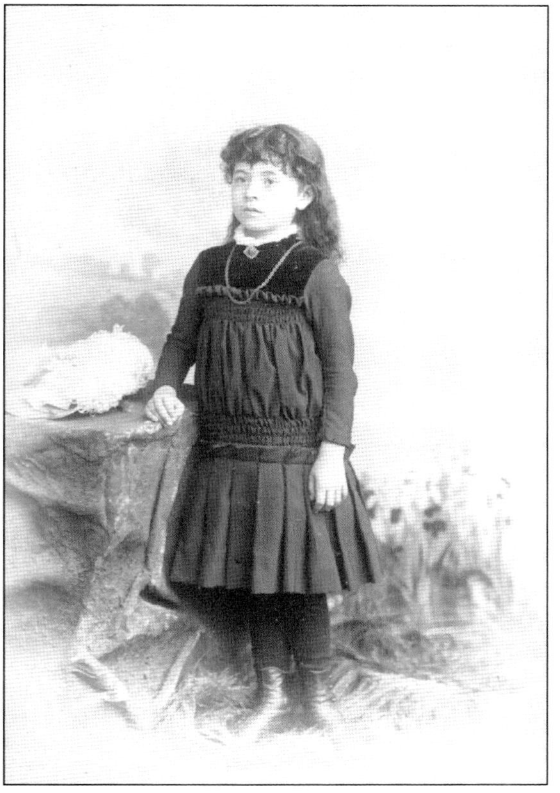

Rock L. Butler. Professor Butler was instrumental in planning and building the new junior-senior high school on lower Nichols Street. Butler's career in education spanned 50 years, 37 of them as a principal.

WELLSBORO SCHOOL

District No. 1

Wellsboro Twp., Tioga Co., Pa.

December 25, 1925

Prof. R. L. Butler,
Principal

Mary C. Coupe,
Teacher

School Board

Louise March   Mr. Harrison
Mr. Sheffer   Prof. Raseley
Mr. Evans

PUPILS

Wayne Smith   Irene Tormey
Delores Bendle
Hazel Hemmons   John Valentine
Beulah Benjamin
Dorthy Mosher   Ruth Henry
La Vonne McCrumb
Geraldine Townsend   Cortland Chilson
James Jackson
Marian Kennedy   Esther Bailey
Robert Wheeler
Richard Love   Rovert Cleveland
Kenneth Smith
Mary Jane Young   Dale Smith
Catherine Gray Bennett
Royce Reinwald   Eleanor Carson
Richard Gee
Harry Webster   Noble Chilson
Mollie Kleiman
Eleanor Green   Nina Bowers
Lester Stebbins
Lucille Bailey   Frederick Husted
Marie Campbell
Donald Clark   Girard Kennedy
Francis Bowen
Dewitt Gerow   Ralph Weller

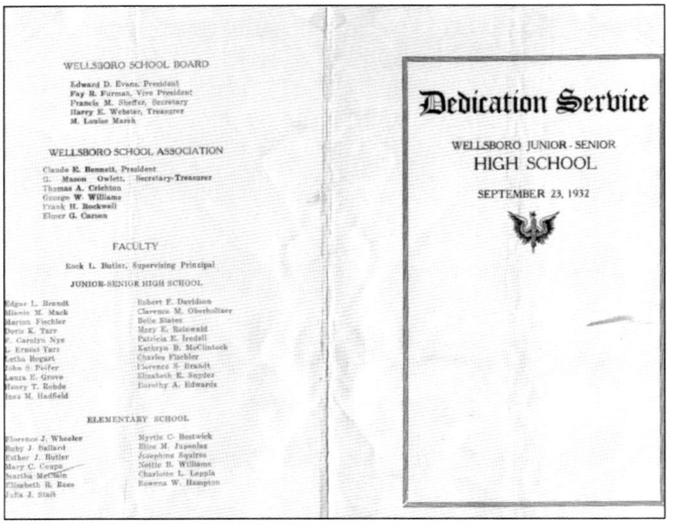

WELLSBORO SCHOOL BOARD

Edward D. Evans, President
Fay R. Furman, Vive President
Francis M. Sheffer, Secretary
Harry E. Webster, Treasurer
M. Louise March

WELLSBORO SCHOOL ASSOCIATION

Claude E. Bennett, President
G. Mason Owlett, Secretary-Treasurer
Thomas A. Crichton
George W. Williams
Frank H. Rockwell
Elmer G. Carson

FACULTY

Rock L. Butler, Supervising Principal

JUNIOR-SENIOR HIGH SCHOOL

Edgar L. Brandt	Robert F. Davidson
Minnie M. Mack	Clarence M. Oberholtzer
Marion Fischler	Belle States
Doris K. Tarr	Mary E. Reinwald
F. Carolyn Nye	Patricia E. Iredell
L. Ernest Tarr	Kathryn B. McClintock
Letha Bogart	Charles Fischler
John S. Peifer	Florence S. Brandt
Laura E. Grove	Elizabeth E. Snyder
Henry T. Rohde	Dorothy A. Edwards
Inez M. Hadfield	

ELEMENTARY SCHOOL

Florence J. Wheeler	Myrtle C. Bostwick
Ruby J. Ballard	Elise M. Jupenlaz
Esther J. Butler	Josephine Squires
Mary C. Coupe	Nettie B. Williams
Martha McClain	Charlotte L. Leppla
Elizabeth R. Rees	Rowena W. Hampton
Julia J. Stait	

Dedication Service

WELLSBORO JUNIOR-SENIOR
HIGH SCHOOL

SEPTEMBER 23, 1932

DEDICATION. The Wellsboro Junior-Senior High School, for grades seven through twelve, was dedicated September 23, 1932. Williamsport architects W.D. Shollenberger and John Y. Roy are acknowledged in the program, as are local heating contractors Bliss & Kimball. Rock L. Butler (father of William Butler, MD) was the supervising principal. (Courtesy GFL.)

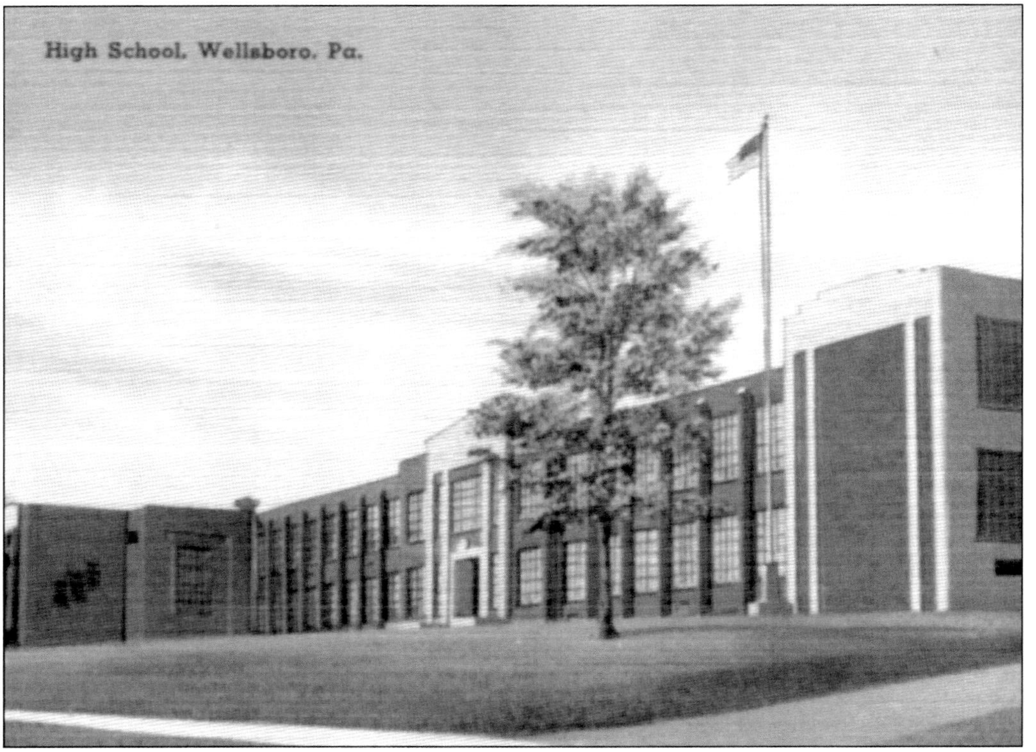

WELLSBORO JUNIOR-SENIOR HIGH SCHOOL. The elegant home of Luther C. Bennet and his wife, Anna, once occupied the site where the new school was built. The Bennets sold the property to Horace A. and Katherine B.C. Field in 1897. It eventually fell into disrepair and was sold at sheriff's sale in 1931. The Wellsboro School Association acquired and then cleared the site. The cornerstone of the new high school included the signatures of all students attending school in 1932. Francis Bacon's well-known quote, "Knowledge is Power," greeted students as they passed through the front entrance. Later reorganized as the Wellsboro Middle School, the institution was rededicated as the Rock L. Butler Middle School on May 23, 1992.

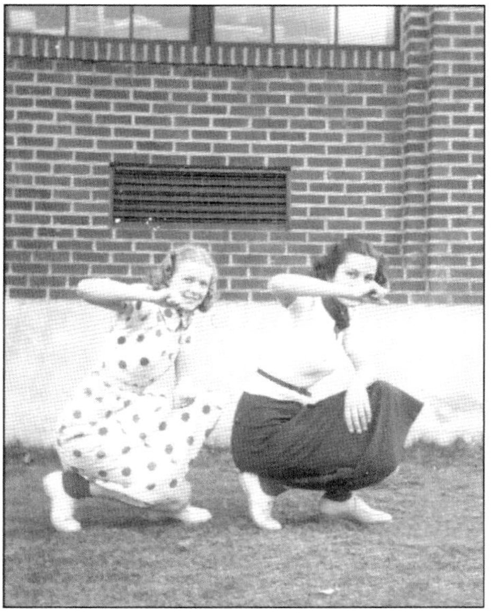

Wellsboro High School Cheerleaders. The 1930 high school yearbook includes the joyful claim that "it cannot be disputed that 'school days' are the happiest days of our lives." These cheerleaders appear to agree as they practice their routines in front of the new high school on Nichols Street in the mid-1930s. (Courtesy Mia Anderson.)

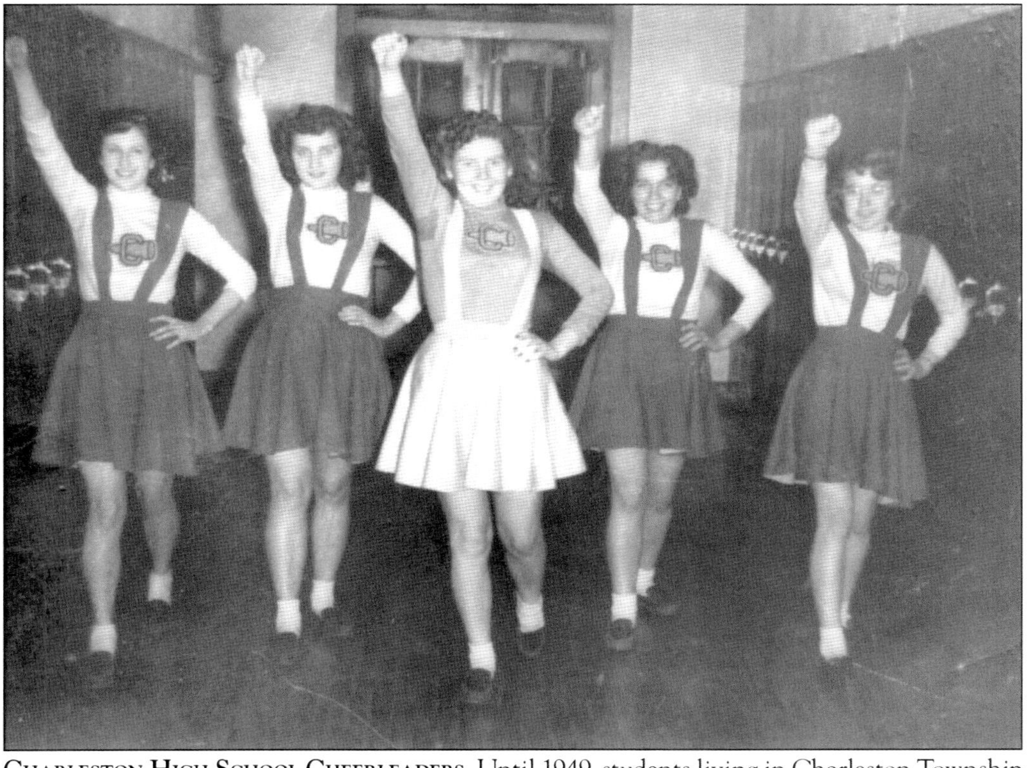

Charleston High School Cheerleaders. Until 1949, students living in Charleston Township attended school separate from the Wellsboro students, first in Dartt Settlement (1909–1936), and later on Route 6 (1937–1956). Under a new state law, the schools of Wellsboro, Delmar, Charleston, Middlebury, Duncan, and Shippen consolidated and became known as the Wellsboro-Charleston Joint School. The photograph shows Charleston cheerleaders in the hallway of the Charleston High School on Route 6 in the 1940s.

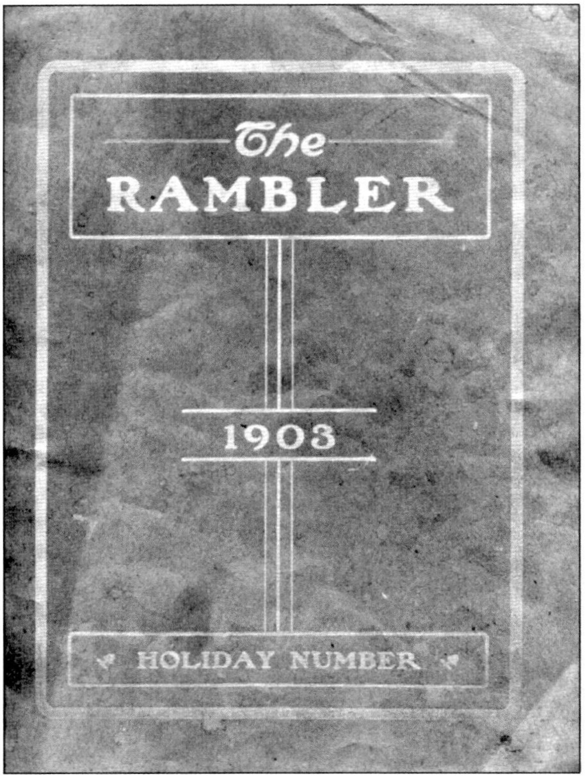

THE RAMBLER. The first *Rambler* appeared in manuscript form in 1902 because sufficient funds were not forthcoming from the business community. The "Father of the *Rambler*," Ivan M. Bernkoff, instead read the students' work aloud in chapel. The class of 1903 succeeded at fundraising, and the first volume of the *Rambler* enjoyed immediate success. The 1924 *Rambler* features student work that ranges from "Frog, Love, Liquor," a story about moonshine, to "The Riddle of the Universe," a metaphysical treatise on the evolution of the soul.

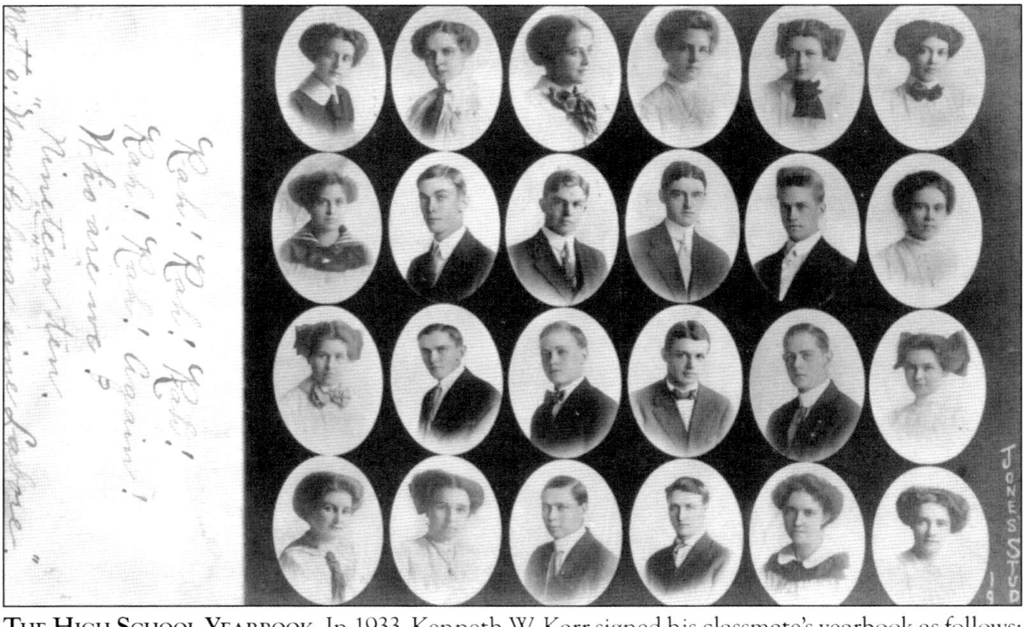

THE HIGH SCHOOL YEARBOOK. In 1933, Kenneth W. Karr signed his classmate's yearbook as follows: "Sempre mi recorda lei carne un buon amica" (I always counted her a good friend). Wellsboro's historical yearbooks show entire editorials composed in Latin. The class of 1910 chose *Non palma sine labore* as its motto; this translates as "no reward without labor."

THE CAULDRON. The school newspaper, the *Cauldron*, "unrivaled in its originality," was published every two weeks. Students and faculty paid 5¢ per copy, money used to finance the school yearbook. The *Cauldron* staff met students at the school door every other Thursday morning, as shown in the 1942 photograph. (Courtesy Mia Anderson.)

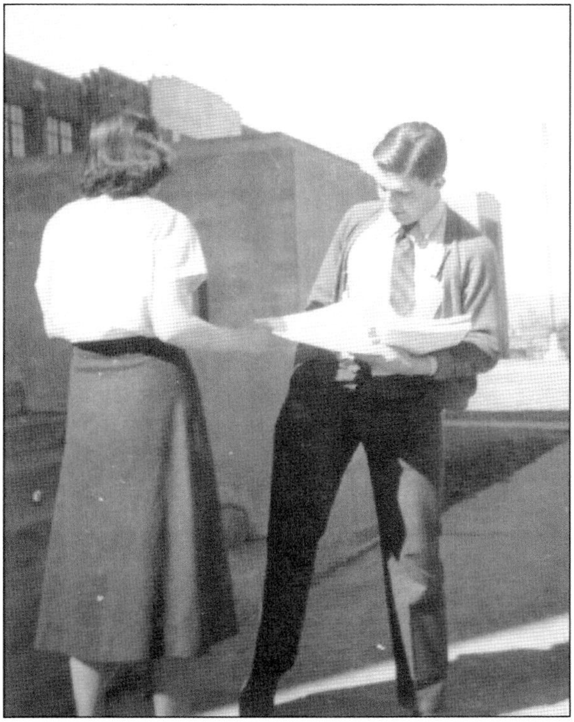

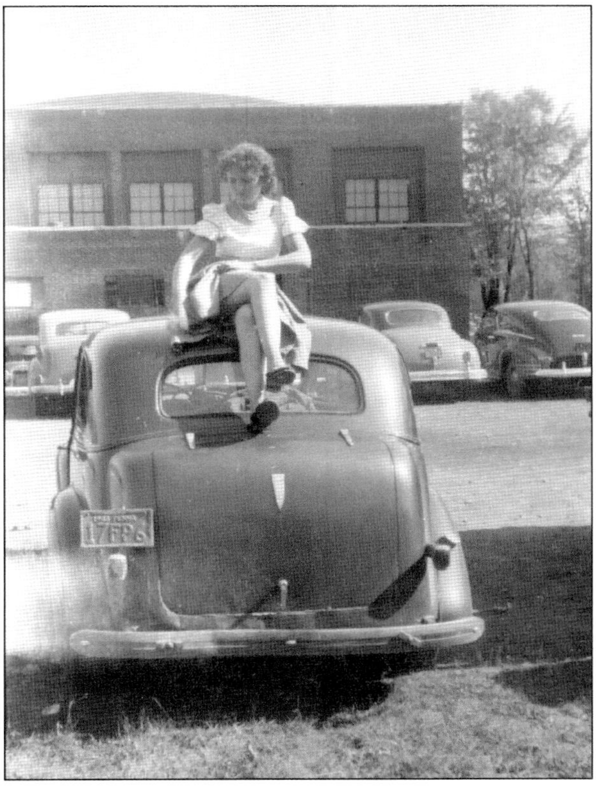

LORENE PARSONS (WEBSTER). Posing atop automobiles seemed to be popular during the 1940s. This photograph of Lorene Parsons (later Webster) was taken behind the high school on lower Nichols Street in 1948.

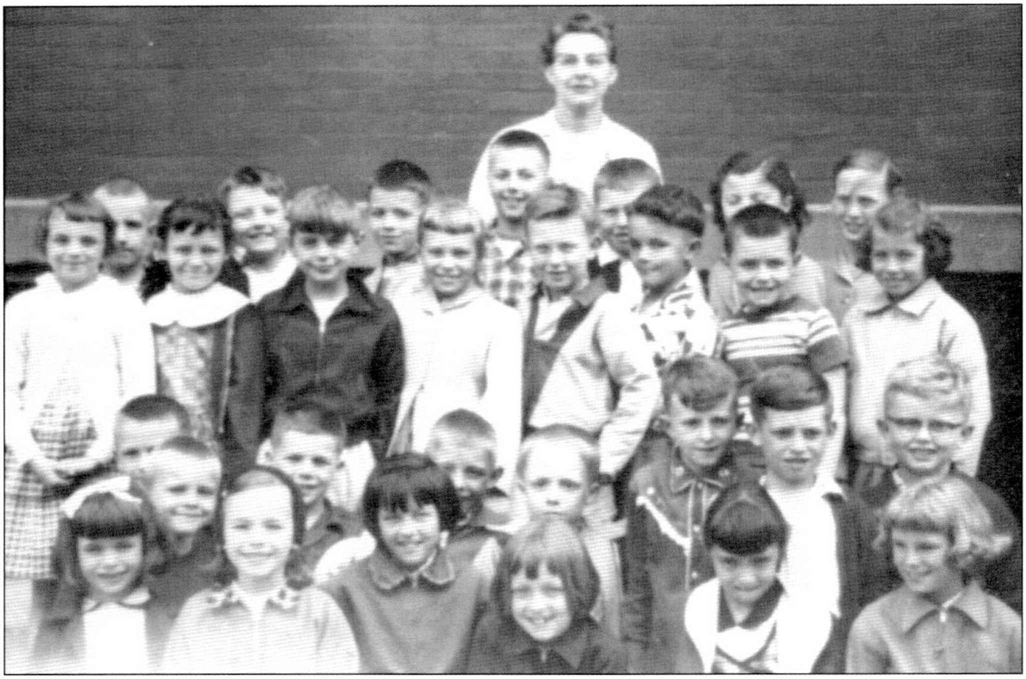

GRANT STREET STUDENTS. A 1955–1956 Grant Street second-grade class includes, from left to right, (first row) Darlene Shelley, Joyce Escott, Connie Briggs, Mary Margaret Fullwood, Diana Howard, and Nancy Davis; (second row) Steve Greenfield, three unidentified boys, James Youdas, Jerry French, Stephen Buchko, and Daryl Nobles; (third row) Gail Satterly, Diana Bliss, David Monks, Susan Stager, James Crooks, Eddie Slatterly, Louis Prevost, and Anne Christ; (fourth row) Thomas Weller, John Dewey, John Campbell, Michael Murtland, Lynn Halstead, Sharren McElligott, and Helen Sunstrom. Behind the students stands teacher Thyra Fischler. (Courtesy Sharren McElligott Hummel.)

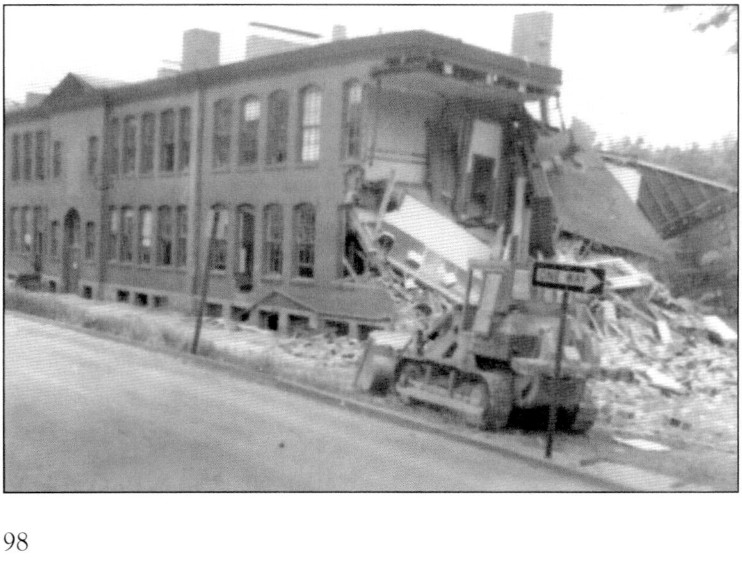

GRANT STREET ELEMENTARY SCHOOL DEMOLITION. The Grant Street School continued to serve students even after most of the elementary classes moved. The property was sold to the borough in 1969, and the building was razed. The town constructed Park Hill Manor, housing for senior citizens, on the site in 1971. (Courtesy TCHS.)

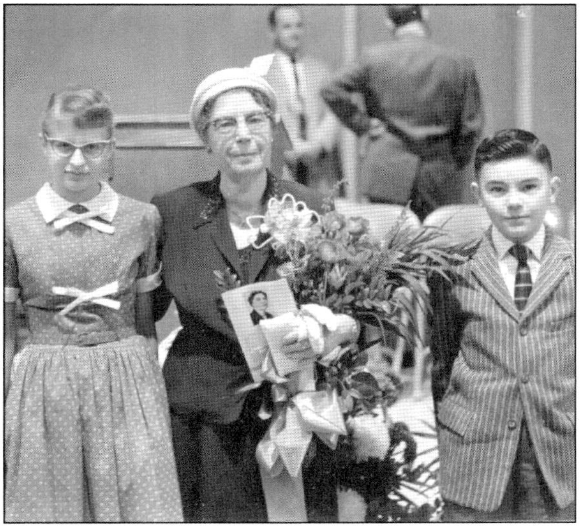

Charlotte Lappla (1884–1968). After moving to Wellsboro with her family in 1893, Charlotte Lappla lived on the corner of Grant Street and East Avenue. Lappla graduated from Wellsboro High in 1903, attended West Chester Normal School, and taught from 1905 to 1955. The borough bestowed her name on the new elementary school. She is pictured at the November 20, 1957, dedication of the Charlotte Lappla School, located on Meade Street, with sixth-grade student representatives Kathy Eaton and Dennis Bliss. The school originally served grades four to six, with only one section reserved for third-grade students. (Courtesy Dennis Bliss.)

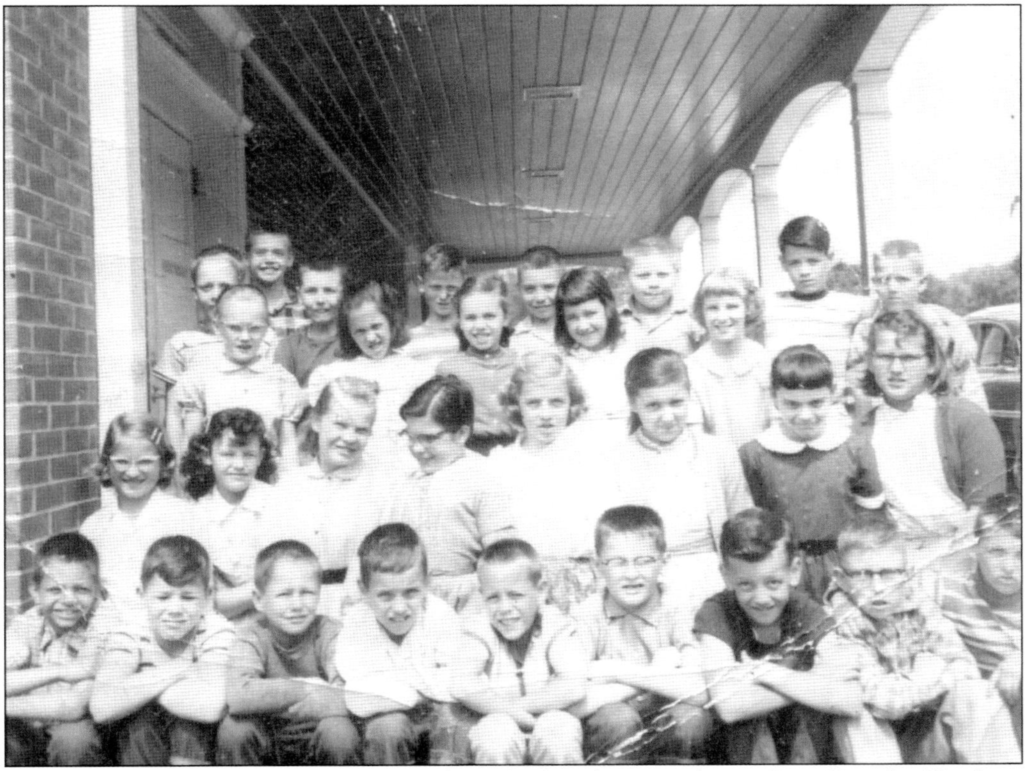

Charlotte Lappla Students. The fourth-grade class that moved in 1957–1958 to the Charlotte Lappla school includes, from left to right, (first row) Alan Wood, LaRue Knapp, Michael Cooney, John Krystoff, Dennis Brucklacher, Marvin Focht, Randy Weller, Lowell Sarber, and unidentified; (second row) Nancy Seamans, Diane Bliss, Carol Buss, Mary Dambly, Janet Niles, Cathy Lytle, Diana Howard, and Frances Zuchowski; (third row) Betty Shumway, Connie Briggs, Joyce Escott, unidentified, and Nancy Davis; (fourth row) James Youdas, Randy Ward, Louis Prevost, two unidentified, Gary Metarko, John Campbell, and Tom Gross.

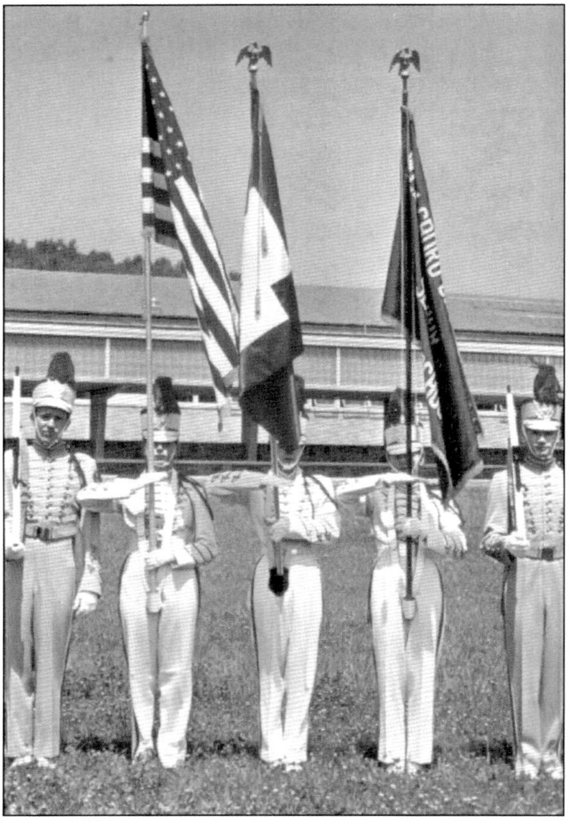

WELLSBORO-CHARLESTON JOINT SENIOR HIGH SCHOOL. Move-in day for the students at the new senior high school on upper Nichols Street occurred on December 17, 1956. The dedication followed on February 24, 1957. The program included a concert led by Lenore "Nodie" Johnson (later Bujno), speeches by dignitaries, and the singing of "The Star-Spangled Banner" accompanied by the band and color guard. Band members then conducted tours of inspection, and the Parent-Teacher Association served refreshments. (Courtesy TCHS.)

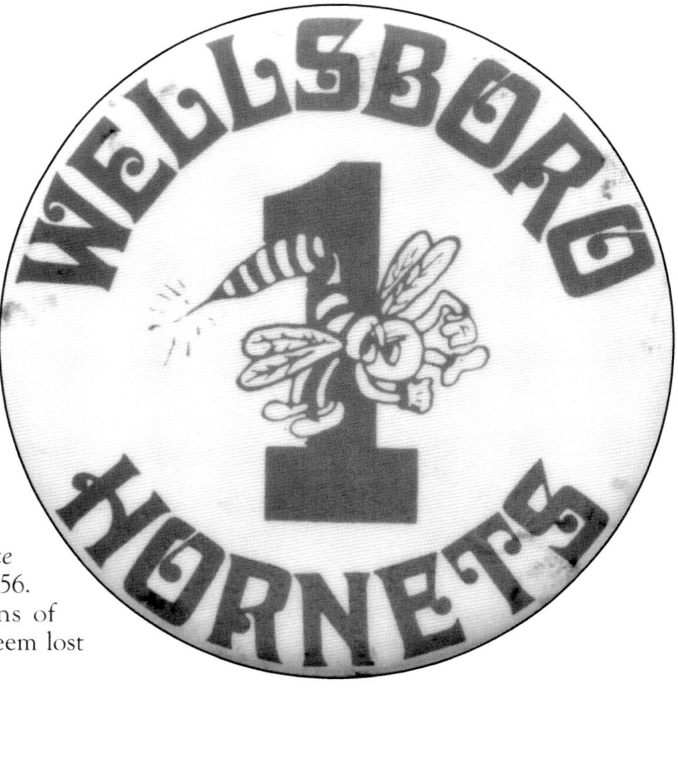

WELLSBORO GREEN HORNETS. *Wellsboro Gazette* columnist Betty Frazier wrote in 1989 that green and white became the official school colors "more than fifty years ago." Robert Grossenbacher, WNBT radio announcer, sometimes receives credit for nominating the name "Hornets," which members of the senior class allegedly chose as their favorite in 1955; the *Gazette* first mentions the Hornets in 1956. Nonetheless, the exact origins of the school colors and mascot seem lost to history.

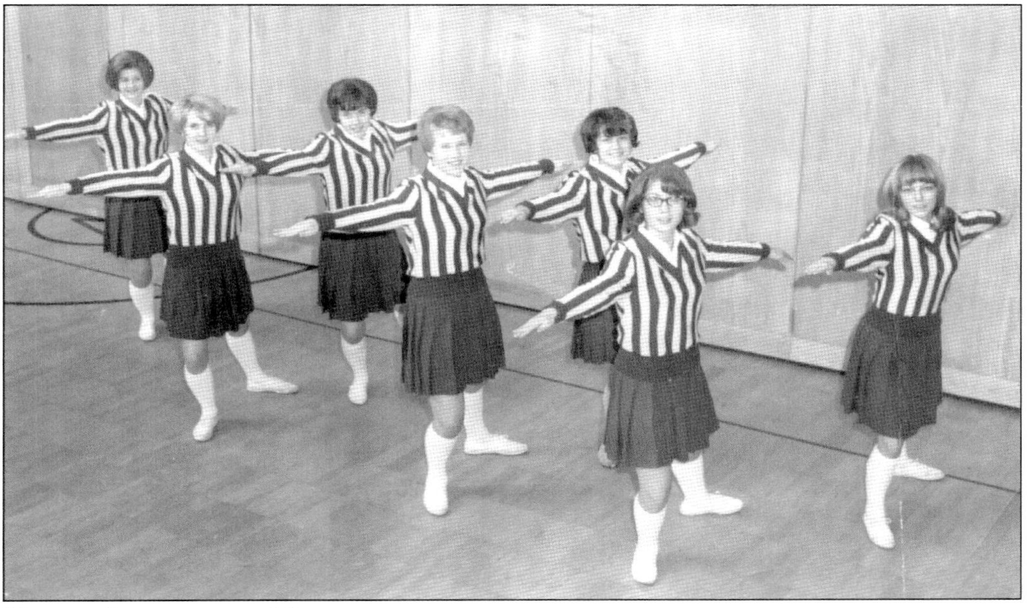

Varsity Cheerleaders. The fall 1966 Wellsboro High School cheerleading squad includes, from left to right, Deborah Dillman, Patricia Clark, Cynthia Wood, Linda Ingerick, Patricia Kerr, Anita Dillman, and Ann Benjamin.

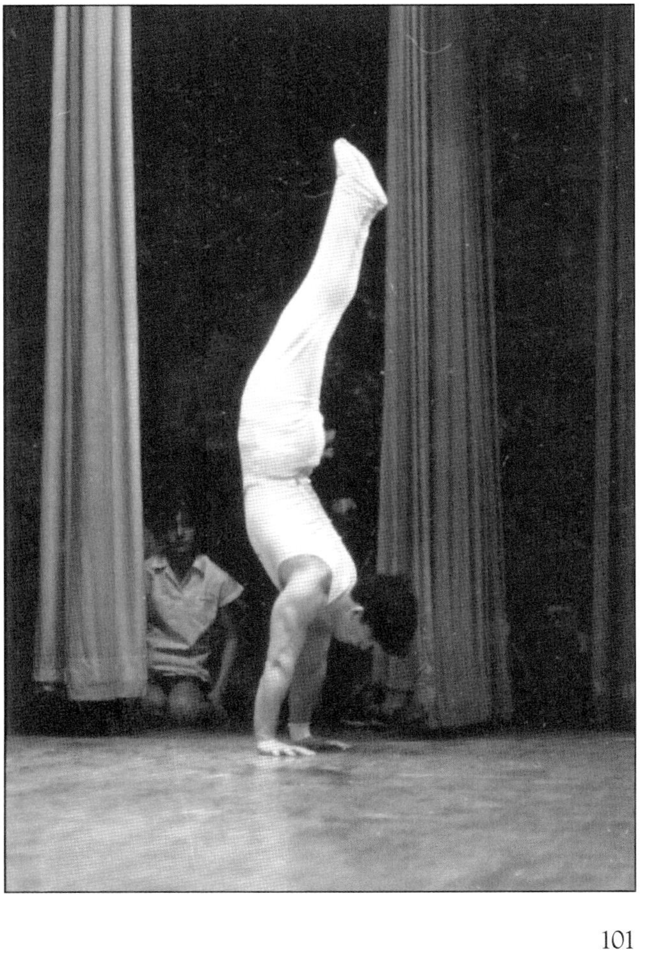

Gymnastic Genius. Archie Laird thrilled his classmates and friends with his athletic skill, particularly as a gymnast. Stories of his death-defying handstands on the railings at Colton Point, which overlooks the canyon, or on cars traveling down Main Street, still circulate. Laird is pictured here performing onstage in the high school auditorium in 1966. (Courtesy Archibald Laird II.)

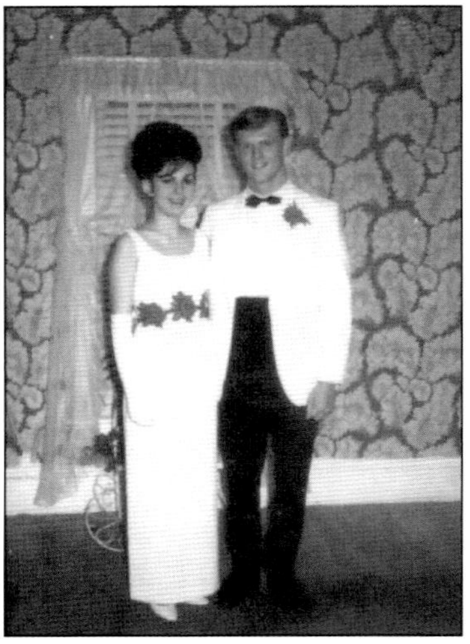

Autumn Leaves. The class of 1967 held its autumn leaves–themed senior prom in fall 1966. Lisa Vaganos Root is shown at her home on McInroy Street with her escort Karl Simonds. (Courtesy Lisa Root Dodge.)

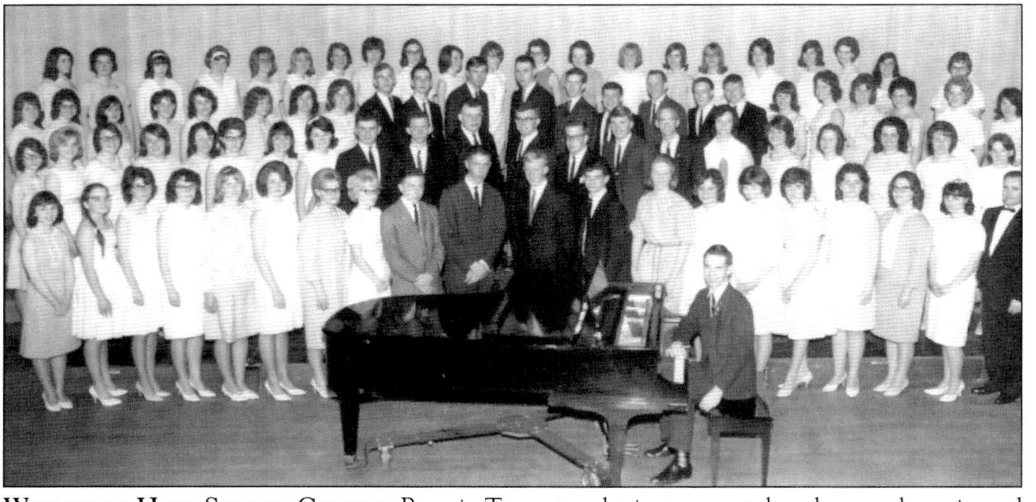

Wellsboro High School Chorus. Bennie Truax taught instrumental and general music and supervised the music department in the Wellsboro schools from 1958 to 1968. This photograph shows Truax at a May 8, 1965, high school concert. Pictured are, from left to right, (first row) Susan Leach, Deborah Fuller, Pamela Slocum, Sherry Tillotson, Joanne Brown, Connie Manning, Esther Walker, Donna West, Lynn Davis, Jock Suhr, Tom Scranton, Carlo Bennett, Linda Simmons, Linda Maynard, Cindy Wood, Ardys Smith, Janet Day, Judy Sheer, unidentified, and Truax; (second row) Sharon Fuller, Cindy Johns, Nancy Sherman, Debby Bronkowski, Diana Howard, Deborah Compton, Maryanne Andrascik, Sharren McElligott, Robert Adams, Mike Butler, Blaine Bush, John "Rick" Kimball, Kermit Shrawder, Barry Kirkpatrick, John Gee, Diana Bliss, unidentified, Bonnie Carpenter, Betty Johns, Cheryl Fisher, and Linda McCarthy; (third row) Roxanne Bellinger, Bonnie Cruttenden, Mary Fullwood, Carol Parker, Toni Smith, Janet Smith, Sherry Cuda, Karen Brooks, Daryl Nobles, Brad Holiday, Mike Murtland, James Warriner, Ronald Boyce, Kevin Maynard, Lawrence Kitts, Pamela Mosher, Ellen Brill, Linda Day, Connie Peer, Mary Adams, and unidentified; (fourth row) Linda Bailey, Jeanne Northrup, Shirley Bliss, Cinda Bryant, Eleanor Kennedy, Pat Clark, Sandra Oates, Martha Powers, Ann Jorgensen, two unidentified, Anne Christ, Patty Brown, Nancy Davis, Brenda Benson, Rhonda Baker, Shirley Brown, Shirley Derbyshire, Glenda Stebbins, Linda Brown, and Pat Kilshaw. (Courtesy Sharren McElligott Hummel.)

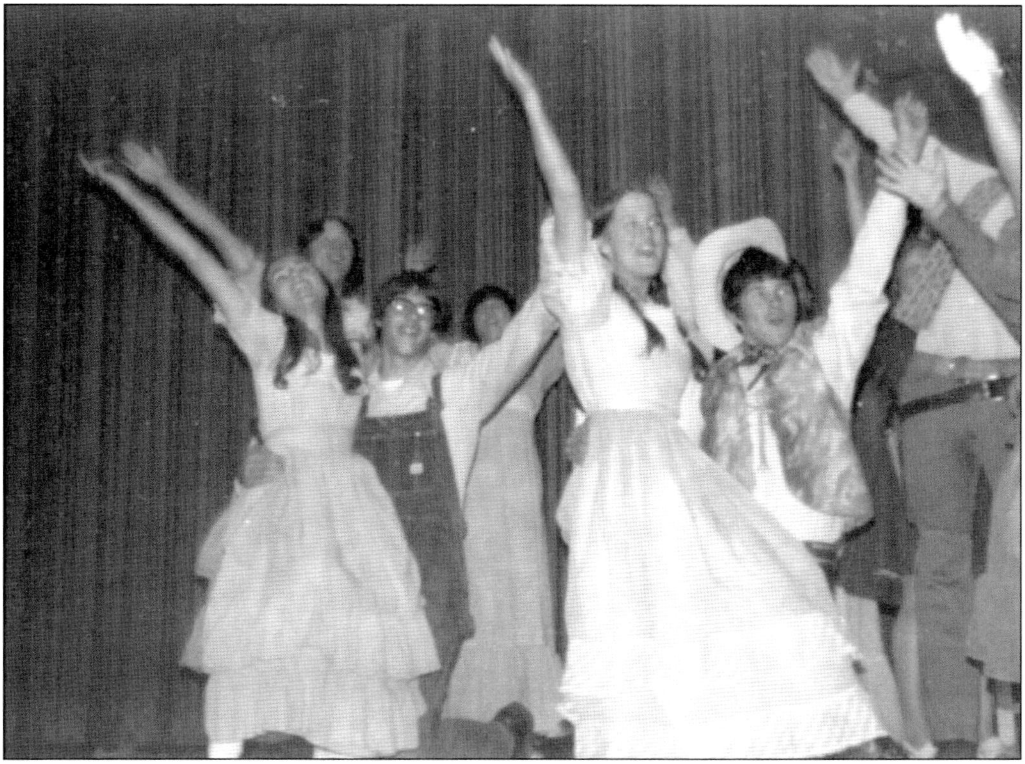

OKLAHOMA! The Wellsboro-Charleston school system benefitted from exceptionally strong arts programs. The music teachers achieved legendary status, including Lenore "Nodie" Bujno, Bennie Truax, and Patricia Brown Davis. *Oklahoma!*—performed in 1975 under the direction of an exuberant, foot-stomping Nancy Williams, with music direction by the talented Patricia Brown Davis—received an enthusiastic standing ovation. Pictured, from left to right and front to back, are Debbie Lada, Brion Antoine, Sally Benjamin, Scott Lindsey, Tracy Walrath, and Joan Brown. (Courtesy Sally Benjamin.)

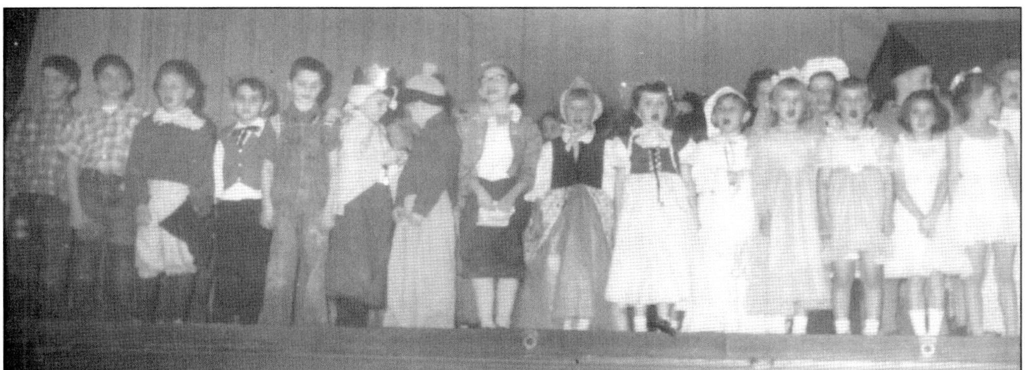

CHRISTMAS PAGEANT. Charleston elementary school students, taught by Leona Harrison, performed *Christmas in the Shoe* in 1957. Performers include, from left to right, Eugene Mosher, Gregory Boyce, Mike Osgood, Lee Drew, Bud Heichel, Bill Lyon, unidentified, Mike Passmore, Ann Benjamin, Shirley Bliss, Judy Sheer, Barbara Banik, Denise Compton, Cynthia Starks, and unidentified. (Courtesy Barbara Lyon Hotalen.)

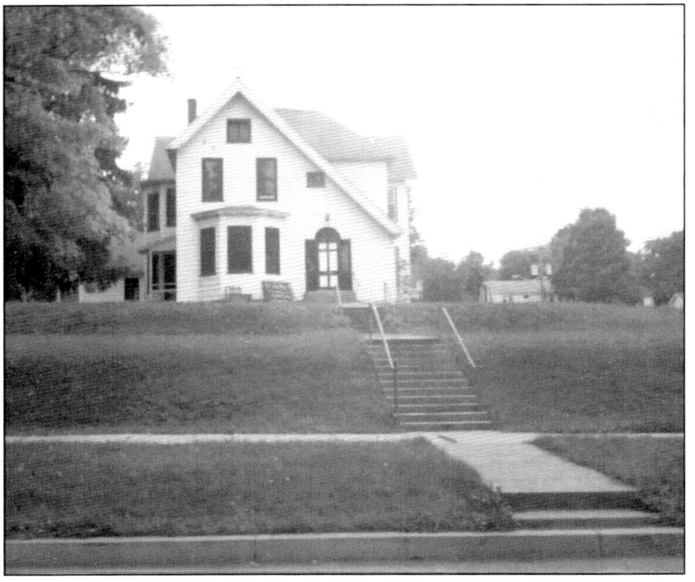

St. Peter's Convent. George C. Bowen built the house at 50 Central Avenue in 1888 and later sold it to Thomas Stone. George Derby, perhaps the most famous owner, played professional baseball for both Detroit (1881–1882) and Buffalo (1883). The house became St. Peter's Catholic Convent in 1945. When St. Peter's built a new church on Central Avenue, the building was razed, and the site became a shared parking lot for the church and for Soldiers and Sailors Memorial Hospital. (Courtesy Sandra Losinger.)

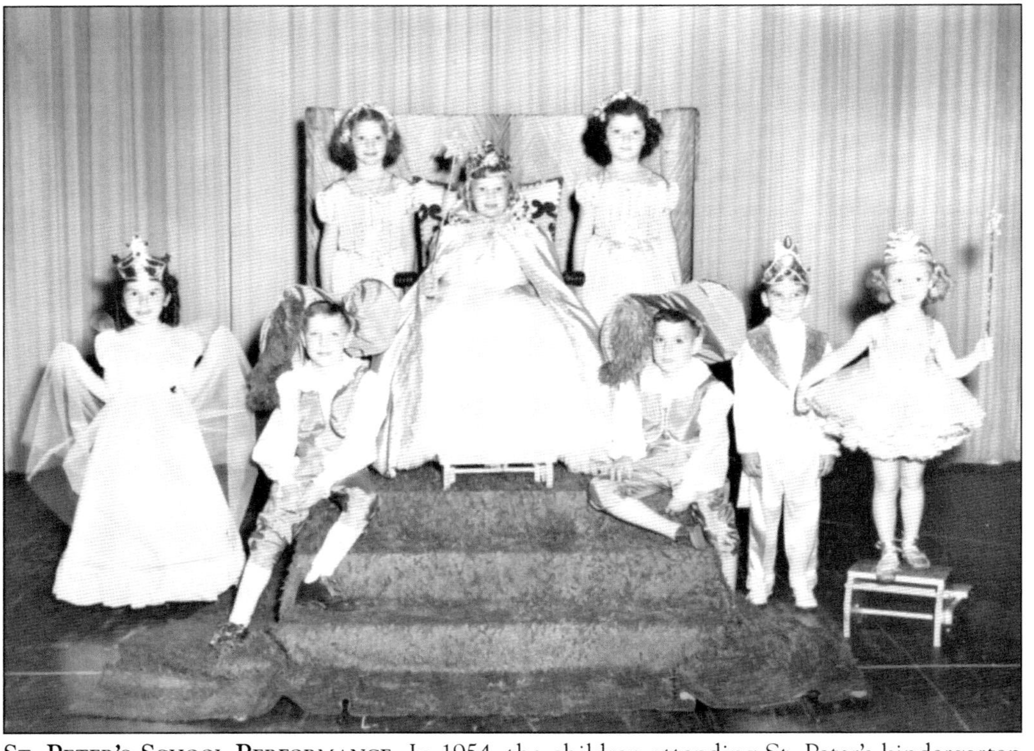

St. Peter's School Performance. In 1954, the children attending St. Peter's kindergarten performed the play "Fairies Are Really True," featuring, from left to right, Patty Harris (Dotty), Jock Suhr (Pageboy), Beverly Copp (Fairy Queen Attendant), Susan Stager (Fairy Queen), Sharren McElligott (Fairy Queen Attendant), Mark Storti (Pageboy), Thomas Callahan (Teddy), and Ann Marie Turchik (Runaway Fairy). (Courtesy Sharren McElligott Hummel.)

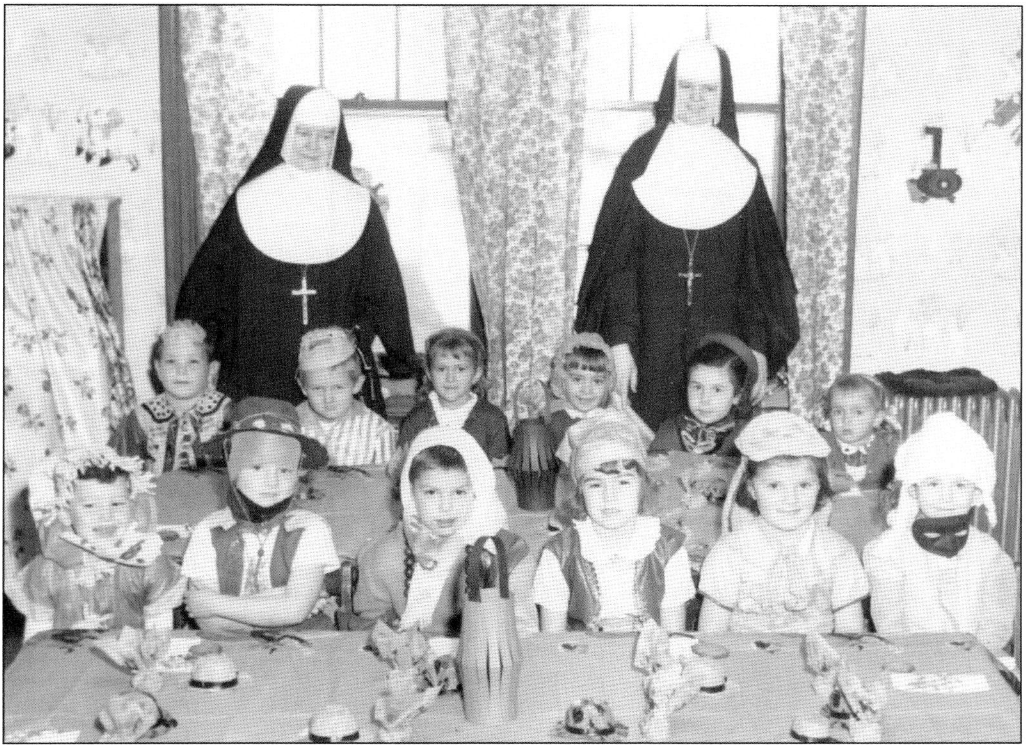

Sisters of the Immaculate Heart of Mary. The sisters, invited by Rev. Thomas Kelley, pastor of St. Peter's, arrived in Wellsboro in August 1945. They taught catechetical classes for hundreds of parish students in addition to opening St. Peter's convent to both Protestant and Catholic children for kindergarten and nursery school. Nursery/kindergarten classes ended in 1976. Among those pictured with Mother Marie Gabrielle (left) and Sister Marie Eugenia (right) in 1953 at a Halloween party are, from left to right, (first row) two unidentified, Richard Dillman, Penny Bailey, Sharren McElligott, and Louis Prevost. (Courtesy Sharren McElligott Hummel.)

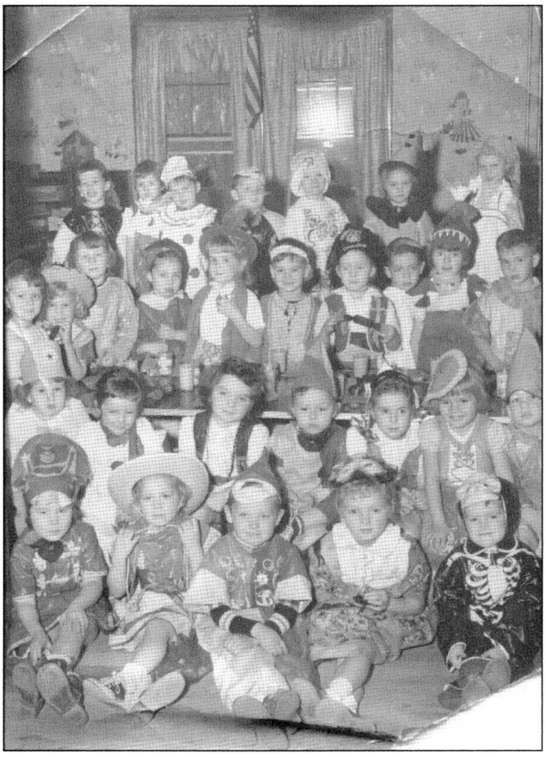

Halloween Party. Classes at St. Peter's would not meet today's group-size requirements. One class, pictured in fall 1952, includes almost 30 young children; the class of 1954 graduated 44 students. (Courtesy Patricia Benjamin Schwab.)

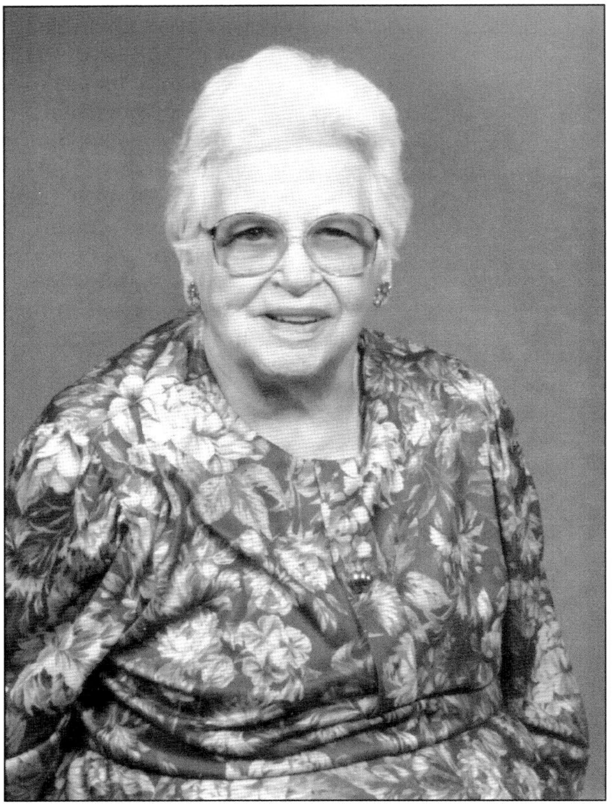

Vera Bailey Blair Ferguson (1917–2007). "Mrs. Blair," the kind lady with the pretty handkerchief peeking from her uniform pocket, managed the junior high school cafeteria. School lunch was always wholesome and tasty; the submarine sandwiches were especially memorable. She was born November 28, 1917, in Wellsboro, the daughter of the late Robert B. and Estella Price Bailey. She survived two husbands, Glenn Blair, who died August 12, 1977, and Herman Ferguson, who died July 7, 1989. Vera died February 24, 2007, at Broad Acres and was laid to rest at Tioga County Memorial Gardens. (Courtesy Robert Blair.)

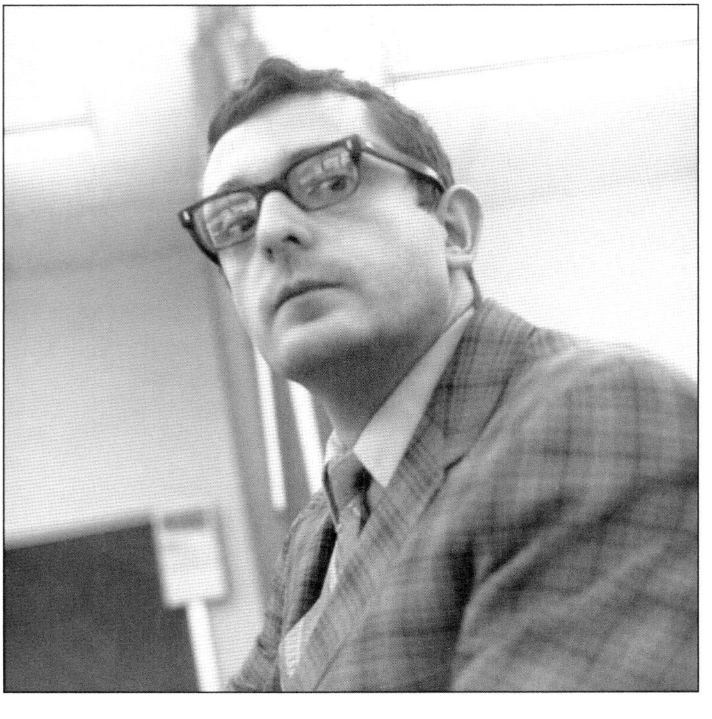

Brian Stahler. Brian Stahler, English teacher extraordinaire, inspired generations of Wellsboro students, particularly aspiring authors. Mr. Stahler retired after serving the Wellsboro school system for 37 years and currently resides in Mansfield, Pennsylvania. (Courtesy Sally Benjamin.)

Seven

NAMES AND FACES

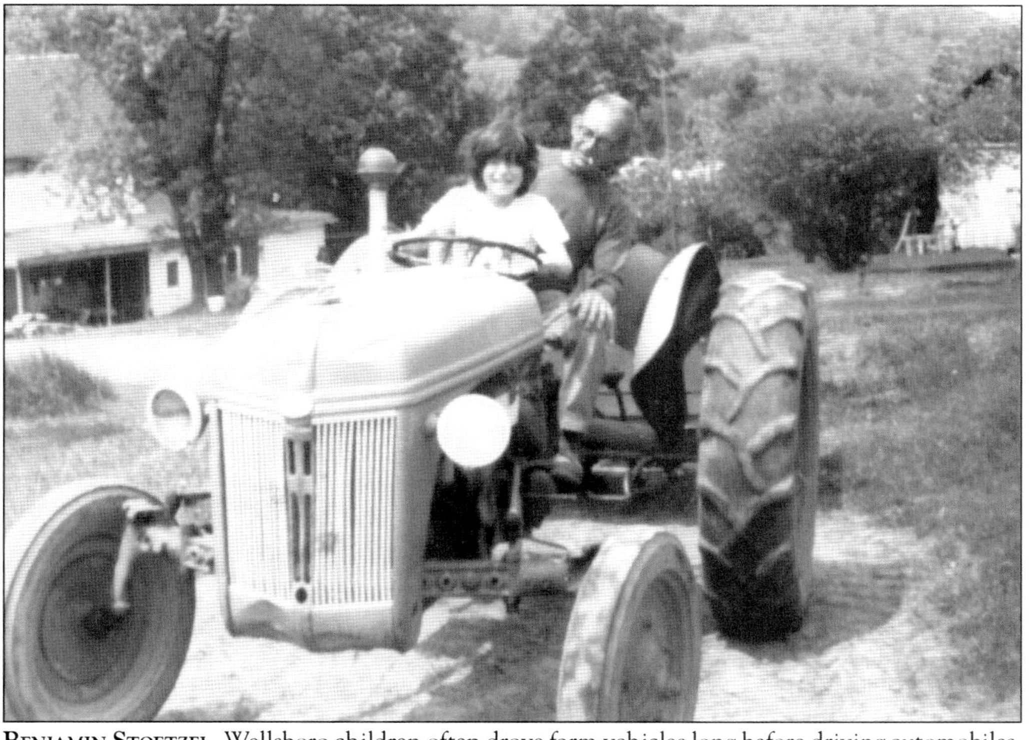

BENJAMIN STOETZEL. Wellsboro children often drove farm vehicles long before driving automobiles. The photograph shows Ben Stoetzel, nicknamed "Sassafras," happily steering a vintage 8N tractor, with a little help from his delighted grandfather N.J. Benjamin. Perhaps the most popular utility tractor of all time, the 8N featured a light gray frame and a red body. The Ford Motor Company produced this tractor from 1947 to 1952.

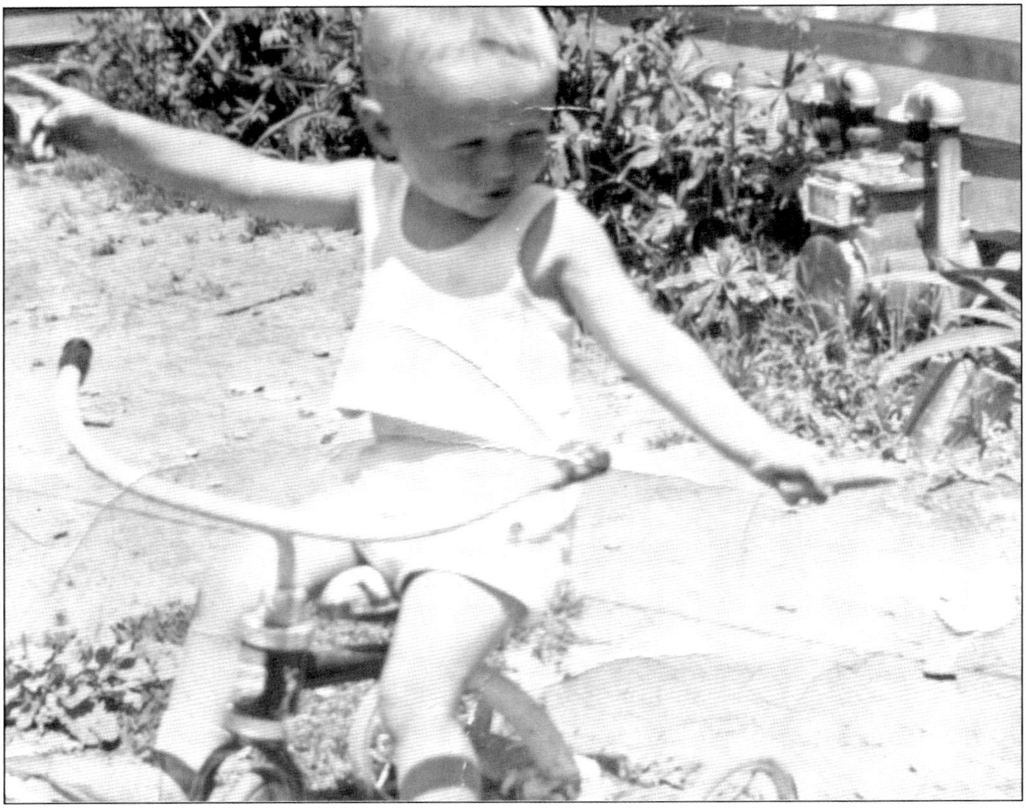

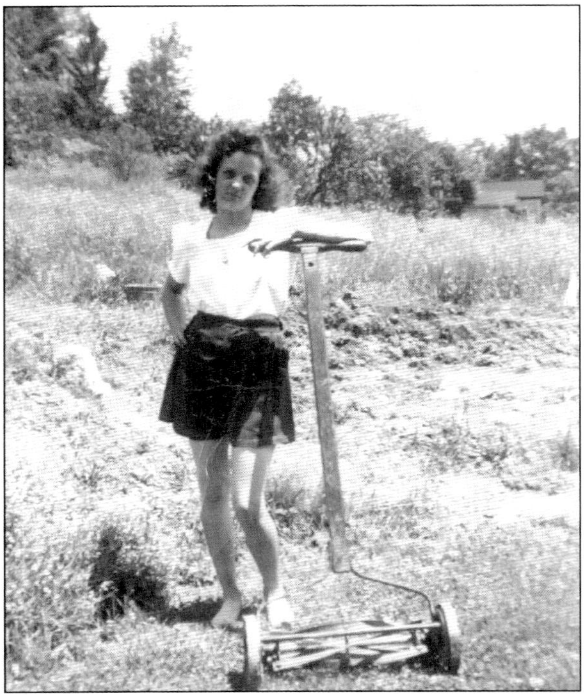

Michael Joseph Cooney. Mike has lived in Wellsboro for 65 years, the first 17 spent at his home on West Water Street. This photograph shows Mike riding his tricycle; he later graduated to a dirt bike, and still later to a Harley-Davidson, which he intends to ride indefinitely—but without the hot dog.

Virginia Wilcox (Cooney). After marrying in 1941, Virginia and John Cooney moved to 8 West Water Street, where they raised John Jr., Michael, Ann, Timothy, and Christopher. A nurse at Soldiers and Sailors Memorial Hospital, Virginia, a devoted mother, also sewed for her daughter, crocheted doilies, and prepared hot breakfasts each morning for her family. She is shown taking a break from mowing the lawn when she still lived on Wetmore Street.

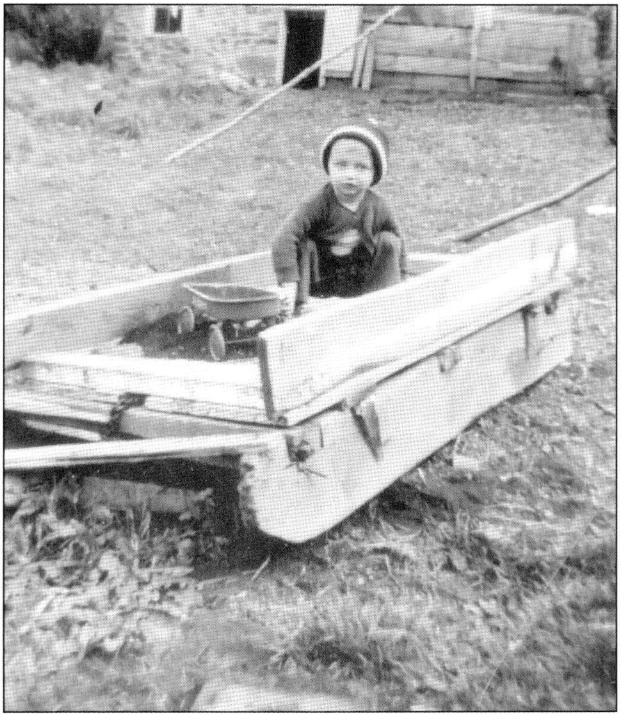

Dennis Eugene Gillespie (1948–1986). Denny grew up in Round Top, attended the Charleston Elementary Schools, and graduated from Wellsboro High School in 1966. He worked at Corning Glass Works as a "hiker," making and sealing boxes of Christmas ornaments and lightbulbs. (Courtesy Ruth Benjamin Dartt.)

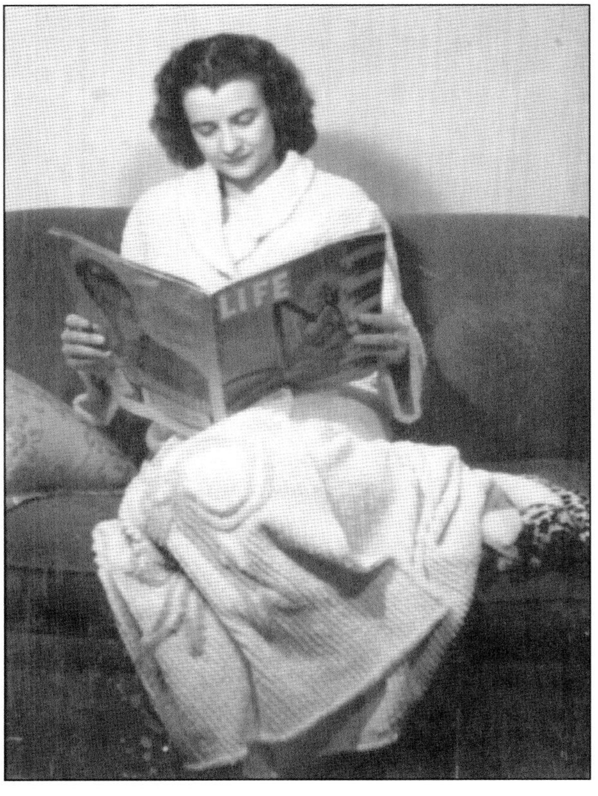

Frances Benjamin (Gillespie) (1923–2011). Born in Welsh Settlement, "Frannie" was the second of four children born to Frank and Ruth McMahon Benjamin (Dartt). In her later years, she worked as a physical therapist at Soldiers and Sailors Memorial Hospital. This photograph calls attention to classic indicators of life during the 1940s—*Life* magazine and a chenille bathrobe. (Courtesy Ruth Benjamin Dartt.)

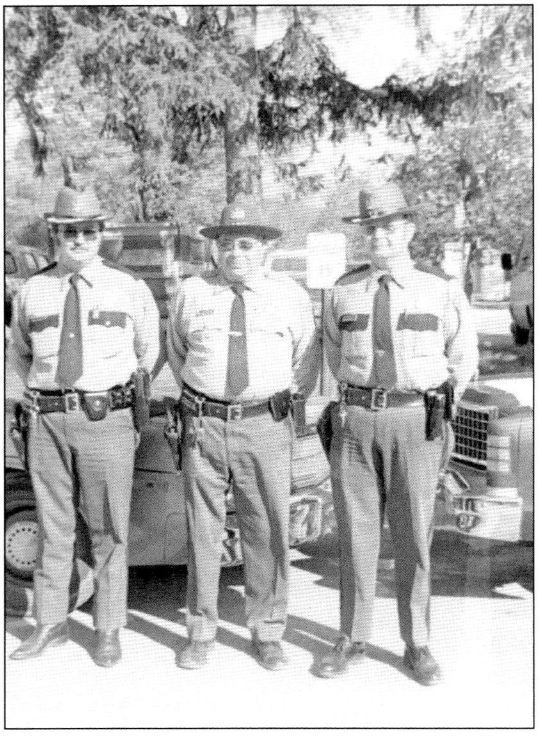

The Wheeler Family. Three members of the Wheeler family served with the Wellsboro police force. Pictured are, from left to right, Richard, who joined the force in 1969 and served for 23 years; John W., Richard's father, who was hired in 1973 and worked part time; and John E. Wheeler, Richard's brother, who became an officer in 1971 and served as police chief from 1987 to 2001. (Courtesy John E. Wheeler.)

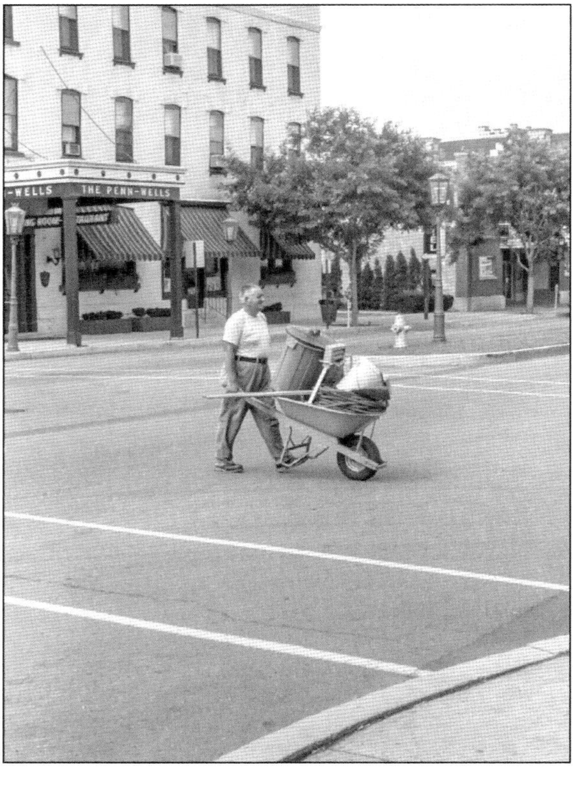

Tom Sticklin. Hardworking, dedicated, and highly recognizable, handyman Tom Sticklin washed windows, mowed lawns, and helped where he could, using tools as needed from the wheelbarrow that he pushed around town. When Sticklin was not working, he could be found at St. Peter's Catholic Church or riding his bicycle. (Courtesy Bill Bachman.)

Robert C. Bair. Dr. Bair opened an office in Wellsboro in 1957 and retired in 1986. In addition to being the chief surgeon at Soldiers and Sailors Memorial Hospital, Dr. Bair volunteered to give team physicals and to act as team physician for all athletic district activities in Wellsboro. (Courtesy Bill Bachman.)

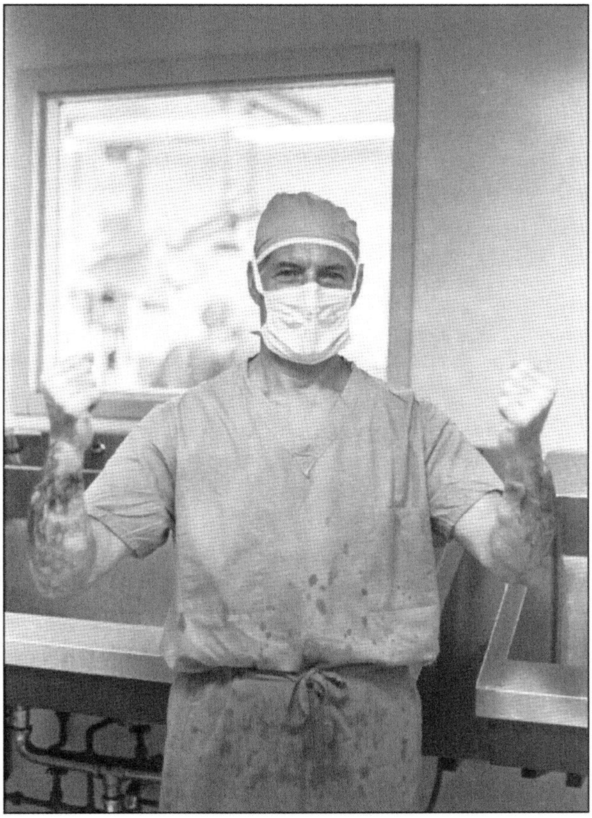

Jack Wilcox. Sheriff Jack Wilcox, first elected in 1966, served until 1982. He also served two terms as county treasurer, 1954–1958 and 1962–1966. Sheriff Wilcox lived on Eberenz Street. (Courtesy Bill Bachman.)

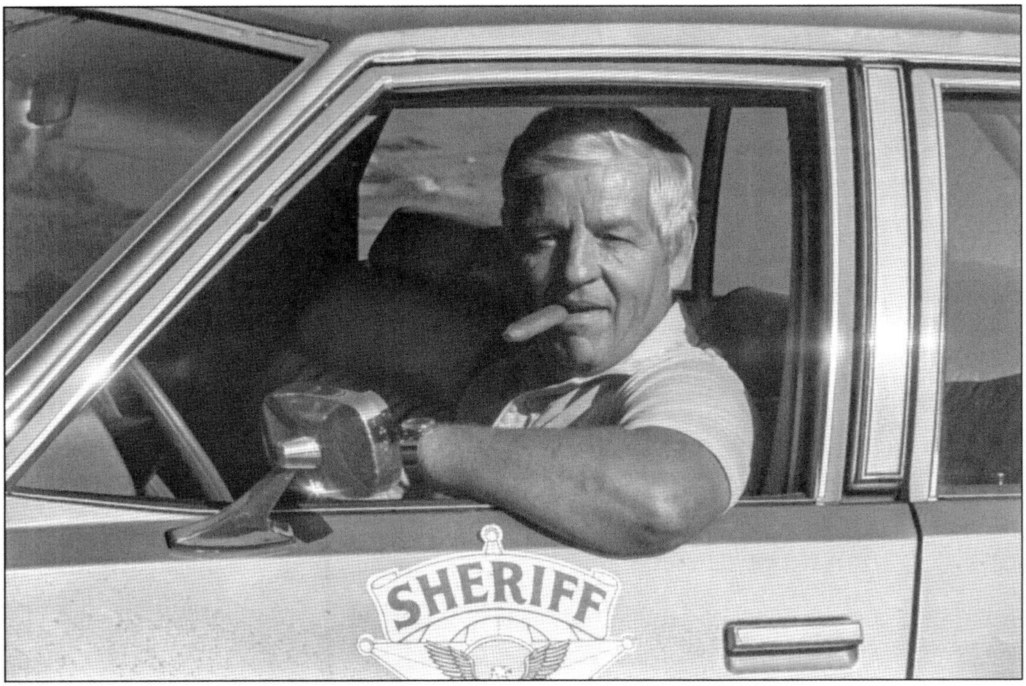

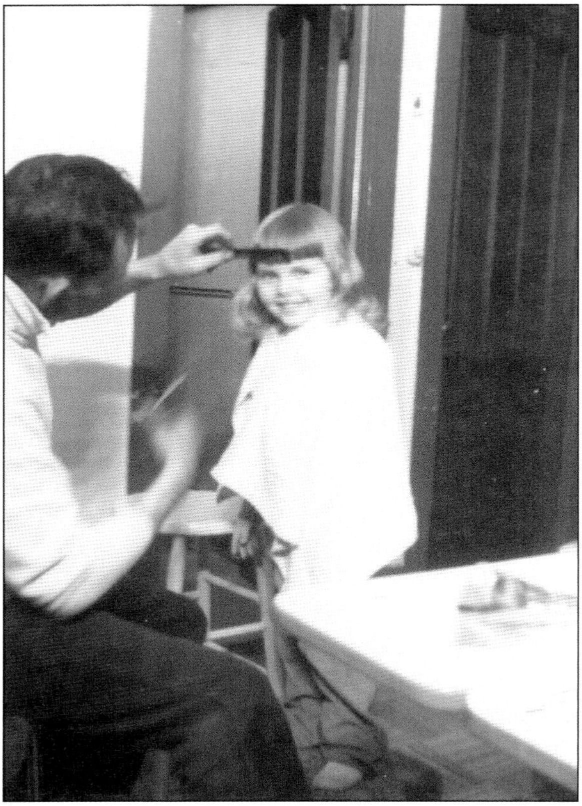

RUTH BENJAMIN (WIDRIG). A 1979 alumna of Wellsboro High School, "Ruthie" Benjamin later graduated from Mansfield State College and from Washburn University. A dedicated health care professional, she currently works as a radiation therapist at the Guthrie Healthcare Center/Robert Packer Hospital in Sayre. Ruth's adventures include running in marathons and hiking in the mountains of New York and New Hampshire This 1966 photograph shows five-year-old Ruthie standing obediently while her father trims her bangs. (Courtesy Ruth Benjamin Widrig.)

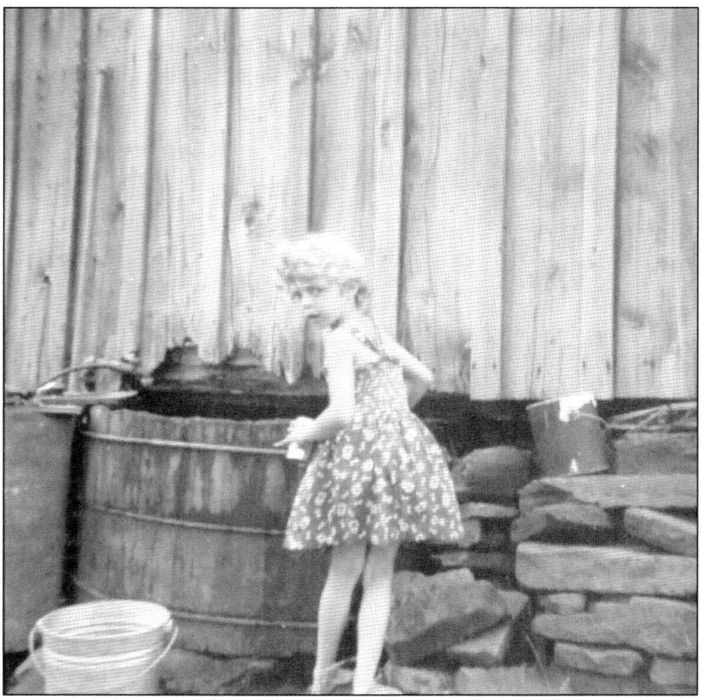

SUE ELLEN BENJAMIN. In 1992, Sue Ellen Benjamin returned to her family's Round Top farm, which today produces organic fruit and vegetables marketed through Community Supported Agriculture (CSA). Sue, also a gifted textile artist, participated for years in local and regional events, including the Laurel Festival, the Tioga County Fair, Dickens of a Christmas, and Hickory Fest. She is pictured on the farm in 1959, near the sheep shed, where a spring-fed trough provided water for the animals. (Courtesy Sue Benjamin.)

Patricia Benjamin (Schwab). Patricia "Pat" Benjamin was elected president of the Wellsboro High School art club in 1963, the year that the art club float, "Puff the Magic Dragon," won first place in the Laurel Parade. An accomplished equestrian, Pat competed in area horse shows, including Holliday and Wetmore Hill. An elementary school teacher for many years, she graduated from Mansfield State College and later from Nazareth College. This baby photograph was taken in Round Top in 1948. (Courtesy Patricia Benjamin Schwab.)

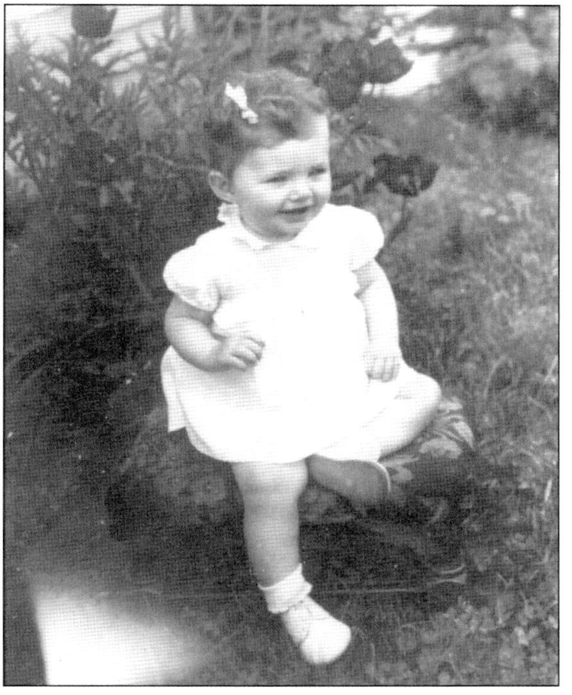

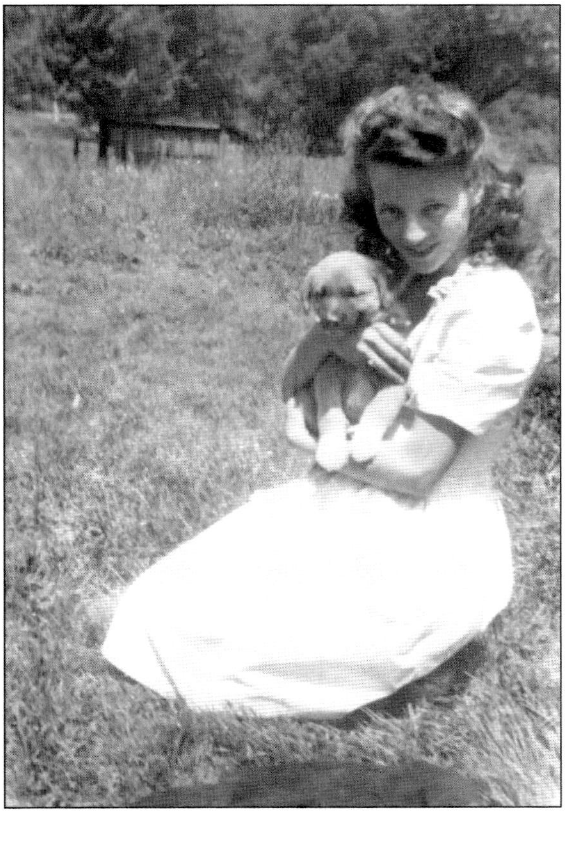

Lucille Jauquet (Benjamin) (1922–1981). "Lou" Jauquet, a native of Green Bay, Wisconsin, met Norton Benjamin, a Wellsboro native, in Denver, Colorado, while both were serving during World War II. They returned from the war to live in Round Top, where they raised five daughters—Patricia, Ann, Sue, Sally, and Ruth. After raising her girls, Lou worked at Corning Glass Works. She volunteered in the Soldiers and Sailors Hospital gift shop and served as president of the Women's Hospital Auxiliary.

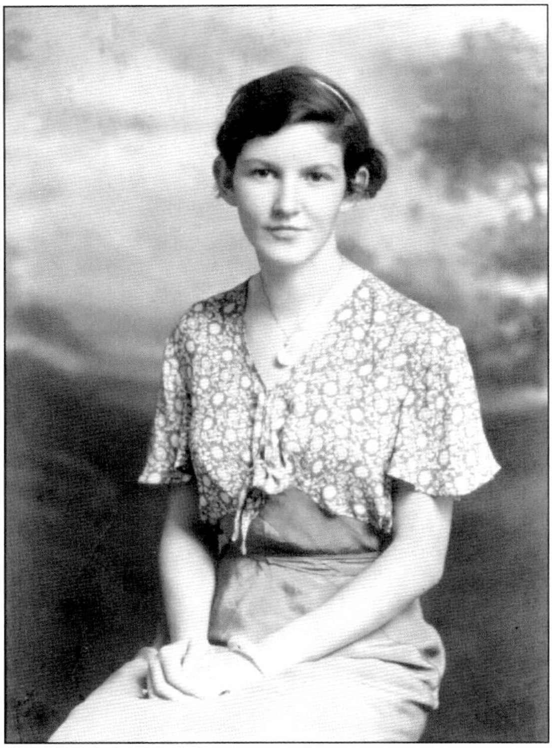

Elsie Watkins (Tanner) (1918–1982). Elsie Watkins, born June 10, 1918, to Leon W. and Edna Hotchkiss Watkins, grew up on a farm near Pine Creek Gorge. A 1935 WHS graduate, Elsie attended the Williamsport School of Nursing, followed by employment at Blossburg Hospital. She married William Jennings Tanner and left nursing to raise sons Frank and Donald. Corning Glass Works transferred Bill Tanner to Danville, Kentucky, where daughter Nancy was born in 1957. The family later returned to Wellsboro. Nancy recently founded Paws 'N Home Pet Sitting Services, located in nearby Covington. (Courtesy Nancy Tanner Bowen.)

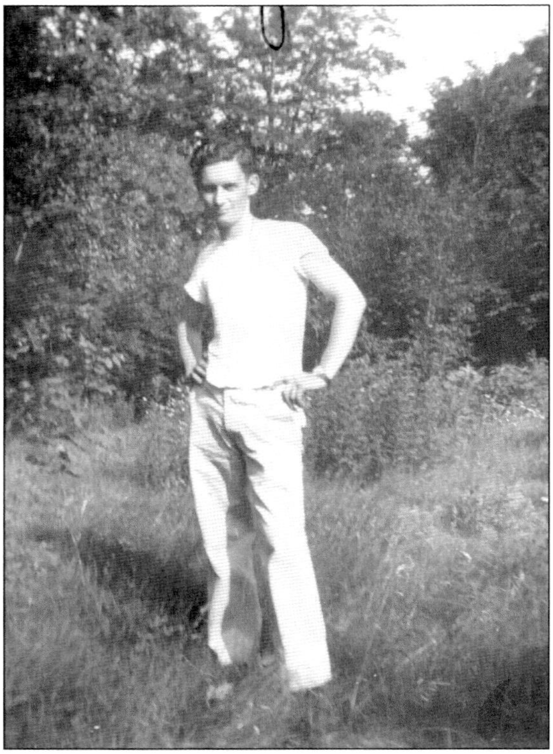

John Patrick Cooney (1919–2008). John Cooney graduated from Wellsboro High School in 1938. He worked as a ribbon-machine mechanic at Corning Glass Works. He enjoyed hunting with his friend Gus Zarvis, who owned the Candy Kitchen. The photograph shows Cooney posing on Rectory Lane while home on leave during World War II.

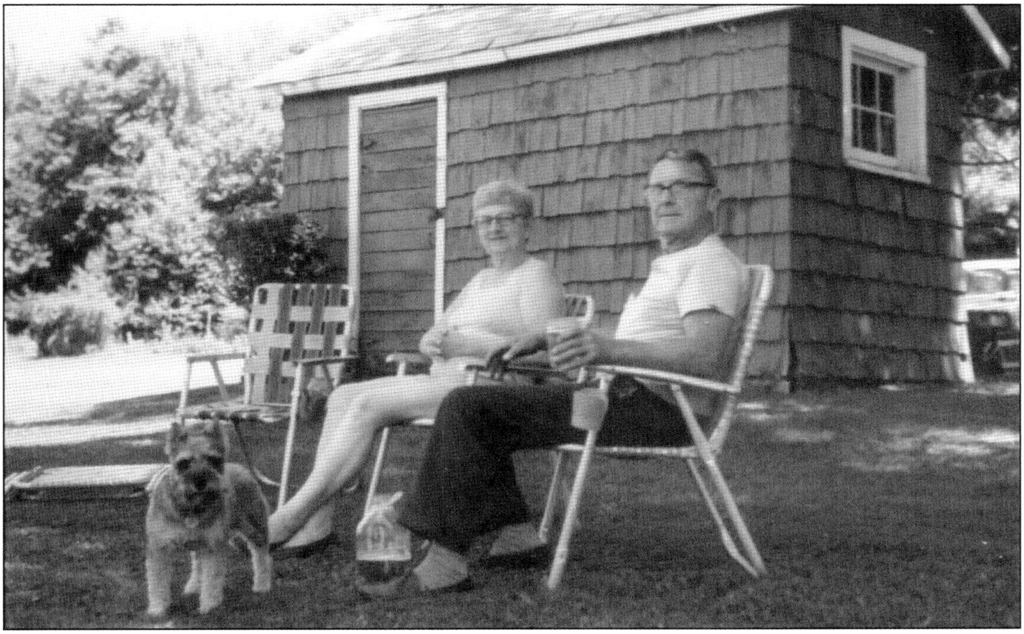

Jerry and Naomi Day. The Days lived for many years at 89 Pearl Street, where they raised four children—Judy, Janet, Linda, and Max. They operated Day's Service Station on Tioga Street. This photograph shows them relaxing at their "camp" on Swede Hill in the 1960s. (Courtesy Sally Benjamin.)

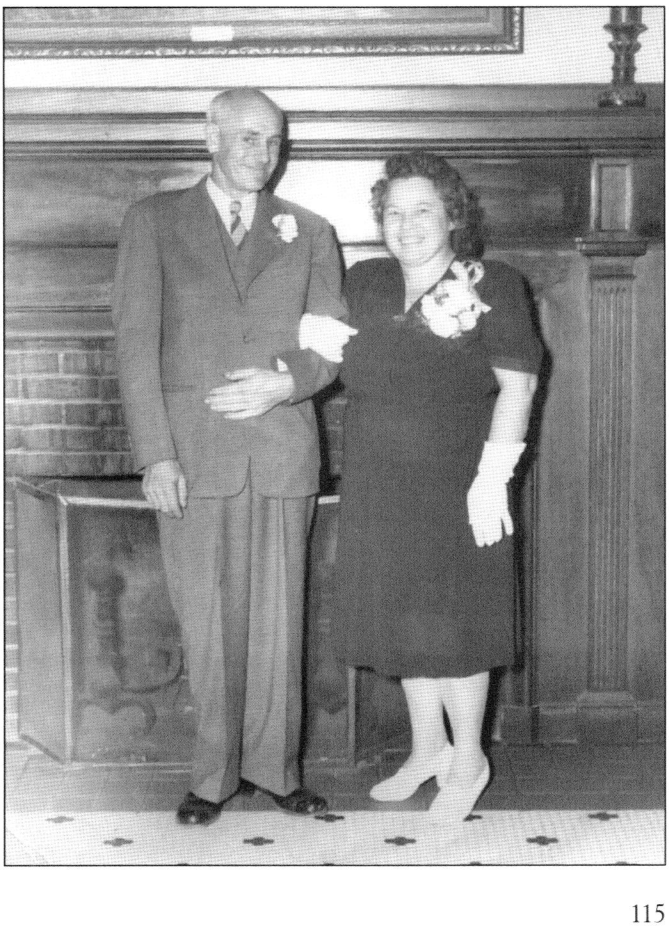

Vern and Margaret Wilcox. The Wilcoxes pose in front of the fireplace in the Penn-Wells lobby. They are celebrating their daughter Eleanor's marriage to Harry Atherton on July 4, 1947. The Wilcox family lived at 6 West Water Street.

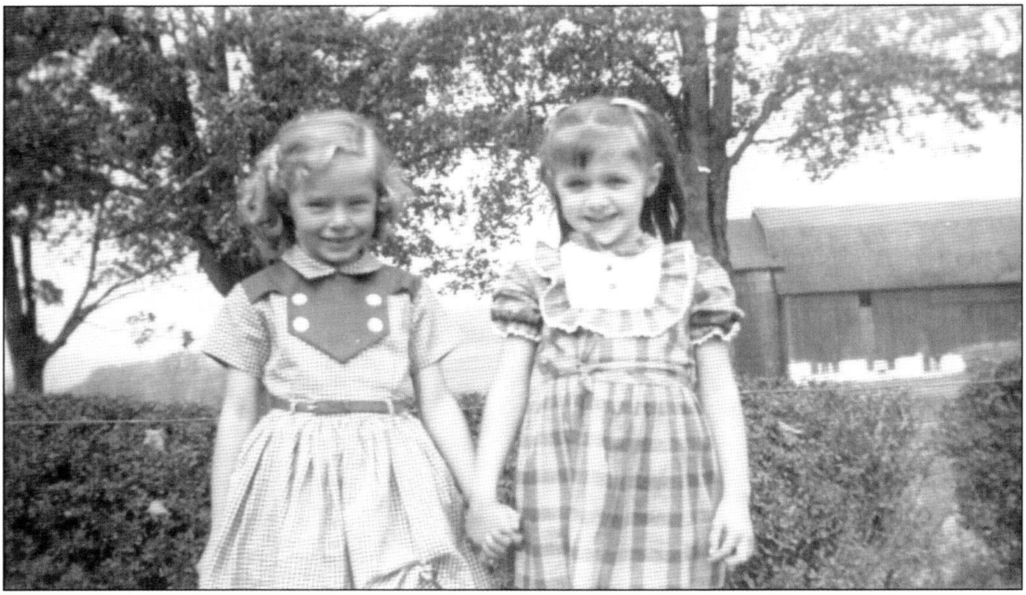

Ann Benjamin and Shirley Bliss (Olmstead). Ann and Shirley became best friends as toddlers and remained so throughout their school years. Shirley stayed in Wellsboro and married Michael Olmstead, chef at the Penn-Wells Hotel and at the Steak House. The Olmsteads also operated Olmstead's Family Restaurant in Middlebury Center for several years. Shirley Olmstead taught second grade at Don Gill until she retired in 2013. This photograph was taken on October 13, 1955, on the playground of the Charleston School in Dartt Settlement.

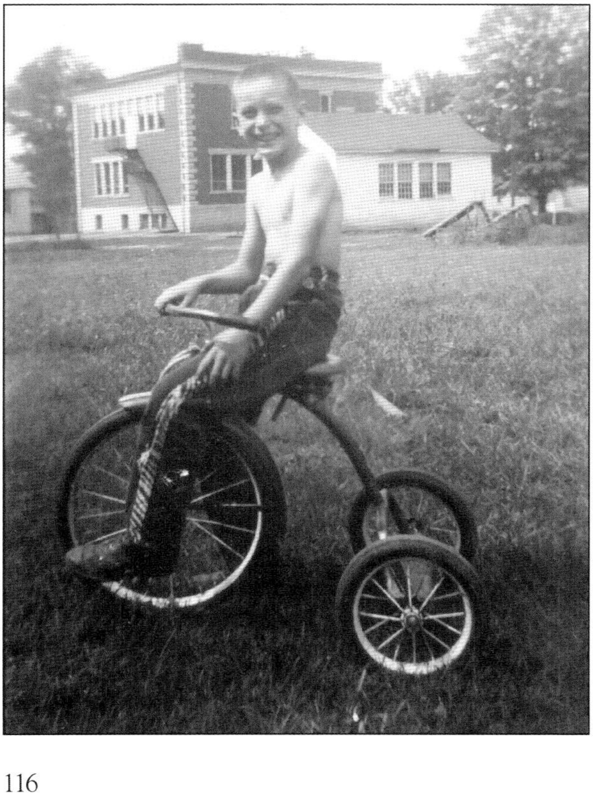

Dale Hollenbeck (1946–1972). Son of Dorothy and Charles Hollenbeck, Dale grew up on the family farm located next to the old Charleston School. The school is pictured in the background, flanked by two smaller buildings, one of which was the last one-room schoolhouse in Tioga County. Dale attended the Charleston Schools before graduating from Wellsboro High School in 1964. (Courtesy Cheri Hollenbeck Bartolotti.)

Eight

NESSMUK'S LEGACY

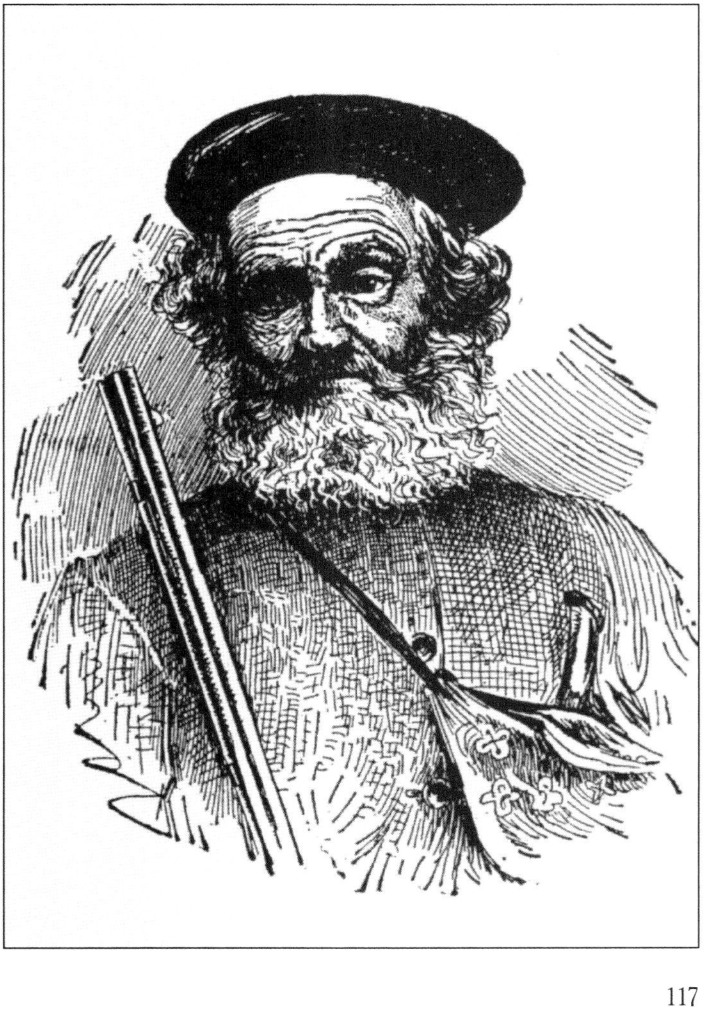

NESSMUK. George Washington Sears adopted his nom de plume, Nessmuk (meaning "wood drake"), from a Narragansett Indian who befriended him as a child in his native Massachusetts. Nessmuk's national fame resulted from freelance work as a sportswriter and from *Woodcraft*, a handbook for "outers" (those who enjoy the outdoors) published in 1884, which served as the basis for the *Boy Scout Handbook*. Although describing "the capital I as a pronominal catastrophe," Nessmuk wrote, "I love a horse, a gun, a dog, a trout and a pretty girl. I hate a pothunter, a trout-liar and a whiskey-guzzling sportsman."

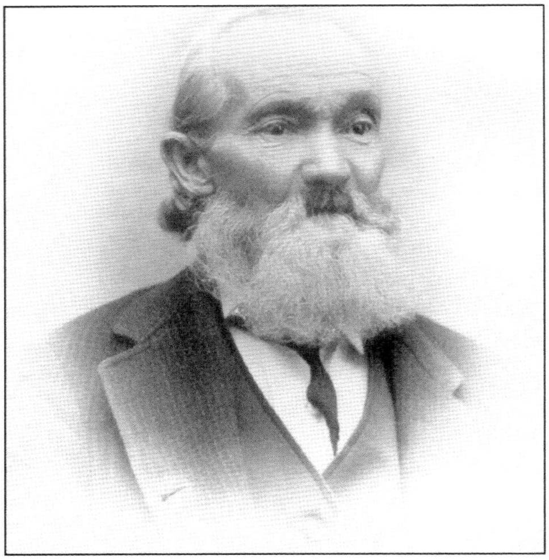

George Washington Sears (1821–1890). A legendary woodsman, pioneer conservationist, and brilliant author, George Washington Sears introduced the Pine Creek Gorge to a national audience in 1860. His descriptions of canoeing in the Adirondacks, published in *Forest and Stream* during the 1880s, catapulted him to national prominence. Sears, who preferred the solitude of the deep woods, wrote some of his finest poems on birch bark while indulging his love of the outdoors.

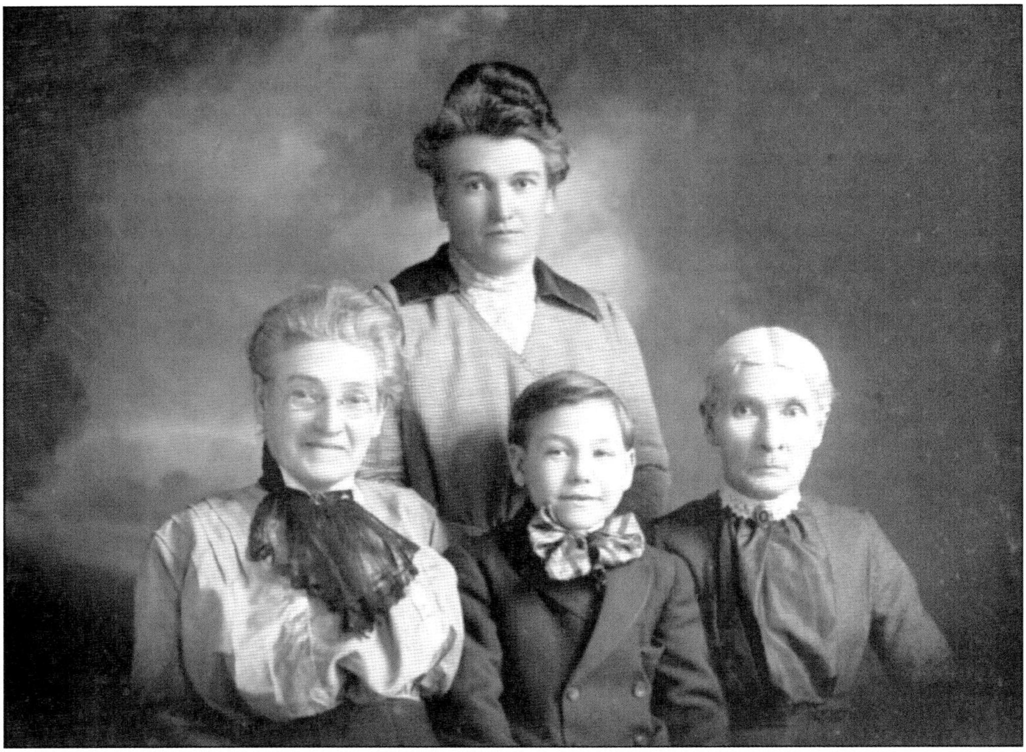

The Sears Family. The Sears family left Webster, Massachusetts, in 1838, arriving in Wellsboro in 1848. Peter Shumway, a relative from Webster, had settled in the region 40 years earlier, in Charleston Township. The Sears men worked as cobblers. Sears, known in Wellsboro as "Bacchus," married at age 35 and fathered three children—Margaret (Anderson), Jennie (Madison Boucher), and George. Sears joined the legendary Bucktails, organized June 12, 1861, but was discharged early after injuring his foot while at camp in Harrisburg. Sears worked briefly as editor of the *Tioga County Agitator*. Members of his family pictured here are, from left to right, (seated) Jennie Sears Madison (daughter), R. Bruce Taylor (great-grandson), and Marietta Butler Sears (wife); (standing) Mary A. Madison Taylor (granddaughter). (Courtesy Nancy Taylor Walker.)

Pioneer Conservationist and Social Critic. Ironically, Wellsboro's most celebrated citizen openly criticized the prosperous lumber barons who denuded the "Black Forest," so called because sunlight could not penetrate its dense canopy. In "Lumbering in Tioga County," a speech delivered at the 1904 centennial, Leonard Harrison confessed that "the rapidity with which the forests are disappearing . . . is at last causing some anxious thought as to the needs of the future."

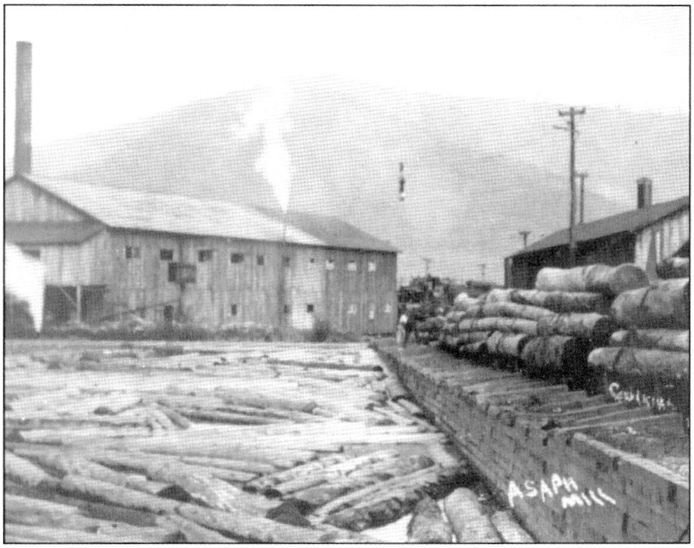

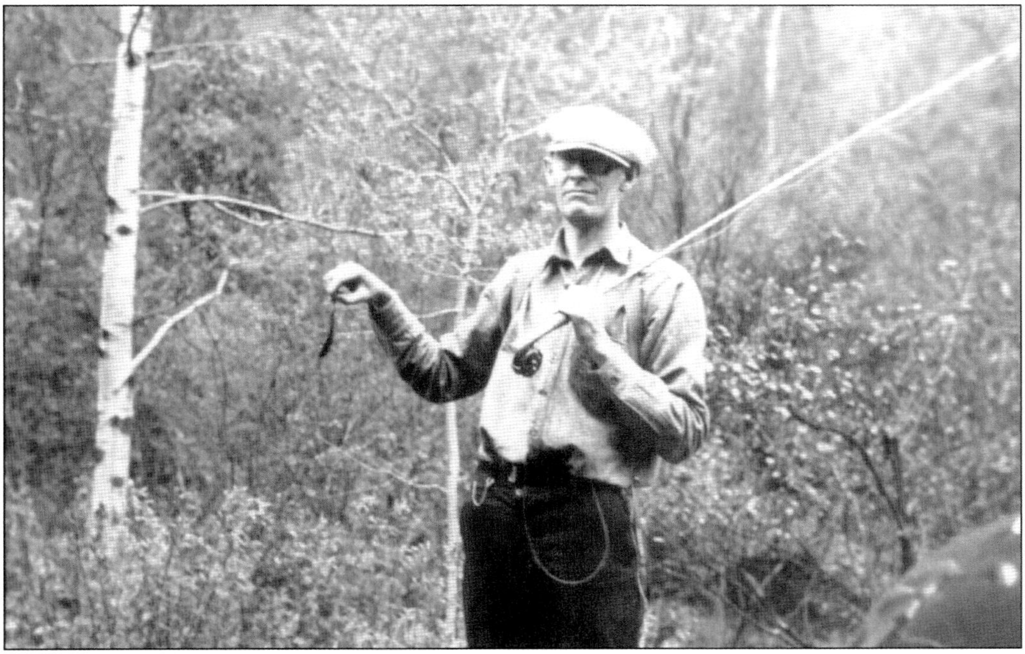

Pine Creek Pollution. Sears also brought suit, unsuccessfully, against the tanneries for their assault on the hemlock and for "poisoning and depleting the purest trout streams in the land." By 1916, affluent Wellsboroans, including Hon. Robert K. Young and Lloyd Smith, railed against the tanneries' "flagrant disregard of the law" and "wanton destruction of game fish by [pouring] acid and refuse" into the steams. Coal companies contributed to the problem by discharging mine water into Tioga County tributaries. Governor Stone's autobiography reports that brook trout had all but disappeared by 1918. A severe drought in 1923, which dramatically threatened the region's water supply, redefined the issue. The motivation to halt pollution abruptly shifted from saving game fish to saving people. The photograph shows fisherman Ransom Phelps with a disappointing catch in about 1930. (Courtesy David Gustafson.)

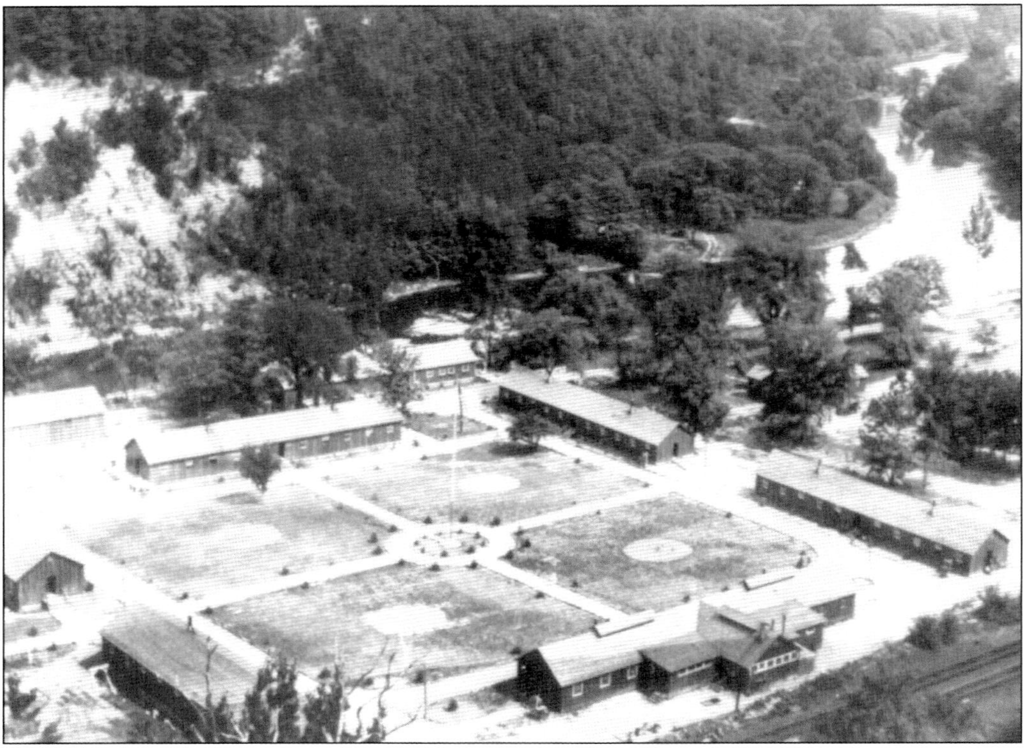

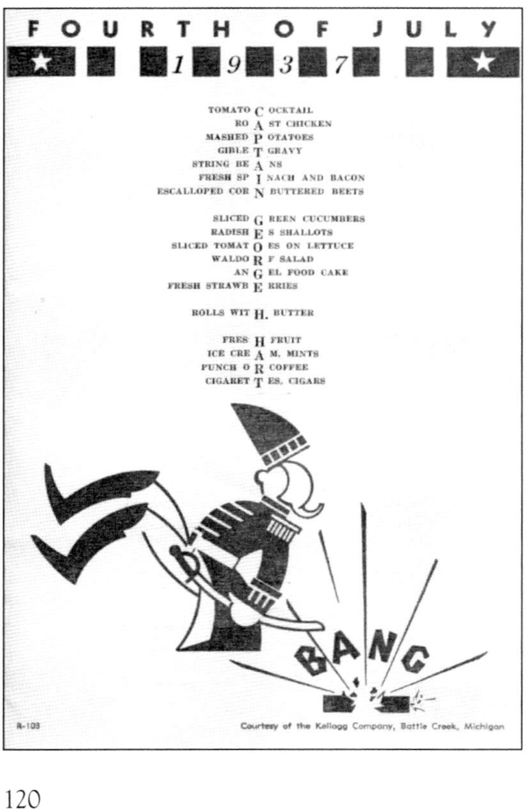

FOURTH OF JULY

1 9 3 7

TOMATO C OCKTAIL
RO A ST CHICKEN
MASHED P OTATOES
GIBLE T GRAVY
STRING BE A NS
FRESH SP I NACH AND BACON
ESCALLOPED COR N BUTTERED BEETS

SLICED G REEN CUCUMBERS
RADISH E S SHALLOTS
SLICED TOMAT O ES ON LETTUCE
WALDO R F SALAD
AN G EL FOOD CAKE
FRESH STRAWB E RRIES

ROLLS WIT H. BUTTER

FRES H FRUIT
ICE CRE A M, MINTS
PUNCH O R COFFEE
CIGARET T ES, CIGARS

R-103

Courtesy of the Kellogg Company, Battle Creek, Michigan

"ROOSEVELT'S TREE ARMY." The effects of the Great Depression, which began in late 1929, were muted in Wellsboro, in part due to the Civilian Conservation Corps (CCC). Pres. Franklin D. Roosevelt, inaugurated in 1933, acted immediately to provide relief to Americans. "Roosevelt's Tree Army" not only buffered the impact of the Depression but also reversed the pernicious effects of deforestation. The US Army ran the camps, but foresters directed the work. Five barracks housed 40 men; officers and state forestry personnel occupied a second building. Additional structures included an infirmary, a mess hall, a canteen, a bathhouse, a latrine, and a garage. The photograph shows the CCC camp at Darling Run. (Courtesy James Losinger.)

FOURTH OF JULY CELEBRATION. Malnourished boys who joined the CCC rapidly gained weight and strength. Enlistees ate well, as shown by this 1937 Fourth of July menu. Note how the menu honors the commanding officer, Capt. George Hart.

CCC Camps. Local camps included Asaph (burned on Christmas Day 1934), Darling Run, Dixie Run, Watrous, and Leetonia. The CCC cleared Colton Point and also built the pavilion at Leonard Harrison State Park, located on opposite sides of Pine Creek Gorge. The archival materials pictured list the officers, personnel, enrollees, and members of Camp S-155.

1354TH COMPANY

Civilian Conservation Corps

CAMP S-155 WELLSBORO, PA.

OFFICERS

HART, George H., Capt. Inf-Res., Commanding Officer
FOLTZ, Jonathan C. Jr., 1st Lt. FA-Res., Executive Officer
CLARKE, Lester E., 1st Lt. Inf-Res., Adjutant and Mess Officer
O'CONNOR, Arthur J., 1st Lt. Med-Res., Camp Surgeon and Exchange Officer

ECW PERSONNEL

GARDNER, Frank L., Project Superintendent
MILLER, O. N. Jr., Engineer
KILMER, Frank, Junior Forester
BRIGHAM, Edward, Blacksmith
BANKER, Wayne, Machine Operator
McDONALD, John, Mechanic
FULLER, Theodore, Foreman
BARTHOLOMEW, Lee, Foreman
APGAR, Monta, Foreman
CURRY, Shelton, Foreman

ENROLLEES

LEADERS

CAMPBELL, John R.
DIEHL, Glenn
LOUDON, Merle
KLINE, Walter R.
MURTLAND, Richard C.
REAGLE, Boyd A.
STRUBINGER, Albert
WAGAMAN, William

ASSISTANT LEADERS

FORNAL, John
KAMINSKI, Stanley
KURTZ, Benjamin
MOWERY, Edmund
MUSHALLA, Michael
KEVINSKI, Stephen
PORAMBO, Joseph
RANKIN, Robert M.
SHERIFF, Elwin A.
SPEISER, Richard G.
SUPPES, Peter J.
STACOVITZ, Ben.
THOMAS, Carl F.
WARD, Kenneth

MEMBERS

ABROMITIS, Albert
BALDWIN, Kenneth
BALKO, Emil
BALLARD, James A.
BALTZLEY, Robert P.
BASKOWSKI, Joseph
BEISWENGER, Leo F.
BEZDZEICKI, Stanley
BISBEY, Bernard A.
BLUCAS, Frank P.
BORN, John D.
BOOR, John
BROWN, William
BUCKLEY, Harry J.

MEMBERS (Continued)

BURKE, Leo E.
BYRNES, Norman F.
CAMPBELL, Augustus B.
CARPENTER, Andrew
CEREP, John D.
CESCHINI, Mario S.
CHAPPEL, John H.
COCHRAN, Roland R.
COLBY, Gerald L.
COLONY, William
COVER, Jerome B.
CRUSAN, Leslie D.
CUSHMAN, Michael
DAVIS, Stephen H.
DAVIS, Elwood A.
DAY, Samuel
DE HART, Roy
DENNY, William
DICK, Charles W.
DIPOFI, Nicholas D.
DORNING, William
DUTZIK, Clarence
EASTON, Albert
EDWARDS, Alfred D.
FEIST, Edwin C.
FAVORITE, Raymond
FIZEL, Thomas
FLACK, George
GAINER, Robert
GARTNER, Alfred
GIERULA, Edward J.
GLEASON, Frank
GROSS, Mervin A.
GROSS, Melvin I.
HEATLEY, James J.
HEITZMAN, Matthew S.
HENDRIX, Marvin
HENNINGER, Robert
HENSEL, Edward A.
HOLTZ, Raymond
HRICKO, James R.
HUBBA, Peter J.
HUFF, Woodrow
HUTTER, Alfred J.
IGO, Frank
INGRAM, William B.
JASPER, Robert M.
JOHN, Henry
KEENER, John Alvin
KELLY, John
KENNEDY, Aaron
KLEBON, Nicholas
KLIPOLA, Stephen
KOLAT, Frank
KOYTON, Andrew
KUTSKO, Joseph
KUTZER, Metro
KUZNIESKI, Stanley
LANCASTER, William A.
LAURIE, George J.
LEONI, Peter W.
LULIS, Walter
LUVARO, Joseph
LYNCH, George J.
MARTIN, John J.
McCARTY, James
McCUE, John
McMICHAEL, Charles B.
MELCHER, Leonard
MELTON, Clifton
MOCK, Torrance
MEDFISH, Anthony
MOYER, Lawrence I.
MURPHY, Emory E.
NEWTON, Eugene
NILON, William
McCARREN, Laurence
MICHALONIS, John
OGRODNICK, Theodore J.
ONCIDI, Ferdinand
PALLA, Julius
PETRO, Steve
POPLAWSKI, Joseph
PONTEFRACT, Harry
QUIMBY, Robert L.
RACZKOWSKI, Stanley
SABOXL, John F.
SATKOWSKI, Anthony
SHADEL, Raymond J.
SHALINSKY, John
SHUTT, Merl L.
STONER, Richard L.
STROLIS, Albert
SUTCAVAGE, Adolph
TAYLOR, William
TOMEL, John
TELEWSKI, Anthony
TELFORD, Alger
TOMSIC, Andrew F.
TRUMAN, James
TURNER, Earl
TURPIN, Clem
SWEDIC, Wassel
WASILCZYK, Alfred
WILLSEY, Wilbur
WILLSEY, Harold C.
WORTHINGTON, Harley
YANEVICH, Edward
ZELINSKI, Joseph
URBAN, William M.
GUSTAITUS, Peter

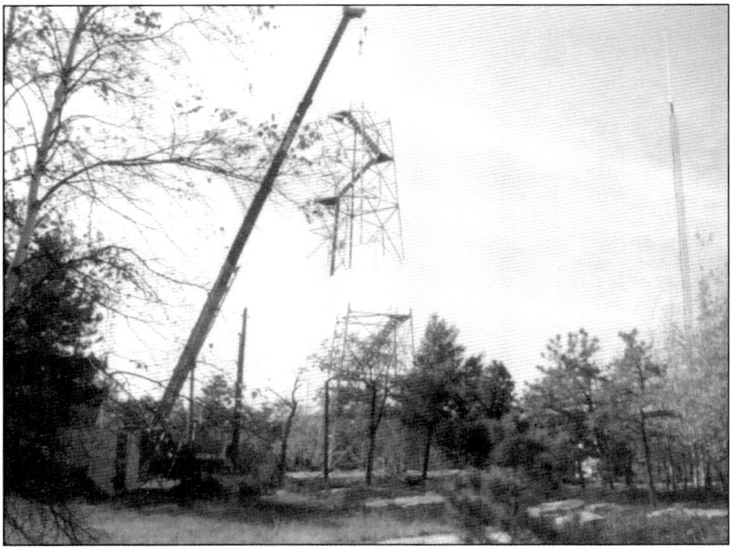

Baldwin Run Fire Tower. The State Department of Forestry ordered a new 47-foot steel fire-observation tower to replace the wooden structure built in 1899. A CCC addition and improvements to the forest roads and trails continued through 1935; fireplaces and picnic tables were also added. In Pennsylvania, the CCC planted 50 million trees and built 86 observation towers. (Courtesy PDF.)

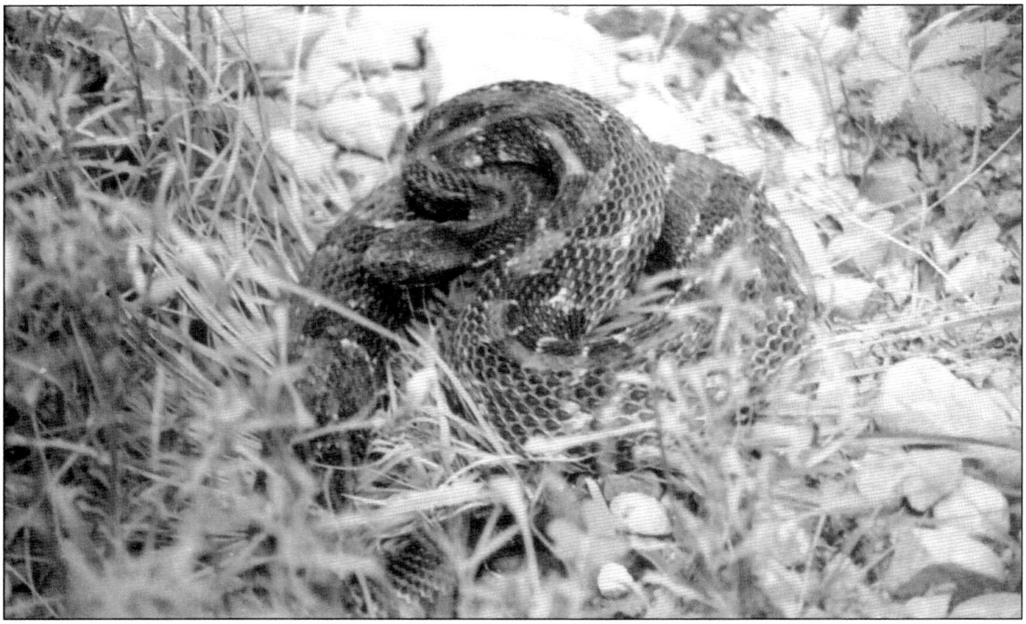

Rattlesnakes. After the lumber companies destroyed the forests, berry bushes proliferated. So too did the timber rattlesnake. Berry pickers, including children, were often bitten, sometimes fatally. Primitive cures for snakebite included placing the slain snake upon the wound, or in the absence of the snake, a dead chicken sufficed. Bounties were paid for rattlesnakes and, by 1951, the population was dramatically reduced. Pennsylvania began implementing protections in the late 1970s, eventually listing the rattlesnake as a candidate for federal protection. This photograph was taken near Landrus in 1978. (Courtesy Sally Benjamin.)

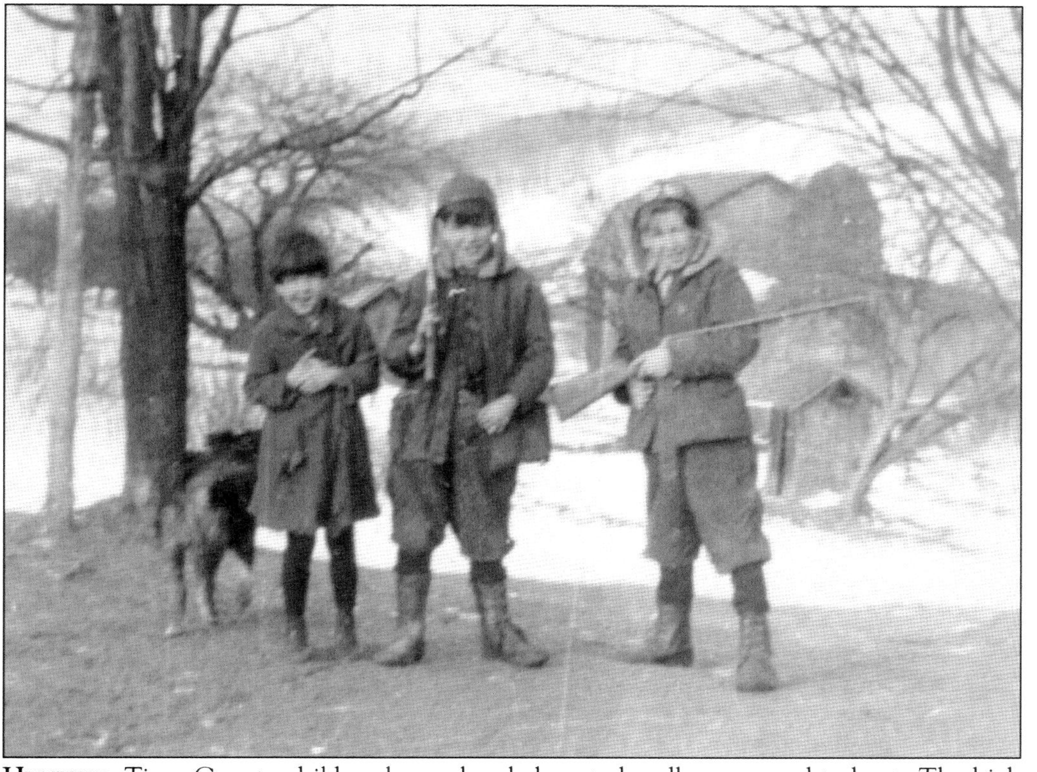

HUNTING. Tioga County children learned early how to handle a gun and to hunt. The high school sponsored a rod and gun club; pickup trucks with gun racks were commonly seen in the school's parking lot. Pictured here are children who lived out toward the Pine Creek Gorge in the 1930s—from left to right are Eleanor Ruth Watkins, Frank Lyle Watkins, and Bruce Leon Watkins. All three died tragically before their time—but not from gunshot wounds. (Courtesy Nancy Tanner Bowen.)

FISHING. Learning to fish came as naturally to Wellsboro's children as learning how to walk. In 1951, when university biologists discovered that trout were competing unsuccessfully with "trash fish" for food, they suggested giving children worms instead of flies for fishing. They reasoned that children would reduce the population of competitors and thus save the trout from starvation. Four-year-old Ann Benjamin, pictured here in 1953, often fished with her father—using worms.

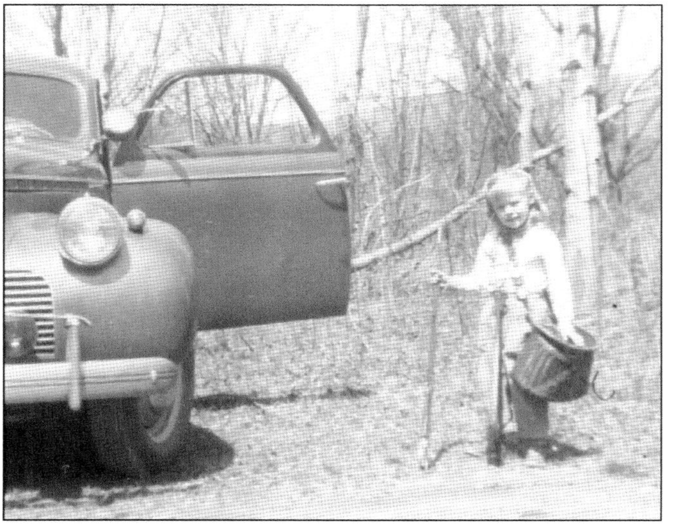

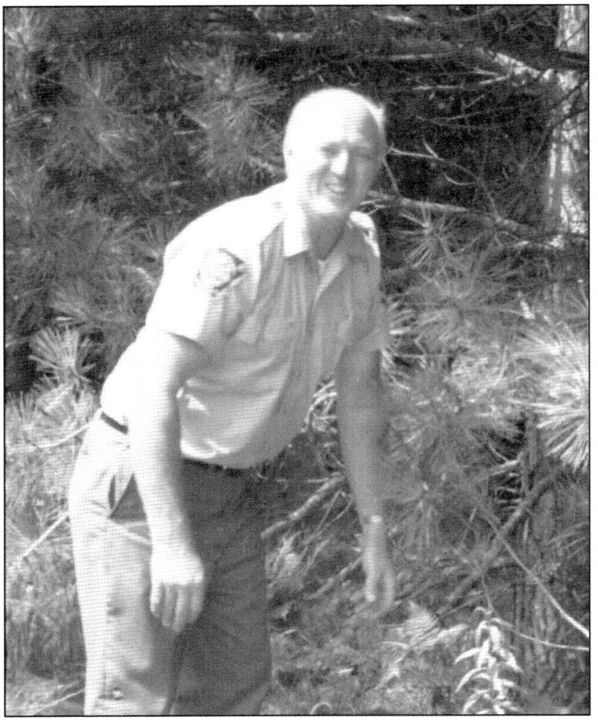

ARNOLD HAYDEN (1933–2001). The Pennsylvania Game Commission's wildlife biologist Arnold "Arnie" Hayden led the acclaimed "trap and transfer" program, which for 28 years studied the eastern wild turkey and contributed greatly to its restoration across Pennsylvania. Memorials to Hayden include the Arnie Hayden Memorial Chapter of the National Wild Turkey Federation, a scholarship for conservation students, a memorial on Armenia Mountain that acknowledges his "hearty laugh," and a memorial bench located near the Wellsboro Diner. This photograph shows Arnie setting up a cannon net on Armenia Mountain in 1978. (Courtesy Sally Benjamin.)

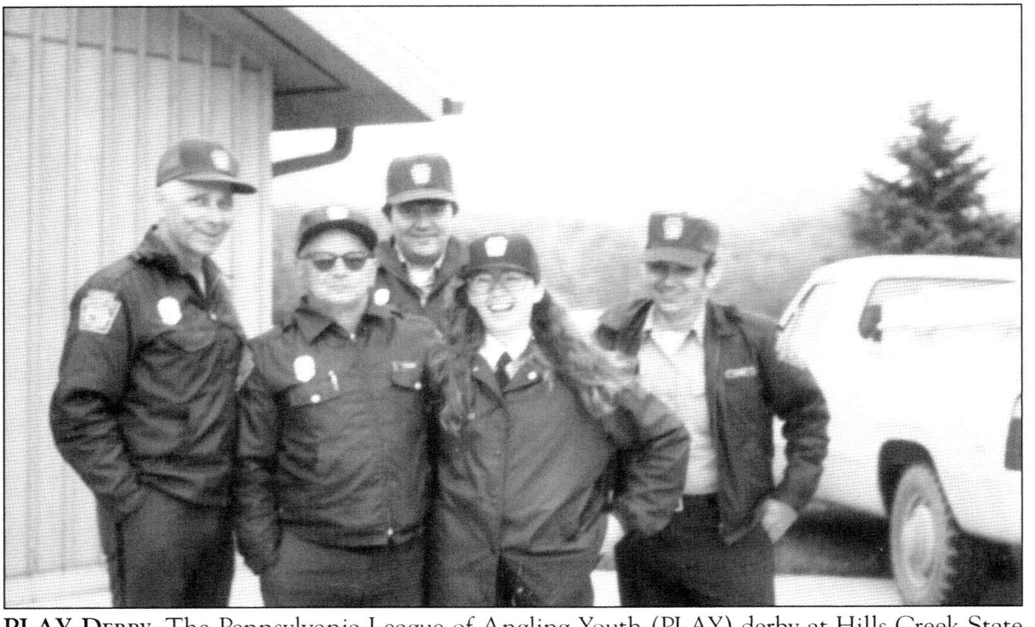

PLAY DERBY. The Pennsylvania League of Angling Youth (PLAY) derby at Hills Creek State Park, sponsored by the Pennsylvania Fish Commission, encouraged children ages six to twelve to hone their fishing skills and learn outdoor ethics while also competing to win fishing rods. This 1982 photograph includes, from left to right, Ray Hoover, district fish warden of Tioga County; Deputy Donald "Wimpy" Knaus; Deputy Gary Hall; Sally Benjamin, PLAY derby coordinator; and Deputy Willard "Jake" Confer. (Courtesy Sally Benjamin.)

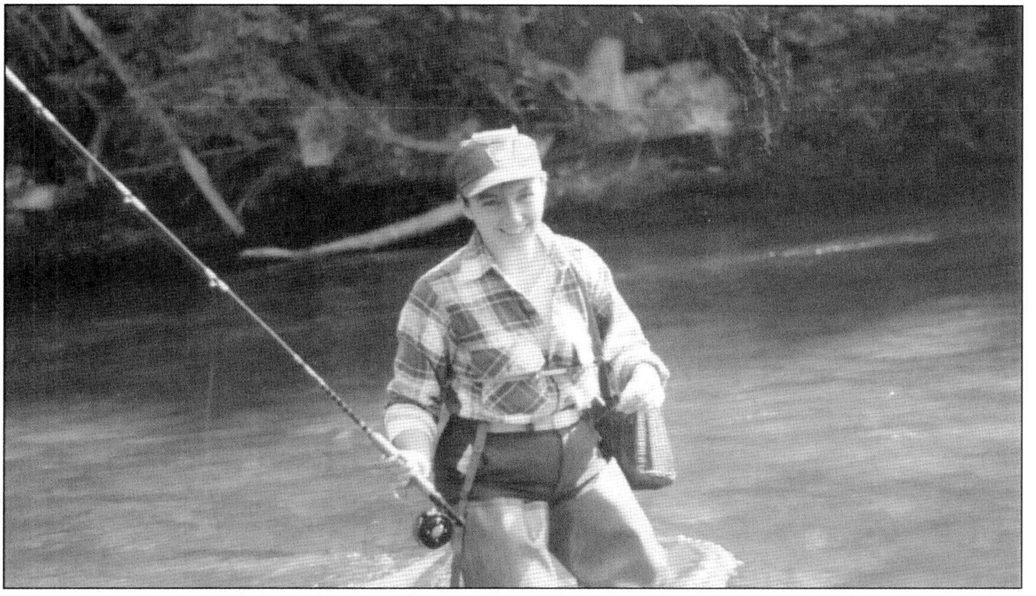

Local Heroes. Wildlife biologist Sally Benjamin heard biologist Arnie Hayden speak at her seventh-grade Earth Day assembly. Benjamin met Ray Hoover, district fish warden of Tioga County, on a class field trip in tenth grade. She recalls Hoover saying, "You know . . . girls can be biologists, too." This photograph shows Benjamin dry fly-fishing for brown trout at the confluence of Darling Run with Pine Creek in the spring of 1983. (Courtesy Sally Benjamin.)

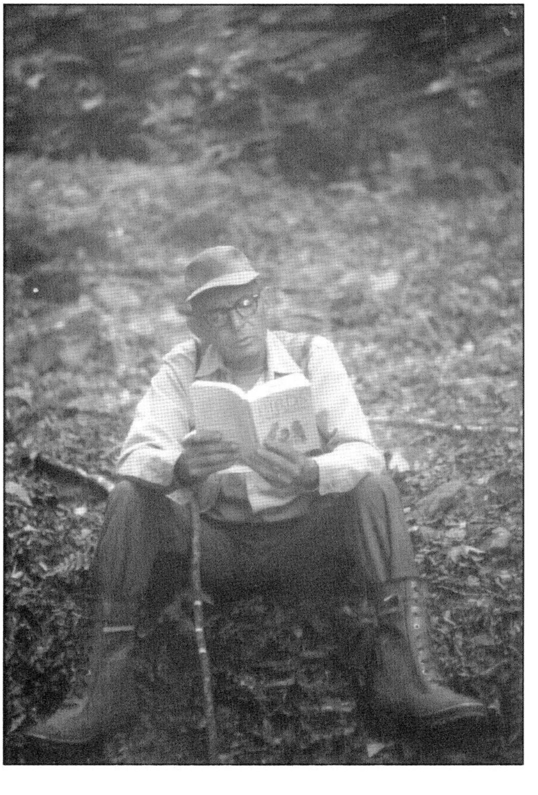

Audubon Society. The Audubon Society was established in Wellsboro in April 1906. With 25 members, the group chose "I know a hawk from a handsaw" as its motto. The publishers of *Forest and Stream* magazine, which published Nessmuk's famous handbook *Woodcraft*, founded the National Audubon Society in 1886. The first volume of the *Audubon* magazine, published in February 1887, promotes *Woodcraft* on the back cover. This image shows outdoorsman Norton Benjamin consulting his bird book at Sand Run Falls in 1975. (Courtesy Sally Benjamin.)

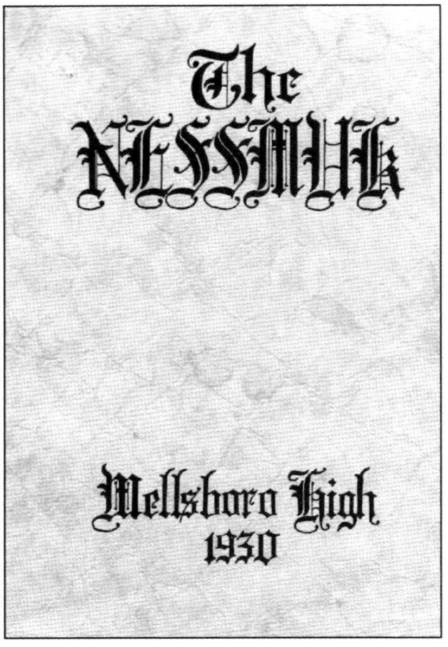

THE NESSMUK. In 1929, Wellsboro High School decided to replace the *Rambler* with a new yearbook. Students protested because they loved their old yearbook. "Conceived in adversity and fostered by dissention," the proposed publication would take a new form and therefore required a new name. The staff announced a naming contest and offered a prize of $2 to the winner. The faculty chose *Nessmuk*, suggested by Carmer McClintock.

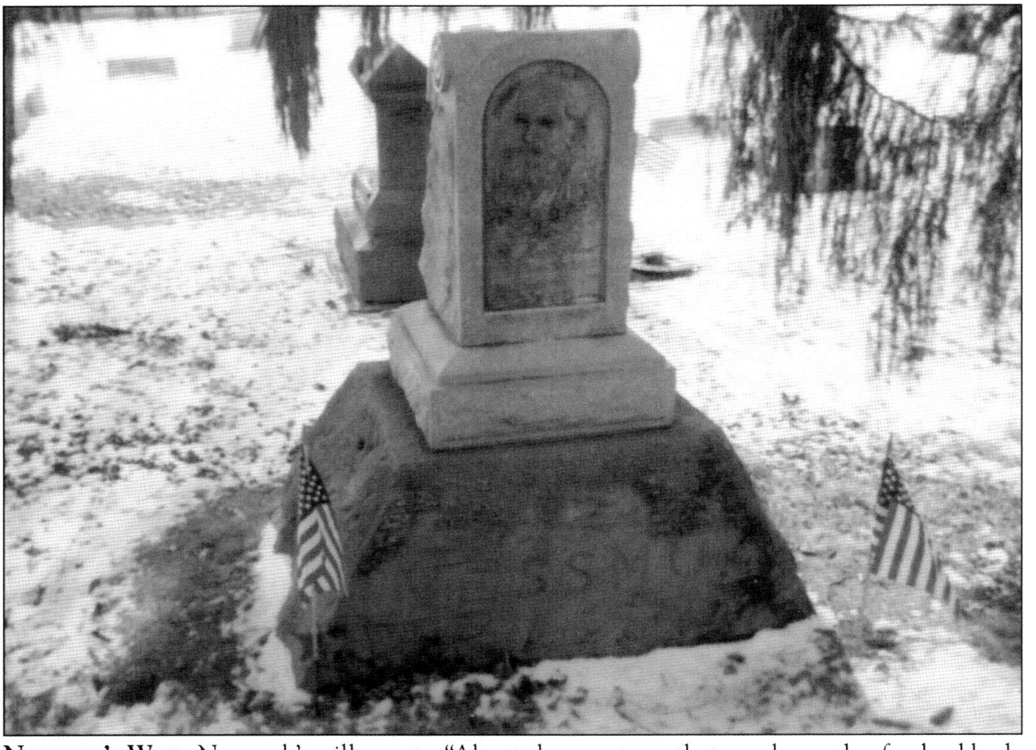

NESSMUK'S WILL. Nessmuk's will asserts, "About the worst use that can be made of a dead body is to bury it in the ground leaving it to rot slowly while poisoning the earth, air, and water." Nessmuk wanted an autopsy so that the results might benefit the living. He bequeathed his body to Dr. Charles W. Webb, directing him to "articulate" and then preserve his bones "where the blessed sunshine can sometimes reach them." The disposition of Nessmuk's body was not carried out according to his will.

Bibliography

Alberts, Robert C. *The Golden Voyage: The Life and Times of William Bingham 1752–1804*. Boston: Houghton Mifflin, 1965.

Bickham, Stephen. *The Story of St. Peter's Parish, Wellsboro, Pennsylvania: 1879–1979.* Available from St. Peter's Rectory, Central Avenue, Wellsboro, PA, 16901.

Fischer, David Hackett. *Albion's Seed: Four British Folkways in America.* New York: Oxford University Press, 1989.

Gitchell, Scott. *Wellsboro: The First Two Hundred Years, 1806–2006: A Pictorial History*. Virginia Beach: Donning, 2008.

Hardt, Anton. "The Railroads of Tioga County." Papers and proceedings of the Tioga County Historical Society, 1909.

Jewett, C.F., and G.H. Walker. *County Atlas of Tioga Pennsylvania from Recent and Actual Surveys and Records*. New York: F.W. Beers, 1875.

Laird, Archibald. *Twentieth Century Wildcats—A History of the Pennsylvania National Guard Medical Units in Tioga County, 1920–1963.* Wellsboro, PA: Doll House, 1966.

Largey, Gale Peter. *Life in Wellsboro, 1880–1920, A Socio-historical Portrait*. Lycoming, PA: Lycoming Printing, 1980.

———. *Life in Wellsboro, 1920–1960, A Socio-historical Portrait*. Lycoming, PA: Lycoming Printing, 1988.

Meginness, John F., John Meagher, and David Craft. *History of Tioga County Pennsylvania.* Harrisburg: R.C. Brown, 1897.

Owlett, Steven E. *Seasons Along the Tiadaghton*. Petaluma, CA: Interprint, 1993.

Roy, Arthur M. *Tioga County Centennial Celebration*. Wellsboro, PA: Centennial Commission, 1905.

Ruppert, Elfriede Elizabeth. *A Historical and Folklore Tour of the Pennsylvania Grand Canyon*. Philadelphia: Dorrance, 1964.

Sexton, John L. *History of Tioga County Pennsylvania with Illustrations, Portraits, and Sketches of Prominent Families and Individuals*. New York: W.W. Munsell, 1883.

Stone, William A. *The Tale of a Plain Man*. Philadelphia: John C. Winston, 1918.

Tioga County Bicentennial Committee. *Tioga County, Pennsylvania: The First Two Hundred Years.* Virginia Beach, VA: Donning, 2004.

Tubbs, Charles. "Wellsboro and the Wells Family." Papers and proceedings of the Tioga County Historical Society, 1909.

Wallace, Paul A.W. *Indian Paths of Pennsylvania*. Harrisburg: Pennsylvania Historical and Museum Commission, 1965.

———. *Indians in Pennsylvania*. Harrisburg: Pennsylvania Historical and Museum Commission, 1981.

Webb, Charles G. *The First Twenty-Five Years*. Elkland, PA: Elkland Journal Press, 1965.

Young, Robert Kennedy. "Indians in Tioga County: Inquiry as to the Last Aboriginal Inhabitant of Tioga County." Papers and proceedings of the Tioga County Historical Society, 1907.

———. *Tales of Tioga Pennsylvania and Its People*. Philadelphia: J.B. Lippincott, 1916.